LIFESTYLE MARKETING

Reaching the New American Consumer

Ronald D. Michman,
Edward M. Mazze, and Alan J. Greco

Westport, Connecticut
London

Library of Congress Cataloging-in-Publication Data

Michman, Ronald D.
 Lifestyle marketing : reaching the new American consumer / Ronald D. Michman,
Edward M. Mazze, and Alan J. Greco.
  p. cm.
 Includes bibliographical references and index.
 ISBN 1–56720–640–9 (alk. paper)
 1. Market segmentation—United States. 2. Target marketing—United States. 3.
Consumers' preferences—United States. 4. Consumer behavior—United States. 5.
Lifestyles—United States. I. Mazze, Edward M. II. Greco, Alan James, 1950– III. Title.
HF5415.127.M535 2003
 658.8′343—dc22   2003057995

British Library Cataloguing in Publication Data is available.

Library of Congress Catalog Card Number: 2003057995

ISBN: 1–56720–640–9

First published in 2003

Praeger Publishers, 88 Post Road West, Westport, CT 06881
An imprint of Greenwood Publishing Group, Inc.
www.praeger.com

Printed in the United States of America

The paper used in this book complies with the
Permanent Paper Standard issued by the National
Information Standards Organization (Z39.48–1984).

10 9 8 7 6 5 4 3 2 1

For Ruth who willed this book
and to Laura, Marc Ross, and Andy who lived it
Ronald D. Michman

To Sharon, my wife and partner,
and to my daughter Candace and my son Thomas
Edward M. Mazze

Contents

Illustrations

TABLES

FIGURES

Preface

As businesses have grown to realize that the success of their operations is dependent upon an adequate knowledge of consumer behavior, the importance of lifestyle market segmentation strategies has become more significant. A focus on the customer has caused marketers to realign organizational boundaries along customer segments instead of product categories to meet the demand for twenty-four hour and seven-day services. The impact of social and cultural changes on purchasing behavior has changed the way companies do business. For example, years ago women did grocery shopping for the family and now men are also doing the grocery shopping. Many products once sold to the male market such as power tools are now being purchased by women. Gender roles are blurred as more women enter the workforce. The same changes can be said for ethnic markets and other markets segmented by age, income, education, and occupation. Affluent consumers are willing to pay more for conveniences and product dependability and this market has gradually developed over the past few decades.

Lifestyle market segmentation is viewed as one aspect of an overall marketing strategy which allows a company to develop a more lifelike portrait of customers. For example, a bicycle could be purchased for a variety of reasons. The adult exercise segment of the market can be subdivided based upon lifestyle purchase motives. There are fitness buffs, recreational riders, nature lovers, and there are those who jog and cycle. Lifestyle analysis enhances target marketing and makes niche marketing feasible. The course that these changing lifestyles follow influence product development, distribution, pricing, and promotion. Technological changes, along with social changes, have created opportunities for firms to develop differential advantages. A differential advantage is at the heart of a firm's performance in competitive markets. Differential advantages are the unique characteristics in a firm's marketing program that cause consumers to purchase its product and not those of the competitors. Differential advantages can be achieved by the development of a distinctive image and by targeting a precisely defined market segment. Lifestyle market segmentation and technology have made possible more effective niche marketing.

A management-oriented perspective is used to interpret signals of change, to assess the implications of change, and to develop strategies to take advantage of change. This work challenges the viewpoint that strategies derived from lifestyle market segmentation studies can be developed in the short term. A spectrum of successful lifestyle market segmentation strategies that include competitive advantage, competitive positioning and niche, and product line maneuvering are all part of strategic marketing planning.

This book evolved from the authors' research on the impact of consumer lifestyles on purchasing behavior and from consulting for consumer goods companies. Literature that reflects academic thought on changing consumer lifestyles has been documented in end notes. To avoid cumbersome references within the text, much of the source material is listed in the bibliography for those interested in the further study of specific market segments.

This book is divided into nine chapters. The first chapter presents an overview of lifestyle market segmentation strategies and demonstrates how these strategies provide a basis for competition. The next three chapters depict lifestyles and decision making, purchasing behavior, and changing values which reflect changing lifestyles. Chapters 5 through 9 focus on markets such as singles, children, tweens, teens, college, the senior market, and ethnic groups including Hispanics, African-Americans, Asian, Italian, and Jewish markets. Each market is analyzed and strategies are proposed to take advantage of the changes taking place in each market segment.

Consumer lifestyles change from decade to decade. Adjustments to changing consumer lifestyles are vital in order for marketing to progress smoothly. This book provides a starting point for marketing professionals and undergraduate and graduate students enrolled in marketing courses to obtain an insight into the complexities and interrelationships of changing consumer lifestyles and their impact on the development of marketing strategies. Hopefully, this book will prevent mistakes and enable marketers to take greater advantage of market opportunities.

Acknowledgments

This is the result of a team of hardworking individuals who have provided valuable insights and have assisted the authors by providing research, clerical, and administrative help. Special recognition is extended to Kelly Glista, Phyllis Boone, and Marie Garofano who typed many of the chapters. Special thanks must also be given to Kelly Glista for handling the administrative activities in getting the manuscript ready for publication. Ron Michman would like to thank his daughter Laura Michman Dessel for her insights into chapters related to children and ethnic groups, and to his grandsons Marc Ross and Andy for explaining their purchasing behavior. Special recognition is extended to Maxine Berlin who made suggestions to improve the material in all chapters. Ed Mazze would like to thank his wife, Sharon, who reviewed each of the chapters and made suggestions to make the book more meaningful to marketing students and practitioners. Alan Greco acknowledges the support and encouragement of Dean Quiester Craig of North Carolina A & T State University.

Even with a team effort, any errors or omissions are our responsibility.

CHAPTER 1

The Basis for Competitive Lifestyle Market Segmentation Strategies

Forty years ago, firms often produced and sold a single product aimed at the mass market since firms believed all customers had similar needs and wants. This strategy has changed since companies can now narrow their target market. The key to successful market segmentation, and particularly to lifestyle market segmentation strategies, is information that can be collected about consumers. For example, checkout scanners in the supermarket now collect data on consumer purchases. An analysis of these data guides market segmentation strategies because different groups of consumers can be distinguished within broad markets by their activities, interests, and opinions. Lifestyle marketing pinpoints the way in which an individual lives and spends money. The target market is seen as a smaller homogeneous segment. A manufacturer of snack food may direct its marketing strategies to party snackers, guilty snackers, indiscriminate snackers, weight watchers, nutritional snackers, or other categories depicted by data analysis.

Lifestyle, cultural trends, and consumer attitudes influence consumer decisions. Strategies for marketing toothpaste used to be about battling cavities and whitening teeth. Through research, marketers have learned that consumers are now concerned with their gums and their entire mouth. To appeal to this broader definition of dental care, toothpastes such as Colgate Total have been introduced.

Marketing research has revealed information demonstrating how lifestyles are changing. For example, online computer games are soaring in popularity and the growth isn't necessarily coming from people under the age of twenty-one. Many retirees are playing games on the Internet and find it a relatively inexpensive and an easy form of entertainment. Some senior executives are playing Yahoo games as a method to relieve stress. Women who have chosen to be stay-at-home moms are motivated to play online games as an escape from household chores. Other game players are using the computer to make new friends and to retain those friends who live long distances away. Leisure lifestyles are changing and thus causing variations in purchasing behavior of unexpected demand of some market segments for online computer games.

When laptops and the Internet were only a dream, a few marketers with vision realized that traditional market segmentation research was not lending itself to a well-defined picture of target markets. Thus, a basis for lifestyle market segmentation research began to take root. New tools provide a more reliable link between the target market and various forms of lifestyle or existing behavior.

Market segmentation is the process of dividing up the total market into groups with relatively similar product and/or service needs in order to design specifically tailored products and/or services to match segment needs. Segmentation also leads to strategies that aim at the differences among consumers who comprise potential target markets. Effective market segmentation requires a sufficient number of customers, resources to meet the needs of the segment, and the ability to reach these customers.

There are many bases for market segmentation strategies. Segmentation should not be limited to one variable and should be based on multiple dimensions. Behavioristic segmentation divides buyers on the basis of need satisfying benefits (referred to as benefit segmentation) derived from product use, the rate of product usage, the degree of brand loyalty, and an understanding of consumer readiness to purchase the product. Psychological segmentation is composed of personality, motivation, and lifestyle variables—a psychographic variable can be used alone to segment a market, or it can be combined with other market segmentation variables such as demographic measures or geographic markets. There is also occasion-based segmentation where a situation will drive product preference and selection such as a special family event or a holiday.

Market segmentation and lifestyle are two related concepts that are potent strategies for satisfying consumer preferences and organizational objectives. Lifestyle analysis involves identifying consumers' activities, interests, and opinions. Activities are classified as sports, work, entertainment, and hobbies. Interests include job, house, family, fashion, and food. Opinions are classified as to social issues, politics, education, business, and outlook about the future. Demographic factors such as age, occupation, income, education level, geography, and stage in the family life cycle are also used along with activities, interests, and opinions for identifying market segments. Sexual orientation can also influence consumer behavior as significantly as a person's age, gender, and ethnicity. Combining both strategies, a peanut butter manufacturer may direct its appeals to families with children and whose lifestyle reveals them to be theme park visitors and heavy video renters.

Although the term psychographics was first used around the time of World War I to classify people by their physical appearance, it was Emanuel H. Demby who conducted the first study in 1965.[1] Psychographics endeavors to depart from earlier views expressed in behavioral, demographic, and socioeconomic measures. Psychographics is a widely applied technique used in the measurement of lifestyle. Psychographics include social class, lifestyle, personality, and other demographic and behavioral variables. The end result of using these variables is the construction of a psychological profile of a market segment. Psychographic research uses quantitative techniques to measure the psychological apart from the demographic dimensions of consumers. Lifestyle describes how individuals spend their time, what they consider important about their immediate surroundings, their opinions on various issues, and their interests.

Psychographic studies can also use traditional bases of product usage, demographics, and other variables such as product attributes, lifestyle variables along with the psychological variables that include self-image, personality, and attitudes. Statistical techniques such as multiple-regression analysis, factor analysis, cluster analysis, multidimensional scaling, perceptual mapping, and multiple-discriminant analysis provide greater precision than previously available in using these data. The use of probability samples provides a database that is satisfactory for deriving statistically significant results related to a market.

The Stanford Research Institute uses values as a segment discriminator. This has permitted researchers to view a population as composed of individuals with certain feelings and beliefs. It is a formal attempt to link aspects of psychographics with lifestyles. Since marketers use market research for applied purposes, psychographics has come to be intertwined with lifestyle research and with research on consumer activities, interests, and opinions.

The benefits of psychographic and lifestyle studies have implications for marketing planning. Product development can be based upon knowledge of the benefits sought by customers. Competitive strategy can be formulated based upon how well competitors' brands satisfy these benefits. Promotion strategies can be directed to specific market segments. Media selection can be geared to specific audiences. Pricing decisions can be developed based upon customer willingness and ability to pay a price for perceived brand benefits. Product distribution can be selected to match customers' patronage motives. Finally, marketing management may be able to develop improved multidimensional perspectives of key target market segments and to develop a more lifelike portrait or profile of customers. For example, a bicycle can be purchased for a variety of nondemographic reasons. The adult exercise segment of the market can be subdivided based upon lifestyle purchase motives. There are fitness buffs, recreational riders, nature lovers, and there are those who both jog and cycle. The success of market segmentation can only be measured when an identified segment can be reached by a marketing mix aimed at that segment.

The problems involved in obtaining, analyzing, and interpreting psychographic and lifestyle data cannot be minimized. It is difficult to draw valid conclusions based upon single studies; only with replication of these studies can trend data show how consumers' preferences change. A major limitation of psychographic and lifestyle studies is the cost factor because the studies are more expensive than other types of market research.

THE CENSUS

According to the recent census, nearly 75 percent of U.S. households are nontraditional, made up of single parents, unmarried couples, divorced or never-married individuals, or older married couples whose kids no longer live at home. Table 1.1 lists typical segmentation characteristics. Marketers need to use different segmentation variables in conjunction with behavioral variables to define markets precisely. There must be a connection between a segment and some form of existing behavior, lifestyle, or self-image that will validate the segment for a specific product category.

A comparison of the 2000 Census data with the 1990 Census data is important in understanding how segments have changed. Identifying market differences serves as a basis for segmenting consumer markets. A market is composed of individuals and organizations with the purchasing power, the interest, the authority, and the desire to buy a specific product. The lifestyles of the people who comprise the market are an important consideration. The extent of their purchasing power and how they desire to spend their discretionary income are other considerations. Consumer markets are composed of individuals either purchasing for themselves or their households.

Table 1.1
Segmentation Characteristics

Variable	Typical Breakdowns
Geographic	
Region	Pacific, Mountain, West North Central, West South Central, East North Central, East South Central, South Atlantic, Middle Atlantic, New England
County size, Standard Metropolitan Statistical Area, City	Under 5,000; 5,000–19,999; 20,000–49,999; 50,000–99,999; 100,000–249,999; 250,000–499,999; 500,000–999,999; 1,000,000–4,999,999; 5,000,000 or over
Density	Urban, suburban, rural
Climate	Northern, southern
Demographic	
Age	Infant, 0–2, 3–5, 6–8, 9–12, 13–15, 16–18, 19–24, 25–34, 35–49, 50–64, 65+
Sex	Male, female
Family size	1–2, 3–4, 5+
Family life cycle	Young single; young, married, divorced, no children; young, married, youngest child under 6; young married, divorced, youngest child 6 or over; older, married, with children; older, married, divorced, no children under 18; older, single; other
Income	Under $10,000; $10,000–$14,999; $15,000–$19,999; $20,000–$29,999; $30,000–$49,999; $50,000 and over
Occupation	Professional and technical; managers, officials, and proprietors; clerical sales; craftsmen, foremen; operatives; farmers; students; homemakers, unemployed, retired
Education	Grade school or less; some high school; high school graduate; some college; college graduate, beyond four years of college
Religion	Catholic, Protestant, Jewish, Muslim
Race	Caucasian, Black, Hispanic, Asian
Nationality	American, British, French, German, Scandinavian, Italian, Polish, Chinese, Japanese, Mexican, Cuban
Psychographic	
Social class	Lower lower, upper lower, lower middle, upper middle, lower upper, upper upper
Values and Lifestyle	Belongers, emulators, survivors
Personality	Authoritarian, compulsive, gregarious
Behavioristic	
Purchase occasion	Regular occasion, special occasion
Benefits sought	Promptness, service, bargains
User Status	Nonuser, ex-user, potential user, first-time user, regular user
Usage rate	Light user, medium user, heavy user
Loyalty status	None, medium, strong
Purchase state	Unaware, aware, informed, ready to buy
Attitude toward product	Positive, indifferent, negative

Source: Adapted from Statistical Abstract of the United States 2001–2002.

A contrast between 1990 and 2000 census data shows the greatest population percentage growth in the Pacific states, Texas, and Florida. These states have good weather and consumers may enjoy outdoor living more than in other states. Therefore, this presents a market for products such as swimsuits, swimming pools, outdoor furniture, gardening tools, and recreational equipment.

Census data indicate that the population in the United States is living longer. Subsequent census data for 2010 and 2020 will probably reveal a similar trend due to advances in medicine and health care. This means that elderly consumers will become an even more important market segment in the future, especially for financial services, travel, and health-care products. The elderly, in their role as grandparents, will also purchase many more gifts such as toys and clothing for children. The elderly will also engage in a more active lifestyle. The shifting age distribution from the 1990 to the 2000 census indicates that sports and recreation companies should become more interested in the over-forty age group. Moreover, colleges and universities should aim their recruitment toward the older, nontraditional students.

There has been a decline in family size. This means that the adults in the household will be able to purchase more and better clothing for themselves, more recreational equipment, and will not only eat out more but will dine at finer restaurants. There will be fewer children with more influence in family purchasing decisions.

The last decade has seen a rise in the number of wealthy individuals going from 10.8 million U.S. households to 22.5 million in 2000. They are younger, more aggressive, increasingly self-directed and often self-made with annual incomes exceeding $100,000 or assets of at least $500,000.

Educational attainment is another factor that impacts the maturity and sophistication of the American consumer. The college-educated consumer was once limited by its numbers but this has changed dramatically in the last thirty years. Today's consumer is better educated and makes a more rational decision in the selection of goods and services. Value, rather than low price, is a more important variable in making a purchasing decision. Promotional materials will have to provide accurate and useful information in order to be effective. More education on the part of consumers creates demand for such products as computers, books, art, travel, and cultural activities. Moreover, educated consumers demand more precise labeling of product contents and are more concerned about the environmental impact of their purchases since it affects their health and safety.

There have been important statistical changes in ethnic groups in America from the 1990 to the 2000 census. The white segment of the population will decrease by 10 percent by the year 2050 and Hispanic groups should increase by more than 100 percent. In response to this trend, Anheuser-Busch divided Texas into several regions. A cowboy image was used in north Texas while in south Texas a Hispanic image was included in advertising. As a result, market share increased significantly and demonstrated the successful application of regional market segmentation. The black segment is estimated to increase by 15 to 20 percent. Ethnic groups within the cultural mainstream that have unique values and attitudes are referred to as subcultures or microcultures and are based upon race and nationality. Differences in ethnic groups result in considerable variations in consumer buyer behavior. It is not only important to understand these variations but to look for links that can offer an opportunity for a broader target market.

In the past, garlic was the most exotic condiment that was sold in supermarkets. Now, there are over thirty varieties of salsa—the Mexican condiment that has outsold ketchup since the early 1990s. Multiculturalism has become a concrete reality. Census data reveal that nearly 25 percent of the U.S. population identifies itself as a segment other than white alone. There is increasing emphasis on ethnic pride that will cause marketers to reconsider their marketing strategies.[2]

THE USE OF DEMOGRAPHIC INFORMATION

Geographic location has long been considered a basis for market segmentation studies. It was not until the last decade of the twentieth century that marketers realized the importance of regional and local lifestyle market segmentation strategies. Studies indicated that psychographic segments that are developed for markets in one geographic location are generalizable to markets in other geographic locations and that long-distance mobility was a life-event indicator, rather than a lifestyle indicator.[3] Regional marketing and identifying changes in local lifestyles have become more important. For example, Ben & Jerry's, an ice cream producer, directed its earlier efforts to a market segment in New England concerned with the environment. Successful in New England, the company used this same appeal in other areas.

Campbell Soup sells a spicier nacho-flavored cheese soup in California and Texas in order to accommodate subcultural differences. Campbell Soup adjusts its product mix to serve different target markets in diverse geographical locations. It is difficult to understand why more vitamins are purchased in Denver and more shoe polish in Indianapolis but the task of marketers is to develop regional and lifestyle market segmentation strategies based on these local tastes.

Population, its distribution and composition, is not growing evenly throughout the United States. Evidence from the census data indicates that population shifts to the Sun Belt states have been much greater than expected. The growth of the Sun Belt areas means that special products need to be developed for warm weather areas that reflect lifestyles due to climate because consumers will spend more time outdoors than those in the eastern and midwestern states.

There is a continuing increase in the number of senior citizens. Levi Strauss is placing more emphasis on marketing jeans for the mature figure and General Mills and Kellogg are developing products targeted to a senior segment concerned with lowering their cholesterol. Other population trends reflect an increase in immigrants and other minority groups. Ethnic markets represent a challenge for marketers to target lifestyles that vary from existing lifestyles, especially in the short term. These changes result in different marketing strategies.

A blurring of sexual roles is breaking down as men and women are now engaged in activities once deemed the province of the other sex. For example, some years ago women did practically all the grocery shopping for the family. Men are now doing a great deal of the grocery shopping. Women now buy products once sold almost exclusively to the male market, such as power tools. Products that were traditionally marketed only to women such as cooking utensils are now marketed to men. There are still significant differences between women and men in their buying behavior and habits. For example, in the area of dieting, most dieters are female. Among women, dieters tend to be between the ages of fifty-five and sixty-four, white, and college educated. Women start to consider slimming down in their mid-twenties, and the desire grows with age.

Consumer spending is influenced considerably by the family life cycle. Age does have an impact on purchasing decisions. Age also has an impact on marital status, the presence or absence of children in the household, and the ages of these children. Consequently, age and life cycle stages are frequently combined in order to study markets. For example, the full-nest family with the youngest child under age six is at its peak for purchasing homes. Although cash may be low, this group is interested in new products and buys washers, dryers, televisions, baby food, and toys. Nevertheless, age and life cycle can be confusing variables for marketers. To illustrate, the Ford Motor Company targeted its first-generation (mid-1960s) Mustang automobile to young people who desired an inexpensive, sporty-type car. The result was surprising as Ford learned that all age groups purchased the Mustang. The Mazda Miata roadster and the Chrysler PT Cruiser followed a similar pattern. The target market was not necessarily chronologically young but psychologically young.

Life cycle position is an important determinant of buying behavior. The young married couple with the children (full-nest stage) have different needs from those of a couple in their mid-fifties with children not living at home (empty-nest stage). Middle-aged couples without children typically buy better home furnishings, more expensive automobiles, and financial services.

SOCIAL CLASS

There are better determinants to define social class than income. They include education, occupation, and housing arrangements. Consumer spending is roughly similar within social class categories although regional location causes some disparities. People within a particular social class are more likely to interact with one another than with members of different social classes. As more and more double-income families emerge, the distinction between social classes will probably become sharper in the future although Americans do not like to believe that social classes exist in the United States.

Occupation and economic circumstances influence consumption patterns. A blue-collar worker is likely to purchase work clothes and work shoes. A business executive is likely to purchase expensive clothing, country club memberships, and a sailboat. Tastes can evolve through the years as the 1980s were about greed and ostentation, while the 1990s were about values and self-fulfillment. Affluent tastes now seem to reflect the utilitarian, with people preferring a Ford Explorer SUV rather than a BMW sport coupe or sedan. For many affluent consumers the favorite American pastime is no longer baseball, basketball, or football since shopping has surplanted these pastimes and has become a consuming passion.

Educational achievement is another variable that explains purchasing decisions and is closely associated with occupation and economic circumstances. Traditionally, cultural organizations such as museums, operas, ballets, and theater have targeted upper-income groups. Occupation, economic circumstances, and education should be considered when developing lifestyle market segmentation strategies.

SUBCULTURAL STRATEGIES

The power of subcultures and their impact on potential marketing strategies is evident when it is considered that some of the largest cities in the United States, including Baltimore, Chicago, Los Angeles, Miami, San Antonio, and Washington, D.C. have majority populations of Asians, African-Americans, Hispanics, and other minorities. Ethnic groups can be referred to as subcultures because they have values, customs, traditions, and activities that are segment specific. Subcultural differences may result in considerable variations in consumer buying behavior. Marketers may have to modify their product, promotion, price, or distribution systems to accommodate these differences. For example, firms wanting to reach the Hispanic market need to advertise in Spanish and use bilingual labeling to ensure that their products are accepted by this market segment. Campbell Soup sells a product line of Latino foods and uses different campaigns to reach Caribbean Hispanics and Mexican Americans. Burger King uses Spanish-language advertising campaigns.

Ethnicity, religion, and race are also lifestyle market segmentation variables. Marketers realize the potential in mainstreaming ethnic products to nonethnic groups or different market segments. To illustrate, Asian items placed on supermarket shelves include the familiar soy sauce, fried noodles, fresh ginger, and other products. Empire Kosher Poultry has not only targeted the Jewish ethnic market but has broadened its appeal to serve the non-Jewish population as well. Many firms serving ethnic markets have developed favorable images but future marketing will involve not only the targeting of ethnic markets but the inclusion of the nonethnic population to broaden the demand for products and services.

A concentrated marketing strategy can make effective use of lifestyle marketing analysis by appealing to one well-defined market segment with a single tailor-made strategy. The following defines the components of a concentrated marketing strategy:

Niche Strategy	A small unique part of a market segment
Market Segmentation	Subdivide a market into distinct sub-markets of customers that have similar needs
Product Line Segmentation	A group of closely related products with benefits desired by consumers
Differentiated Segmentation	Appeal to two or more well-defined segments with separate marketing mix for each segment

An example of a niche strategy is Lance—a snack food manufacturer who provides consumers with a large assortment of cholesterol-free, low-cholesterol, fat-free, and low-fat products. Niche marketing has made it possible to aim tailored products to a specific customer group. General Mills is introducing a Web site that allows consumers to mix and match more than 100 different ingredients to create and name their own breakfast cereals, delivered to their homes in single-serving portions for a price of approximately $1.00 per serving. Fisher-Price toys introduced a children's camcorder aimed at a youth market aged five to thirteen. Product line segmentation is a broad group of products intended for essentially similar uses. In differentiated segmentation, the firm may operate in several market segments, as General Motors does with different products for each segment.

If market segmentation strategies are used to extremes, market fragmentation can result where there are small distinctions among products that are neither meaningful to consumers nor profitable to marketers. When concentrated strategies are used, the firm's financial capabilities, product characteristics, dealer requirements, and the product life cycle must be considered. Above all, market characteristics such as differences between consumers must be considered in selecting the best strategy for segmenting a market. If not, consumers will be presented with endless product differentiation (such as nine different kinds of Kleenex Tissue and Eggo Waffles in sixteen different flavors) that is not only confusing to consumers but also unprofitable for marketers.

LIMITATIONS OF DEMOGRAPHIC DATA

Demographic data, by itself, do not explain consumer behavior. Demographic data do not consider the psychological or the social dimensions influencing consumers. Demographics have also failed to explain brand-choice behavior.[4] Obviously, there are undeniable demographic patterns to purchasing certain products. A single demographic measure, however, has not proven effective. Instead, when a number of demographic dimensions are combined, a more complete and useful profile can be constructed. Demographic measures do not identify changes in lifestyles or tastes. Segmentation variables alone cannot explain differences in product usage and preferences among people of the same age, sex, income, education, or even ethnic background. When used with behavioral data, demographics are useful for understanding purchasing behavior. With demographic data, a consumer is often classified into the segment of best fit and there are consumers in a segment who might overlap with those in another segment based on personal or market conditions.

The census of the U.S. population is taken every ten years and there are time lags between statistical updates. Unless companies close this gap and collect their own data, researchers are in danger of using obsolete data.

BEHAVIORISTIC SEGMENTATION

Behavioristic market segmentation is the division of consumers into groups based on their knowledge, attitudes, responses, or uses of a product. Buying situations vary depending upon the circumstances that the consumer finds at the time. Purchasing situations have an impact on product benefits sought, product usage, readiness to buy, and purchasing conditions of the moment.

Groups of purchasers have been traditionally identified on the basis of common demographic characteristics. In contrast, benefit segmentation uses causal factors on the supposition that buyers are really differentiated by the benefits they seek. An example of benefit segmentation is the toothpaste market. Toothpaste variations in packaging and use are present as some brands are dispensed from a pump while others from the traditional tube and some whiten teeth, remove stains, prevent cavities, and help control plaque. The children's market is targeted by offering such toothpaste flavors as vanilla. Each type of toothpaste gives a defined benefit to the user.

A particular product attribute, benefit feature, or a combination of these variables explains a positioning strategy. Crest toothpaste positions itself on a cavity-prevention benefit while Aim toothpaste is positioned as both pleasant tasting and cavity fighting. Aquafresh positions itself as a cavity fighter and also provides the benefit of fresh breath. Benefit segmentation is a strong strategy providing that not too many attributes are used so that consumers will not be confused or not believe the claims.

Benefit segmentation is related to purchase occasions, purchase intentions, and psychographics. Benefit segmentation strategy uncovers and ideally explains a cause-and-effect relationship that helps a marketer influence buyer behavior.

The limitations of benefit segmentation strategies include costs that can be exceedingly high in obtaining the services of trained specialists to conduct the analysis. Market segments must be recognizable and accessible to a firm's marketing efforts. Moreover, benefits must be identifiable and offer perceived value to the consumers.

PRODUCT USAGE

Product usage patterns can be used for market segmentation strategies and may also reveal lifestyle characteristics. The most common categories are heavy, medium, light, and nonuser. People who buy the brand over and over again show brand loyalty. This is the product's most important market segment and the most difficult for competitors to penetrate. To illustrate, individuals under age twenty-five spend more than twice the amount of other segments for tape recorders and players than the typical household.

When identifying a market based on usage situations, marketers are able to target different segments even when the customers are similar. For example, a market segment may be price sensitive in one situation, such as purchasing wine for everyday use, and price insensitive in another situation, such as purchasing wine for a special occasion. Therefore, inexpensive table wines may be offered for everyday consumption and more expensive wines for special occasions. It would be a mistake to view heavy users as product loyal. They tend to purchase heavily within a product class but frequently have little allegiance to individual products or brands. Moreover, heavy users do not necessarily make purchases for the same reasons.

Segmenting markets based on product usage can enable marketers to increase consumption among heavy, moderate, and light users. This strategy can also add to other approaches that direct themselves to behavioral and lifestyle analysis. Product usage segmentation as a single variable is difficult to explain by just using demographics. Thus, behavioral and lifestyle analysis are necessary to increase market segmentation precision.

PSYCHOGRAPHIC SEGMENTATION

Psychographic segmentation comprises personality, motivation, and lifestyle variables. It is difficult to accurately measure personality characteristics. Therefore, an approach which utilizes personality as an independent or predictor variable has not proven useful. Psychographic segmentation makes it possible to divide different markets on the basis of lifestyle and values. Market segments within the same demographic group can demonstrate different psychographic profiles. For example, Chrysler, in seeking to attract an upscale market, now appeals to golfers. Golfers have a very high average income, are usually multiple car owners, and are much more likely to purchase a new automobile than the average household. Consequently, Chrysler sponsors the Greensboro Scramble Golf Tournament.

Lifestyle is an important psychographic category composed of a combination of factors such as activities, interests, and opinions. Lifestyle patterns are changing. Marketers need to implement proactive strategies to satisfy these markets. New morning routines are creating opportunities for cereal companies. Many families, in which both spouses are employed outside the home, have long commutes and just getting the family off to school and work in the morning is a challenge. Many commuters skip breakfast or hold the steering wheel of an automobile with one hand and grasp a bagel, biscuit, muffin, or doughnut with the other hand while talking on the cell phone. General Mills and Quaker Oats have developed snacks in response to changing consumer lifestyle breakfast patterns. General Mills's Chex Mix and Quaker's Chewy Granola Bars have made inroads into the Kellogg's market share of the breakfast cereal market.[5]

GROUP DYNAMICS AND PURCHASING INFLUENCES

Group dynamics influence consumer behavior in many ways and specifically by the patterns of interaction among its members. Kurt Lewin, an authority on group behavior, stated that "the essence of a group is not the similarity or dissimilarity of its members but their interdependence."[6] Group behavior is based upon the premise that two or more individuals share a set of norms, values, or beliefs. A group may be defined as two or more people who interact to accomplish either individual or mutual goals.

Primary groups are characterized by face-to-face relationships among members. Examples are family, children's play groups, and community groups. These groups provide many of the individual's economic, social, and psychological needs. Secondary groups are larger, more impersonal, and interaction with other group members may be only occasional. Secondary groups include formal organizations, professional associations, and religious institutions. The critical distinction between primary and secondary groups is the perceived importance of each to the individual. The frequency of interaction may be an important variable. Work groups, for example, might serve as a major purchasing influence on their members.

Reference groups emerge from either primary or secondary groups. These groups serve as a frame of reference for individuals in their purchasing decisions. The norms and standards of the reference groups are used as a guide for the individual in developing his or her own consumer behavior patterns. These reference groups guide members' purchases and may be extended to formal social groups such as veterans and religious organizations or informal groups such as interior decorators, travel agents, doctors, and organizations such as Weight Watchers. It is important to ascertain whether the group is a reference group or a membership group for the individual.

The functions of reference groups help to develop the socialization process in individuals. That process makes individuals aware of the behavior and lifestyles of other group members. A second function of reference groups is a comparison function that allows for evaluation of one's self-concept. Reference groups can provide a normative function that is a device for obtaining compliance with societal norms. And, reference groups also serve as a source of product and/or brand-related information.

How consumers learn about group members' lifestyle behavior is important for marketers to understand. Internalized psychological variables such as motivation, attitudes, learning, and values play a significant role in understanding buyer behavior. The impact of socializing agents can change over time. Parents have substantial influence over children, but their influence diminishes as children grow older and interact more with their peers. When teenagers join a social group, they learn about how the group dresses, their athletic activities, and their recreational pursuits in addition to the group's values and norms. Another example involving learning, attitudes, values, and motivation would be when new residents of a neighborhood learn what their neighbors expect in the way of home maintenance, landscaping, interior decoration, and entertaining.

Reference groups provide a means of social comparison and are a motivating force for understanding lifestyle behavior patterns. This concept suggests that the individual's purchasing behavior be compared to other members of the reference groups. For example, manufacturers sell products such as "Ivy League suits" or "executive shoes." An individual may be influenced by a variety of reference groups. Furthermore, the normative function produces conformity among individuals to the approved patterns of behavior of the reference groups. Norms exist for both small and large groups and subcultural groups such as teenagers, singles and elderly people. Although the degree of influence may vary in particular situations, lifestyle-purchasing behavior can be swayed by group norms.

The importance of reference groups' influence varies among products and brands. Reference groups may have the greatest influence on lifestyle purchasing patterns when the product is envisioned as a luxury and its consumption is visible to others. Some products are highly susceptible to social influences such as wristwatches and automobiles. An important variable is the conspicuousness of the product which can be related to its visibility. The fewer consumers who own the product lends itself to an exclusivity benefit. Product visibility and exclusivity are determinants for high reference group influence. For example, golf clubs, snow skis, sailboats, automobiles, and diamond jewelry purchases are affected by lifestyle purchasing patterns. Some consumers will purchase a used BMW priced from $27,000 to $38,000 rather than purchase a new model of another brand priced from $38,000 to $56,000 just to own a BMW. In contrast, the purchase of a mattress or a trash compactor may have little group influence.

FORCES SHAPING AMERICAN LIFESTYLES

A core of attitudes and values can be used as the foundation for a framework to define market segments that may be significant to a product class. Lifestyle is a systems concept that both influences and is influenced by the market. There is a lifestyle hierarchy that is influenced by the relationship between culture and society, groups and individual expectations and values, lifestyle patterns and values, purchase decisions, and the market reaction of consumers. Although the basic relationships and variables often remain constant, specific parameters are constantly changing. These influences continue throughout a lifetime. A few of the current values and lifestyles that have characterized American culture have been conservation rather than consumption, childless marriages, single parenthood, single-person households, divorce, remarriage and extended families, dual-career families, a longer life span and working life, casual, more informal lifestyles, and a trade-off of leisure time for the opportunity to earn more money.

Values were once considered to be relatively permanent and passed from one generation to another within a culture. It has become increasingly apparent that some changes in values and lifestyles are occurring at an accelerating pace. Consider the transition from formal wear at work to "dress-down days." Brooks Brothers, once characterized by conservatism in dress, is currently walking a tightrope with their older customers who feared that this conservatism and personal service would end when the store tried to broaden their market appeal. After years of selling its famous button-down oxford shirts, purple gingham shirts and turquoise-striped ties were added to the product line. Brooks Brothers is trying to change an image of more than a hundred years to reflect changing lifestyles and values. Brooks Brothers originally missed out on the trend for apparel to be worn on casual days or dress-down days. However, Brooks Brothers now sells khaki pants, casual shirts, and selection of brightly colored shirts and ties to make its merchandise more appealing to a new generation with different values.

There is a temporal dimension that indicates a relationship between changes in cultural values, how it affects marketing strategy, and the various times and periods that it has encompassed. In the Brooks Brothers illustration related to dress-down days in the workforce, the temporal dimension not only shows a development of changes in cultural values, but reflects a marketing strategy developed to meet the needs of different ways of thinking and different times. It is becoming clear that organizations should give cultural influences much more consideration in the decision-making process.

Milton Rokeach defined values as centrally held and enduring beliefs that direct actions and judgments across specific situations and beyond immediate goals.[7] Values are shaped by culture and individuals adopt cultural values. Since the aftermath of World War II, cultural values have changed rapidly. World War II caused women in the United States to enter the workforce in large numbers, and in each decade the distinctions between the roles of men and women have grown less pronounced. There is a trend toward more liberal sexual attitudes reflected not only in the movies but in television programming as well.

Everyone is aware of the numbers: people are marrying later and having fewer children; more married people are getting divorced; and more women are in the workforce. The percentage of suburban households occupied by married couples has declined as the percentage of single-parent households and apartment dwellers has increased. Marriage and the family are important institutions that influence individual values and lifestyles. These values and lifestyles are manifest in purchasing expenditures. Since the marriage age is rising, consumers have increased financial resources and are more experienced purchasers. The increasing number of families with two incomes and the greater number of women in the workforce are causing socioeconomic changes that affect spending patterns. Marketers find that families with working wives welcome labor-saving appliances such as slow cookers, microwave ovens, and improved versions of these products. Moreover, working wives become more interested in life insurance, credit cards, rental cars, and travel. Family and household size have declined and single-person households have increased significantly. The growth of the singles market has provided marketing opportunities for the home furnishings industry. Elderly consumers are forging a new lifestyle in active retirement. As our society ages, the theme expressed is that one is as young as one feels. Today's customer, no matter what age, sex, or marital status, wants access to products and services twenty-four hours a day and seven days a week when they are at home, at work, or on the road.

The dynamic marketing environment is one of the most difficult dimensions of marketing to comprehend. Since marketing is eclectic, it is influenced by numerous events of a rapidly changing world. Demographics, economic conditions, culture, and legislation impact all business organizations. An uncontrollable external event such as the bombing of the World Trade Center and the Pentagon on September 11, 2001, triggered many changes in lifestyles for Americans. Many vacationers are eager to avoid air travel and long airport lines and are deciding that it is important to visit with family and friends closer to home. Therefore, there is increased demand for many traditional destinations such as Cape Cod, Massachusetts; Hilton Head, South Carolina; and Lake Tahoe, California–Nevada. Even less-traveled locations such as Ogunquit, Maine and Alligator Point, a Florida panhandle resort, are in demand as vacationers seek safety. How long this behavior will affect tourism remains to be seen.

VALUES AND LIFESTYLES

The values and lifestyle program (VALS), a consumer psychographic segmentation tool, was introduced in 1978 by SRI International, known today as SRI Consulting-Business Intelligence. VALS categorized consumers in the United States by their values, beliefs, and lifestyles rather than by traditional demographic variables. In 1988, VALS2 was introduced which is a more refined psychographic segmentation tool.

Changes in values, beliefs, and lifestyles have had a significant impact on consumer behavior. For example, the emphasis on various aspects of self-fulfillment has increased the markets for cosmetics and beauty aids, health clubs and tanning parlors, weight reduction products, and self-improvement courses. Alert marketers gain by responding to changes in values and lifestyles. Values change in response to generational changes and what is most important at a particular point in time. In contrast, attitudes and opinions change relatively quickly as there is an attempt to reconcile long-held values with new information. If marketers use values instead of attitudes to segment markets, recognition must be made that values do not predict all types of purchase behavior. Instead, values are best used to segment markets for durable goods such as houses and automobiles and symbolic products such as food and clothing. The use of value segmentation for lifestyle-defining activities such as vacation travel, and books and media selection is also beneficial.

David Riesman, in *The Lonely Crowd*, grouped people by major types of social behavior.[8] Inner-directed behavior ensures conformity by instilling early in life a propensity to follow an internalized set of goals. Other-directed behavior ensures conformity by instilling sensitivity to the expectations and preferences of others. The 1978 VALS system elaborated on Riesman's work by focusing on the consumer's state of mind instead of on demographic factors by using four core categories and nine subcategories. The four categories were as follows: the need-driven, who were primarily elderly, the young, and many female single head of households; the outer-directed who were composed of middle America and accounted for more than two-thirds of the adult population who desired social approval; and the inner-directed who purchased products that reflected their own inner needs; finally, there were the integrateds who had a good balance of outer-directedness and inner-directedness but constituted no more than 2 percent of the population.

The VALS2 typology classifies the American population into eight distinctive market segments. The objective of VALS2 was to correct outdated classifications. Changes were made to reflect the aging of the baby boomers, the greater diversity of ethnic groups, and greater media choices such as TV and interactive media. The VALS2 typology explains why and how consumers make purchase decisions. Emphasis is placed on self-orientation that reflects self-image and consumer resources that include educational background, self-confidence, income, and health. Generally, a blending of demographic and lifestyle factors are better for identifying potential market segments.

The most important tendencies of each segment are as follows:

- *Actualizers.* Successful, sophisticated, active, "take-charge people with high self-esteem." Purchases frequently demonstrate cultivated tastes for relatively upscale niche-oriented products. Sometimes guided by principle or to make a change. Image is important as an expression of taste. Possess a wide range of interests. Continue to seek challenges.
- *Fulfilleds.* Mature, satisfied, comfortable, reflective people who value order, knowledge, and responsibility. Conservative, practical consumers concerned with durability, functionality, and value in products. Leisure activities center on their homes. Their decisions are based on strongly held principles.
- *Achievers.* Successful, career and work-oriented. Value structure and predictability. Favor established products and services that reflect success. Social lives revolve around family, church, and work. Respect authority and the status quo.
- *Experiencers.* Impulsive, young, enthusiastic, and rebellious. Interested in exercise, sports, outdoor recreation, and social activities. A high percentage of income is allocated to clothing, fast food, music, movies, and video. Highly ambivalent about beliefs.

The most important tendencies of the four groups with fewer resources are as follows:

- *Believers.* Traditional and conservative beliefs. Favor established brands and familiar products. Follow established routines. Lives revolve around family, religious, and/or social organizations. Education and income are modest, but sufficient to satisfy needs. Tend to purchase American-made products.
- *Strivers.* Seek approval and are insecure. Try to emulate those with greater resources. Money may define success. Desire to be stylish. Easily bored and impulsive.
- *Makers.* Practical and self-sufficient. Desire products with a functional purpose such as tools, utility vehicles, and fishing equipment. Live in a traditional context and suspicious of new ideas.
- *Strugglers.* Elderly, low-skilled, and are concerned about health. Loyal to favorite brands, but represent a modest market for most products and services.

Values and purchasing behavior vary among market segments. To illustrate, achievers tend to have a high purchase rate of imported wine and their activities reflect visiting museums and galleries. In contrast, the strugglers are not a market for imported wine and show little interest in museum activities. Lifestyle categories are not applicable to all situations. For example, food preferences of consumers might be categorized as diet concerned, sophisticated consumers, or natural-food enthusiasts. Market segments can be defined by the products that consumers currently use or need. A market segment must have a characteristic that distinguishes the market segment from the overall market—for example, a certain market segment might want pollution-control equipment. A market segment must also be measurable. This means that the market potential should be of significant size and possess sufficient purchasing power to be profitable to a company. Once a market segment has been identified and measured, the next factor is whether it is accessible. The market segment should be reachable through distribution, pricing, or promotion efforts. Finally, the market segment should favorably respond to a specialized need or benefit for that segment.

There has been an effort to link products and brands with the relationships between attributes, benefits, and values referred to as mean-end chain theory.[9] Volkswagen has been praised for demonstrating how the Beetle can offer fun and excitement, which is a consumer value, and also showing how the Beetle can be agile and lively, which are product benefits. This theme developed in their advertising campaign has made it difficult for competing brands to use similar positioning and a competitive advantage has been created.[10]

Perrier: A Case Study

One of the most important changes in the soft drink industry has been the decline of diet drinks and colas. Many consumers are becoming more health-conscious and favor drinking bottled water. Coca-Cola and Pepsico did not foresee changes in consumer behavior patterns and allowed Perrier and the bottled water industry to gain a foothold in the soft drink industry.

Perrier has successfully used a product positioning strategy to capture a larger share of the soft drink market. Perrier positioned its product in consumers' minds as an alternative to soft drinks. A product's position is the complex association of perceptions, impressions, and feelings that consumers maintain for the product as compared to competing products. For Perrier to accomplish its objectives, the product had to be sold to supermarkets and displayed in the same aisle as soft drinks. Previously, Perrier was sold only in health food and gourmet shops. Perrier managed to overcome obstacles to motivate independent soft drink bottlers and beer distributors throughout the United States to distribute Perrier and continually replenish store shelves.

Perrier is now marketed with natural flavor in variations of lemon, lime, orange, and berry. The product is calorie-free and natural. Perrier is competing with soft drinks by offering flavored water. Perrier has met the consumer need for convenience by also making the product available in cans that can be taken to work, picnics, or consumed at poolside. Perrier is environmentally responsible by providing glass and plastic bottles that are recyclable. The world of the one perfect soft drink for everyone is gone. The bottled water industry has come a long way since Canada Dry started marketing water as a mixer in other drinks in the early 1980s. Bottled water sales have tripled in the past ten years to $5.7 billion in 2000. And, women constitute the majority of bottled water drinkers.

ALTERNATE APPROACH

An alternative to VALS is the List of Values (LOV), which was developed at the University of Michigan Research Center. Nine values including self-respect, security, warm relationships with others, sense of accomplishment, self-fulfillment, sense of belonging, being well-respected, fun and enjoyment in life, and excitement were defined. Researchers disagree as to which approach, VALS or LOV, is superior in certain situations.[11] Marketers find VALS2 a useful tool in market segmentation, new product development, and in preparing advertising campaigns. For example, identification of heavy, medium, and light users can be applied to VALS2 profiles which was done with two brands in the ibuprofen analgesic category. It was found that Advil was favored most by experiencers and Nuprin by achievers.

It is unlikely that the market for any particular product can be segmented on the basis of the value system alone. The value system, rather than a single value, will provide a more complete understanding of buyer motivation. The integration of LOV and VALS2 is more effective when used along with demographic data.

Another alternate lifestyle segmentation approach is geodemographic segmentation. The underlying thesis is that people who live in close proximity to one another are likely to have similar financial means, tastes, consumption habits, and lifestyles. Neighborhoods based upon postal zip codes are classified into lifestyle groupings. Cluster data can then be used for direct-mail campaigns and to select sites for retailers. Marketing strategies can then be developed.

This technique is useful if the market segment in terms of lifestyle is isolated rather than composed of a broad cross-section of consumers.

Geodemographics is one of the most promising developments in multi-attribute segmentation by the market research firm Claritas, Inc. and uses a rating index by zip code markets, referred to as PRIZM. This grouping employs thirty-nine factors in five broad categories: (1) education and affluence, (2) family life cycle, (3) urbanization, (4) race and ethnicity, and (5) mobility. To illustrate, one of the PRIZM clusters has the title, Cashmere and Country Club. This title includes the aging baby boomers that live in the suburbs and are likely to buy a Mercedes. They would be likely to subscribe to *Golf Digest*, use salt substitutes, enjoy European getaways, and buy high-end television sets. Median income is over $65,000.[12]

MANAGING CHANGE

An effective market segmentation strategy can be developed when demographics are used in conjunction with psychographic and lifestyle data. To illustrate, in tracing changing cultural values and lifestyles, marketers must recognize the importance of subcultures based upon social class, ethnic origin, race, age, and geographic location. Subcultural values assimilated by society frequently provide market opportunities. The current interest in ethnic and health foods is an example of marketers responding to changing cultural, behavioral, and demographic patterns.

Traditional market segmentation research has performed an inadequate job in targeting consumers. Lifestyle market segmentation research has closed many gaps, but inadequacies still exist. For example, in 2001 many consumers had lost money in the stock market and were still recovering from the devastation of the World Trade Center and Pentagon terrorists acts. Yet consumers continued to spend by buying new cars that reflected flash, glamour, and luxury such as the Chrysler Sebring Convertible, the Mercedes-Benz CLK, and the Cadillac Escalade SUV with sales up respectively 287, 76, and 169 percent.[13]

Nearly one in four American adults lives by a new set of values.[14] This market segment is referred to as "cultural creatives" and tends to be affluent, well-educated, and believe in environmentalism, feminism, global issues, and spiritual searching. This group is more likely than average to live on the West Coast and to be on the cutting edge of social change. More women than men are found in this market segment. Cultural creatives tend to buy more books and magazines than the average consumer and read periodicals such as *Consumer*

Reports. They do gourmet and ethnic cooking, and try natural and health foods.

Today's consumers are driven by four fundamental core values.[15] The first core value is the shrinking American day as many are endeavoring to cope with time-crunched lifestyles. Many consumers will try to reduce time expended on unpleasant tasks such as housework and spend more time on pleasant activities such as dining out. The purchase of brand names will make buying decisions faster and easier. There will be an almost relentless pursuit of free time. Various consumer market segments will desire the best and fastest service, and forgo much comparison shopping. The desire to simplify lifestyles will be an important consideration.

The second core value is referred to as the connectedness craze. Consumers will turn to the Internet as a source of information, as a method of contacting sellers of merchandise, services, friends, and family. The Internet will not necessarily become a mass medium, but rather a niche medium. The interactive features of the Internet will be used to satisfy very specific, individualized needs. The use of computers or an Internet-accessing appliance in households, or a hand-held PC away from the home will become a way of life facilitating access to a college degree and medical, financial, and entertainment information. Computer use will also allow payment for purchases and the negotiation of buying terms between buyer and seller.

The third core value is known as the body versus soul uncertainty. Paradox will pervade the beginning of the twenty-first century. Consumers will enjoy eating nonfat cookies and at the same time consume rich premium ice cream. Consumers will continue on a fitness agenda but also buy junk food. More time will be allocated for home enjoyment, but consumers will desire the outside world to provide more entertainment. A higher value will be placed on the spiritual things as consumers search to satisfy physical pleasures.

The fourth core value is the triumph of individualism. Marketers will no longer just target a woman, but instead a single mom, an ethnic minority, a buyer of full-size fashions, a bicycling enthusiast, and a purchaser of mutual funds. Individualism will also encompass ethnic markets. The Hispanic market with their own tastes and preferences will double in size. Moreover, fashion trends will be driven by the expansion of ethnic markets. Furthermore, the elderly consumer market with its significant increase in size will not only dictate fashion trends but will influence the lifestyles relating to continuing education, vacation, travel, and financial services.

The twenty-first century has presented important change processes that affected buyer behavior. Market-oriented firms that support active dialogue with customers will further lifestyle market segmentation strategies. To illustrate, Internet companies such as Amazon.com have adapted well to the new customer. The company recommends books based on the buyers' previous purchases and on other customers who have bought similar books. As preferences change, Amazon makes suggestions to reflect these changes. A customer's search for information to make decisions can be managed as Microsoft has e-mail and Hotmail services for more than 30 million subscribers. Co-creating personalized experiences is a strategy as firms aim toward microsegmentation—namely, the market of one. Customers have already become co-creators for such products as greeting cards and flower arrangements by selecting from a menu of features. Organizational flexibility becomes the thrust as firms endeavor to satisfy changing customer desires.[16] Market segmentation research is designed to identify market segments within a larger market and to recognize the needs and wants of one or more groups so that the marketing mix can be directed toward the satisfaction of their needs. The study of buyer behavior is helpful in learning about the characteristics that consumers exhibit in searching for, purchasing, and evaluating the goods and services they seek. The study of buyer behavior is interdisciplinary. It is based upon disciplines such as psychology, sociology, social psychology, cultural anthropology, and economics. Buyer behavior has been intertwined with both market segmentation and lifestyle market segmentation strategies.

NOTES

1. Emanuel H. Demby, "Psychographics Revisited: The Birth of a Technique," *Marketing News*, 2 January 1989, 21.

2. Joan Raymond, "The Multicultural Report," *American Demographics* 23 (November 2001): 3–7.

3. Jack A. Lesser and Marie A. Hughes, "The Generalizability of Psychographic Market Segments Across Geographic Locations," *Journal of Marketing* 50 (January 1986): 18–27; and Michael R. Hyman, "Long-Distance Geographic Mobility and Retailing Attitudes and Behavior: An Update," *Journal of Retailing* 63 (Summer 1987): 187–204.

4. Jagdish N. Sheth, "Demographics in Consumer Behavior," *Journal of Business Research* 5 (June 1977): 129–138.

5. Keith Naughton, "Crunch Time at Kellogg," *Business Week*, 14 February 2000, 52–53.

6. Kurt Lewin, *Resolving Social Conflicts* (New York: Harper and Row, 1948), 54.

7. Milton J. Rokeach, *Beliefs, Attitudes, and Values* (San Francisco: Jossey Bass, 1968), 161.

8. David Riesman, Nathan Glazer, and Revel Denney, *The Lonely Crowd* (New Haven, Conn.: Yale University Press, 1950).

9. Marco Vriens and Frenkel Ter Hofstede, "Linking Attributes, Benefits and Consumer Values," *Marketing Research* 12 (Fall 2000): 4–10.

10. D. Welch, "VW: Now That's How to Rebuild a Brand," *Business Week*, 19 June 2000, 216.

11. Wagner A. Kamukwa and Thomas P. Novak, "Value System Segmentation: Explaining The Meaning of LOV," *Journal of Consumer Research* 19 (June 1992): 119–132; and Thomas P. Novak and Bruce MacEvoy, "On Company Alternative Segmentation Schemes: The List of Values (LOV) and Values and Life Styles (VALS)," *Journal of Consumer Research* 17 (June 1990): 105–109.

12. Christina De Valle, "They Know Where You Live—and How You Buy," *Business Week*, 7 February 1994, 89.

13. Sholnn Freeman and Karen Lundegaard, "Behind the Buying Binge," *The Wall Street Journal*, 9 November 2001, W1, 16.

14. Paul H. Ray, "The Emerging Culture," *American Demographics* 19 (February 1997): 29–34, 56.

15. Annetta Miller, "The Millenial Mind-Set," *American Demographics* 21 (January 1999): 60–65.

16. C. K. Prahalad and Venkatrom Ramaswamy, "Co-opting Customer Competence," *Harvard Business Review* 78 (January–February 2000): 79–87.

CHAPTER 2

Lifestyles and Decision Making

Lifestyles emerge from various social influences. They are also derived from the individual's personal value system and personality. Marketers need to study the way consumers live and spend their money as well as how they make purchase decisions. For example, blue jeans may serve as inexpensive, functional clothing to blue-collar workers, but as fashionable, self-expressive apparel to upper-class members. Credit cards may be used as a convenience for the affluent, while others use them as a basis for installment purchases since balances are not paid off immediately. Decisions emanating from lifestyles are learned as the result of many influences such as culture, subcultures, social class, reference groups, and family. Activities, interests, and opinions reflect how consumers spend their time and their beliefs on various social, economic, and political issues. When understood by marketers, these variables can help reduce risk in the decision-making process.

Perception plays a major part in the perceived risk of purchasing a product or service. Perceived risk represents the anxieties felt because the buyer cannot anticipate the results of a purchase. A number of different strategies may be used to reduce risk. First, perceived risk can be reduced by a prepurchase information search—by decreasing the probability of failure. Second, the buyer can shift from one type of perceived risk to another type that is of less impact on the realization of objectives if this method fails. Third, the purchase transaction can be postponed, thus delaying a situation of risk. Fourth, the purchase can be made and the risk absorbed.

How the individual consumer utilizes risk-reduction methods depends partly upon personality and lifestyle variables. The types of perceived risk are time loss, hazard loss, ego loss, and money loss. Time loss involves repairs of merchandise or adjustments in quantities or styles. Hazard loss has a direct relationship to either the loss of health or safety of the buyer. Ego loss occurs if the product does not work properly and others perceive the purchase as a foolish expenditure or an error in judgment. Money loss is a loss due to the improper operation of the product or due to the overexpectation of potential results. Since each perceived loss varies in intensity, a shift from one type of risk to another depends upon the circumstances.

Product endorsements, testimonials, the use of private testing organizations, product ratings, and money-back guarantees and warranties are among the risk relievers that marketers use. If the product is relatively small in size and inexpensive, free samples might be given or mailed to consumers. Brand name is important, particularly when the product has been used previously and has been found satisfactory. Some buyers purchase only well-known brands because they rely on their established reputations. Word-of-mouth, brand image, and store image are important variables that, if positive, increase consumer loyalty. These variables—requiring or maintaining brand awareness, perceived quality and functionality, and positive association—are used to strengthen brand loyalty. Consumer brand loyalty allows marketers to easily launch brand extensions of products because the brand name carries recognition and credibility. Marketers will also have more leverage in bargaining with distributors and retailers since customers will demand the brand. Gap stores now features its name on soap, shampoo, spray perfume, and other products. Honda uses its name on automobiles, motorcycles, snow blowers, and lawn mowers.

Attitudes are shaped by demographics, perception, learning, social factors, and personality. Marketers try to develop positive consumer attitudes toward their products and brands. Attitudes represent feelings toward an object stemming from opinions and beliefs. Consequently consumers develop opinions and beliefs about products and their attributes as well as about retail stores where they shop.

Attitudes reflect the decision whether to buy a specific product or service and the selection of a particular brand. One of the best-known approaches to relating attitudes to buyer behavior is used by the Survey Research Center at the University of Michigan. Consumer spending intentions for large-value items are analyzed. For example, consumers are asked if they have a definite intention to buy, a probable intention to buy, an undecided intention to buy, or a definite intention not to buy a new automobile, home, or a major appliance over a definite period of time. The results are interpreted in items of short-run demand for consumer durable-goods spending.

Attitudes are often difficult to change, but marketers may be able to accomplish attitude change through communications, particularly if buyers' perceptions about the brand are incorrect. Buyers' attitudes toward brands are important because these attitudes do influence consumer behavior. Attitude change revolves around changing the motivational function associating the product with a special group or event or changing beliefs about competitors' brands. The functional approach is a theory that shows how modifying basic motivations can change attitudes. Consumers today develop new attitudes as the Internet, new technology, and environmental trends change or modify their beliefs and the importance they attach to product attributes such as speed, convenience, and ease of use.

SELF-CONCEPT

The way individuals see themselves and the way they believe others see them is called the self-concept. The self-concept affects the choice of lifestyles and, consequently, influences the consumer's purchase-decision process. More simply, the self-concept is the individual's perception of oneself and denotes subjective rather than objective analysis.[1] Although the self-concept may change over time, the consumer gains identity which will provide for consistent and coherent behavior through a indeterminate time-span depending upon the individual.[2] Self-image has four components. First, there is the real self, or the way individuals actually are. Second, there is the way that others perceive the individual. Frequently, this is referred to as the "looking-glass self." Third, there is the way the individual would like to be. This goal may or may not be viewed realistically and is called the ideal self. Fourth, the way the individual sees him or herself is referred to as the self-image. It is a combination of the real self and the ideal self. Self-image is learned largely from social interaction. Perception is the core of self-identification. For example, jewelry and apparel can manifest symbolic expression within ourselves. These symbols may reflect our worth as a person, help to achieve a mood and send symbolic messages to others. Within the self-concept are a variety of motives such as the desire for love, power, achievement, status, or symbols that represent wealth or beauty. Marketers need to capitalize on self-image theory by designing products and promotional campaigns that establish a product image in accord with the self-image of the consumer. This may be reflected in an advertising campaign that shows positive change in the individual brought about by an exercise program.

When implementing a self-concept strategy in marketing campaigns, efforts were made to associate self-concept with work. This strategy worked when targeting baby boomers but not Generation X. Generation Xers do not necessarily have a self-concept that is fully associated with their work. Self-fulfillment comes only partly from the workplace.[3] There may be a shift in product preferences between the ideal self-concept and the actual self-concept. For example, a male baby boomer may purchase comfortable but not fashionable apparel to wear at home on weekends but also buy expensive high fashion exercise clothing, envisioning himself as a young active mobile man. This same individual may drive an old pick-up truck weekends but a foreign sports car to work.

LIFESTYLE GENERATIONAL MARKET SEGMENTATION

Among the most attractive market segments of the 1990s were the yuppies, Generation X, and Generation Y, because each segment depicts variations in lifestyle. The baby boomers and yuppies were born between 1946 and 1964 and account for 40 percent of the total adult population. Baby boomers number approximately over 70 million and yuppies compose about 3.5 million of the population. "Yuppies" is an acronym for young, urban professionals who are well-educated college graduates interested in their personal fulfillment.[4] Yuppies are an attractive market because of their affluence. They participate more in physical fitness activities, utilize convenience products and services, are interested in satisfying their personal needs regardless of price, and are emotionally secure relying on themselves. They tend to be materialistic and desire the best of everything. At the same time, they value home and family and have a strong concern for work and career. Baby boomers are a lucrative market segment because of their market size and their demand for goods and services. Baby boomers are living longer due to advances in medicine. The Yuppie market segment can be divided into segments such as the following:

- *Satisfied Selves.* Optimistic about life, receptive to new ideas and experiences.
- *Contented Traditionalists.* Conservative, home-oriented, and concerned about the impact of social change.
- *Worried Traditionalists.* Poor self-image, insecure about their employment and very upset about the increasing crime rate.

- *Sixties in the Eighties.* Have a relatively lower standard of living than the yuppies and tend to lead a casual life.

The lifestyles of the people who comprise each segment are an important consideration. The extent of their purchasing power and their decision-making process in allocating their discretionary income are of paramount concern. Generation segmentation is pursued further by marketers targeting Generation X. Generation Xers were born from 1965 to 1975 and are more interested in tennis shoes and camping equipment than in BMWs or ocean-front condos. There are individuals within Generation X who have feelings of alienation because of the tight job market when they entered the workforce. The intensity of this alienation varies from individual to individual, but nonetheless income levels tend to be below expectations and some believe that they will not be able to match or surpass their parents' level of success. These feelings of alienation are translated into consumption patterns that include rap, hard rock music, and the "grunge" look which includes earrings, body piercing, and tattoos. Generation X is a diverse group and certainly not all of them identify or have such strong feelings of alienation.[5] Generation X came of age during the country's longest economic boom and were part of the dot-com revolution. Many Generation Xers have old-fashioned goals and would prefer to spend their careers with their current companies rather than job hop. They rate companionship, a loving family, and enjoying life as important.

Baby boomers have a tendency to drink Scotch while Generation Xers are more likely to drink Tequila. Generation Xers are more likely to remain single longer than the baby boomers and are able to accumulate more savings before marriage. They tend to spend more on recreation instead of furniture. Generation Xers are typically cynical about hard-sell marketing campaigns. Members of Generation X take pride in their purchasing sophistication compared to baby boomers.

The third group is Generation Y who was born between 1976 and 1994 and is sometimes referred to as the Internet Generation, the Echo Boomers, or the dot-com Generation. This generation already numbers over 73 million and has money to spend. Some of the most successful brands of the past such as Levi's, Nike, and Pepsi are not in favor with this market segment. Generation Yers prefer brands such as Mudd, Cement, and Paris Blues. For this market segment, magazines such as *Sports Illustrated* and *Seventeen* have heavy competition from *YM* and other niche magazines.

Generation Y favors L. L. Bean, J. Crew, Motorola Flex Pagers, and Mountain Dew. Generation Y is comfortable with computers and wireless technology. For this market segment digital technology is no more challenging than the use of a toaster. Fashion trends that used to spread slowly have accelerated rapidly. Hilfiger jeans are now the brand replacing Levi's of an earlier generation. This generation prefers very baggy jeans, power beads, and the Backstreet Boys. Marketers with established brands can no longer rest on their laurels and are racing to communicate via the Internet with the largest generation since the baby boomers.[6]

Buyer behavior and the decision-making process is not necessarily confined to a single individual. Instead, various family members, friends, or coworkers may be involved. One or more individuals may assume the role of an information gatherer. Others may take the role of an influencer. Another individual might assume the role of purchaser and someone else might actually use the product or service. Consumer behavior involves decisions about what to acquire, use, or discard. The reasons to buy or dispose of a product vary in complexity depending upon the price, the frequency of use, and a host of other factors. When to make the purchase and where to make the purchase are other considerations. Additional dimensions of complexity are the buyer's cultural environment and psychological behavior.

MARKETING STRATEGIES

Modern marketing strategy includes segmenting, targeting, and positioning. The determination of a target market is the first step in developing a marketing strategy. This decision depends in part on the options available to the marketer. These options range from the use of mass marketing strategies to targeting one or more segments as illustrated by formulating different marketing programs for the yuppies and Generations X and Y market segments. Firms are finding it increasingly unprofitable to use mass marketing in today's markets.

Positioning strategy is linked to lifestyle market segmentation. Positioning is the process of distinguishing a company or product from competitors along such dimensions as product characteristics or values that are meaningful to consumers. For example, Dior is positioned as a French designer. Positioning strategy aids customers in evaluating product attributes that are of significance or value to them. Mitsubishi, for example, has positioned its vehicles as more attractively styled than competing makes.

A firm differentiates itself from competitors by competitive advantage. Michael Porter, a recognized authority on competitive strategy, refers to this process as the value chain.[7] Porter maintained that every organization is a collection of activities that are directed to design, produce, market, deliver, and support its products. Value, in competitive terms, is the amount that consumers are willing to pay for the bundle of products and services provided. For example, service activities such as installation, repair, parts supply, and product adjustment would be useful in formulating a competitive strategy. Differences in customer needs, if based upon lifestyle analysis, could strengthen competitive strategy. Value-chain analysis helps marketers to separate the fundamental activities a firm performs in designing, producing, marketing, and distributing its products or services. A competitive advantage that can be used in positioning strategy can then be developed from these activities. To illustrate, Volvo offers durability and Jaguar offers elegant styling.

Diversity of lifestyles in the 1960s, 1970s, and especially in the 1980s were notable market changes. The 1990s was a period for marketers to reconsider and develop new strategies to satisfy appropriate target markets. The first decade of the new millennium will be the age of niche marketing as organizations endeavor to satisfy small, but lucrative markets with special needs. Already, the toy industry with retailers such as Zany Brainy are utilizing niche strategies in the educational toy market. Lance was the first major snack food manufacturer to follow a niche strategy by providing consumers with a large assortment of cholesterol-free, low-cholesterol, fat-free, and low-fat products. This innovation in strategy, appealing to consumers with special lifestyle needs, has helped Lance to successfully compete with Frito-Lay, Borden, and Nabisco.

Changes in roles of women and men, blurring lifestyles, and changes in racial integration and attitudes have significantly modified marketing strategies. The rise in the divorce rate with accompanying extended families, openly gay and lesbian relationships, and a significant increase in cohabiting arrangements are among the trends taking place. Society is now more tolerant about sexuality and sexual fulfillment. There has been a rise in the number of people who are able to work at home. It is likely that most of this proclivity for social diversity, which will shape new marketing strategies, will continue in the years ahead. Even in the investment world, profits for the good of society have been intertwined as socially responsible mutual funds have been established.

Many marketing opportunities can be identified and developed from lifestyle analysis. For example, the manufacturer of Porsche automobiles targeted those people who were considered achievers and who had established for themselves extraordinarily high personal and professional goals. Brooks Brothers has used a lifestyle-based marketing strategy to convey conservatism and good taste for

over a hundred years. In recent years, the use of lifestyle analysis
has increased as marketers realize its vast potential.

LIFESTYLE TRENDS AND BUYER BEHAVIOR

A lifestyle priority system can be developed that shows the relationship between culture and society, group and individual expectations and values, purchase decisions, and the market reaction of
consumers.

The following is a list of lifestyle trends that characterize American buyer behavior:

- Cross-Shopping
- Increased Affluence
- Poverty of Time
- Life Simplification Desires

Marketers can better understand consumer behavior by studying
these trends to identify product and service opportunities. These
trends must also be considered in developing marketing programs.

Cross-Shopping

A new consumer phenomenon has developed that has had a profound impact on specialty store and department store retailing and brand
marketing which is referred to as cross-shopping. Cross-shopping means
wearing a Liz Claiborne blouse purchased at Neiman-Marcus and a
pair of Levi's jeans purchased at Sears. Cross-shopping behavior is a
distinct lifestyle trend.

The new consumer is better educated and has developed clearer
buying objectives that facilitate cross-shopping. Higher educational
levels coupled with higher incomes allow consumers to spend more
time assessing the quality of products before purchasing. This accounts for the popularity of off-price retailers such as Loehmann's
and Marshalls. Cross-shopping behavior accounts for the purchase
of a virtually look-alike turtleneck sweater at Wal-Mart instead of at
Banana Republic. Gap, with their Old Navy division, is the first specialty apparel retailer to make a concentrated attempt to meet the
cross-shopping challenge by taking market share away from the mass
merchants and discounters such as Wal-Mart, Target, Sears, and J.C.
Penney.

Consumers often want to purchase store-label fashion merchandise. This was not always the case as in previous years consumers
had expressed preference for manufacturers' national brands. Mass

merchants such as J.C. Penney have reduced their inventories of designer labels such as Ralph Lauren and have placed their own labels on clothing. The reason is that many designer-labeled products are now available at much lower prices in stores such as Target, thus encouraging cross-shopping behavior. Since many more merchants and discounters carry designer label brands, cross-shopping has been accentuated. For cross-shoppers it is quite common to purchase scarves at Lord & Taylor and Martha Stewart lounge chairs at Kmart.

The majority of the American population is middle-aged and growing older. As consumers grow older, more self-confidence is manifested, and there is less impulse shopping and less of a fashion orientation. This diminished fashion orientation is reflected, in part, with casual dress workdays in industry. The result has been a growing polarization that favors the low-margin, mass volume retailers on one end and high-prices, haute-service boutiques offering one-of-a-kind or unusual items on the other. Cross-shopping or polarization will cause difficulty for the Gap, The Limited, Benetton, Ann Taylor, and other merchants in the middle unless the threat is successfully addressed. Cross-shopping will increase in the future as consumers are presented with more shopping options. Price competition will mount as consumers navigate the system and make more value purchases.

The Age of Affluence

America has gone through an income revolution that has created a redistribution of wealth.[8] Many families that owned one automobile became two- and three-car families. Home ownership rose as the population relocated to the suburbs. Salaries continued to outpace inflation until the mid-1970s. Soaring double-digit inflation by the mid-1970s found society attempting to adjust to lowered expectations. Families found they could only afford to purchase used cars instead of new ones, home ownership became for many a distant dream. The 1980s found a resurgence in baby births affecting income. Many career-oriented women became more concerned about their careers encroaching upon their childrearing abilities but still entered the workforce. The 1990s demonstrated a sharp contrast between double income families and single income families. Many families enjoyed material goods that were once out of reach. These double income families adopted new lifestyles that not only reflected added wealth but also a poverty of time. The purchase of time-saving products such as wireless communication devices and laptop computers were symbols of the 1990s.

The affluent market is not necessarily a single market segment. Wealth is spread among many niches including the older baby boomers, double income families with and without children, and those families who have been very successful in their careers. These groups are broad markets but can be divided into niche markets. For example, Michelin Tires and Calvin Klein clothes focus on the upper-end market segment, consumers who desire top quality and are not price-sensitive.

The older baby boomers, who were born in 1946, came of age in a period when it was easy to begin a career and afford a home. Older baby boomers can now be characterized as middle-aged, established family members with a number of automobiles and at least one mortgage. This market segment is important to marketers because of their numbers, wealth, and departure from established lifestyles. There are fifty-year-old baby boomers wheeling strollers and some who are retiring early, often cashing in on past investments. This market segment is better educated than previous generations and is expected to inherit more wealth than in previous history. There are products that have specifically addressed the needs of baby boomers. Many boomers, for example, grew up wearing jeans and desire to continue this practice. Since waistlines have expanded with age, companies have introduced larger sizes with different styles to conform to the middle-aged physique.

Many baby boomers are obsessed with aging and desire to maintain a youthful appearance. Consequently, many boomers monitor waistlines and diets. Boomers are good prospects for spas, health clubs, cosmetics, beauty salons, vitamins, and health foods. Gray-haired men and women are used as models in television commercials to sell cars, dishwashers, soap, cooking oil, and laundry bleach. Manufacturers are trying to develop products aimed at this market for removing wrinkles or easing baldness. Baby boomers have an active lifestyle and are increasingly the buyers of leisure products and services such as educational seminars, travel and sporting goods, and recreational equipment. Baby boomers might be differentiated by subgroups based upon age from 1946 to 1951, 1951 to 1956, and other five-year periods. Boomers in these subgroups share common life experiences or events that might be useful in targeting these groups. Therefore, the oldest and the youngest baby boomers would appear to have the most differences and would likely require different marketing programs.

Ben & Jerry's ice cream company, founded by two baby boomer bohemians, expresses a lifestyle that blends with the corporate establishment. This merged lifestyle of boomers has been expressed by corporations like Apple and Gap which cite Gandhi and Jack

Kerouac (an author who successfully depicted the drug age in his books, *On The Road* and *Dharma Bums*, first published in the late-1950s) in their advertisements. Ben & Jerry's has directed many of its appeals to a market segment that is concerned with ecological environmental challenges. For example, the proceeds from its Rain Forest Crunch ice cream flavor went to save the Amazon. Aware of environmental concerns, Ben & Jerry's packing materials are recycled. Ben & Jerry's constructed a water treatment plant in 1989 and is also noted for its energy conservation within the manufacturing process. The corporate structure is still the antithesis of the large corporate bureaucracy since fun and a laid-back atmosphere are promoted and encouraged even though Ben & Jerry's is now part of Unilever.

The baby boomers have established a mixed-up lifestyle as bankers sit in coffee houses listening to alternative music while others are dominated by a culture that is both bourgeois and bohemian. The Yuppie attitudes of the1980s have merged with the hippie attitudes of the 1960s. Thus, the culture reflects the Woodstock 1960s, the Reagan 1980s, and attitudes toward work, sex, pleasure, ambition, and even God and Buddha are shaped by these historical periods. The antimaterialistics are now submerged in stock options and the bohemian world of creativity. Now it is management that talks about changing the status quo and thinking outside the box.

Toy manufacturers and retailers have established a niche to satisfy the affluent baby boomers who are well educated and desire to purchase toys that promote creativity and learning in their children. A niche is a narrowly defined group whose needs are generally not well served. Niche marketers and retailers presumably understand this small market so well and serve the market so well that customers are willing to pay a premium. Zany Brainy and Noodle Kidoodle were the retail innovators of the 1990s. Zany Brainy established its first store in 1991 and Noodle Kidoodle in 1993. Both chains competed directly with one another and carried creative and nonviolent children's products, such as toys, books, games, video and audiotapes, computer software, crafts, and learning products. Instrumental to the success of each organization was the selection of its locations. Zany Brainy selected sites in southern New Jersey, suburban Philadelphia, and Washington, D.C., while Noodle Kidoodle situated itself in northern New Jersey, Long Island, Connecticut, Texas, Oklahoma, Florida, and the Boston, Chicago, and Detroit metropolitan areas. The recent merger of the two firms, now named Zany Brainy, has given added strength to the sale of educational toys.

Although niche stores provide a unique selling message, niche strategies also present special challenges. Zany Brainy has worked with manufacturers to create toys that develop intelligence and promote creativity such as building toys and puzzles. Zany Brainy cannot compete with Toys "R" Us on the basis of price. If Zany Brainy is to succeed, there must be customer-relationship building and exceptional service. This relationship building is a key strategy. A staff of former teachers and learning specialists are in the stores to provide insights on product selection. The stores provide superior customer service while providing an entertaining shopping environment through interactive play areas and frequent in-store events.

The age of affluence is here. Yesterday many households possessed only one telephone, and perhaps not even a single computer. Tomorrow, there will be household ownership of multiple computers situated in different rooms, fax machines, and high-definition television sets. Galbraith coined the phrase "the affluent society" and many consumers spend more time shopping than reading. Many affluent consumers have a crazed impulse to acquire material goods and the malls and stores have become instruments of this indulgence. The affluent consumer takes joy in spending.

Baby boomers have also adopted a long-term concern with health that they can afford. Boomers strive for lifelong fitness; the ability to remain active, alert, and independent even as aging advances. Many boomers pay for personal trainers. They will eat more health-oriented goods and desire cleaner air. Many boomers will hold memberships at gyms and choose healthful activities such as walking.

The Role of Women

There has been an expanding role for women in business, government, entertainment, fashion, finance, health care, sports, and theology. Trends reflecting job sharing, flex time, and the growing use of professional women on part-time assignments will encourage and increase opportunities for women. Computers will allow women to complete their assignments while working at home.

The period from 1960 to the beginning of the twenty-first century was notable for the changes in lifestyles that it promoted for women. During this period, the role of women has changed rapidly and we have seen the dramatic rise of women in the workforce as they enter, in increasing numbers, professions such as accounting, law, medicine, and health care. The blurring of traditional female and male roles has prompted marketers to reconsider and develop new strategies in the way products and services are marketed.

The central values of women's emancipation do appear to be in opposition to family values. Underlying the women's movement is the development of individualism, which is in contrast to family values that subordinate individual interests to those of the group. It has become more difficult to reconcile the needs of the family with the development of women's individuality. For example, self-fulfillment develops when a working wife believes that a reward of special vacations and other luxuries are needed for working hard. Career women prize the advancement of themselves as individuals and secondary are the needs of the family, which has been the case for men in the workforce. Because these values are a paradox and conflict with traditional values, some career women decide to temporarily leave their careers in order to support and maintain the family.

The pace of life is more stressful with the advent of new media, more two-income families, random violence in educational institutions, domestic terrorism, and a political climate that has challenged many traditional values. As the pace of life changes, women are increasingly making buying decisions that were once made jointly with husbands or by the husband alone. This larger role is a reflection of the gains made by women in education and the emergence of economically independent women. It is also a reflection of new living arrangements that emphasize the role of women as household heads. As more women opt for the workforce, they make increased efforts to look young and act young. The traditional roles of housewife and mother have changed considerably with smaller families and day care becoming more common. Already, marketers have found it necessary to change their promotional messages for products such as automobiles, insurance, travel tours, tires, and particularly for home appliances in order to communicate effectively with women who are in the workforce. Poverty of time has also had a profound impact. The kitchen shelves are filled with instant potatoes, cake mixes, and instant soups; the freezer is packed with complete dinners. Supermarkets are selling more complete meals. The microwave oven has become the most important time- and labor-saving appliance in the kitchen. Although many two-income families are more affluent, this greater affluence results in less free time because alternatives competing for their time have expanded. Retailers can respond to the poverty-of-time problem by stocking labor-saving devices, increasing store hours, prewrapping gift items, adding special services such as fashion coordinators, and expanding in-home sales efforts such as telephone, direct mail, and Internet-based sales. Televisions will have built-in computers so the shopping can take place on the Internet. Future technology will allow more men and women to work at home, thus modifying many of their lifestyles. The new role of women has caused men to assume new household roles.

Life Simplification

Life simplification symbolizes the yearning of some consumers to return to a less complicated time period and a simpler life. There is little agreement about what constitutes luxury but it is likely to involve product use that leads to comfort, pleasure, health, savings of time, and preserving youthfulness. Even upscale consumers have been described as pursuing aestheticization of taste.[9] This lifestyle trend reflects a quest for material simplicity and durability and a striving for self-reliance. There is a fundamental belief that focuses on ecological awareness and the purchase of inexpensive products. The depletion of natural resources and the adopting of a value system guide buyer behavior to a great extent.

The consumer pursuing life simplification feels overwhelmed by change. Technology is changing so rapidly that many individuals believe that their jobs are threatened. Everywhere there are requests for social security numbers, account numbers, PINs, and zip codes. There is a menu of telephone options without ever speaking to a person. All these circumstances leave an impersonal impression so that a return to simpler, less confusing times is desirable. Family lives have also been affected as there are more extended families. Children grow older faster in a process known as age compression. For example, girls who were once interested in playing with dolls until they were nine or ten years old now lose interest at age five or six. The problem is how to attract or interest older children in products that might be considered nontoys. Thus, toy manufacturers and retailers need to attract adolescents and adults to expand their market.

The major aspect of complexity in modern life has been technological advances in computers, fiber optics, broadband, wireless communications, and their resulting impact on consumer lifestyles. In the future, communications is expected to replace computing as the application for processing chip technology. For example, digital signal processors or DSPs can enable portable, personal, and "always on" high-speed broadband Internet connectivity along with Web access via wireless handsets. Wireless Application Protocol (WAP), a system designed to make Web sites more usable on cell phone screens has become available. Consumers possessing this technology could easily and quickly access prepurchase information on a wide range of products and services.

Market segmentation strategists have long considered personal values as an important explanatory variable in the consumer's decision process. Through the years, personal values have been linked to gift giving, natural food shopping, and choice of leisure activities. For those consumers who desire to return to a much simpler lifestyle, vacation activity preferences is also a concern of value-system based market segmentation. In one study, values in the selection of a vacation destination were linked to cultural activities, outdoor activities, sports activities, and visiting friends and/or relatives. The underlying assumption of the study was that differences in value systems would be a basis for activity preferences of tourists visiting a destination.[10] Therefore, values expressed for life simplification could well be expressed by consumers in the selection of vacations and activities.

The emphasis for those trying to simplify their lives is on living in a way that they consider being outwardly simple and inwardly rich. Values associated with this lifestyle are self-realization and an ecological ethic. These values underscore material simplicity which does not necessarily mean adopting a lower consumption standard but rather valuing products that are handcrafted and also aesthetically pleasing. Another value is that of human scale that implies a preference for smaller living environments and greater value associated with one's contribution to society. An ecological awareness acknowledges the interconnection between people and natural resources. This new consciousness notes the need for the reduction of environmental pollution and is receptive to new products such as bottled water which preserve and maintain the natural environment. The value of personal growth refers to the ability of the individual to clear away external clutter in order to develop the inner life. This will mean an increase in enrollment in adult education courses, spiritual exploration, and more interest in hobbies such as ceramics and other handicrafts.

A new society is emerging. Marketers must adjust to the lifestyle changes in order to predict the dimensions and scope of future market opportunities. Understanding the new directions for lifestyle behavior patterns will enable marketers to more effectively plan strategies to reach their potential target market by uncovering new product opportunities, obtaining better product positioning, and developing improved advertising communications based upon a more lifelike portrait of the customer. To illustrate, Ben & Jerry's has established a foundation that contributes to the peace movement and to a nonprofit program that supports mentally challenged people. The company has, in turn, influenced its suppliers to hire homeless people. Ben & Jerry's created a position of environmental development to direct the company's environmental practices and communicate its social mission.

Many firms that want to target consumers who practice the life simplification lifestyle focus on relationship marketing. Relationship marketing's objective is to build long-term mutual relationships with customers in order to retain their loyalty and patronage. The blurring roles of men and women have also contributed to a desire for more clear-cut behavior. For example, before the new millennium, there had been a craze for Jane Austen movie versions of *Pride and Prejudice, Emma*, and *Sense and Sensibility*. This period represented civility, politeness, and courtesy. Consumers are looking back nostalgically to a simpler period which represents stability and order. Varying degrees of motivation and the opportunity to make the purchases are considerations. Information exposure and individual understanding of this information will influence buyer behavior judgment. Attitude formation and possible attitude change will be based upon comprehension of information. Cultural factors in the decision-making process may involve regional, ethnic, or social class influences. Demographics such as age and gender also influence the buying decision process. Finally, lifestyle, reference groups, and other cultural and environmental elements have an impact on consumer behavior.

THE BUYER DECISION PROCESS

Consumers actually make different types of purchasing decisions in their daily lives. First, consumers must determine their purchase priorities and how much money to allocate for each product or service. Next, consumers must consider where the purchase should be obtained. Finally, brand and style selection can involve detailed choices. The level of the decision process may vary from routine to complex depending upon past experiences and importance of the product category such as a new home, motor vehicle, or a computer.

The buying-decision process encompasses psychological and cultural factors. The framework used to depict the stages of the buying decision process implies that consumers pass sequentially through all five stages in purchasing a product. This is not necessarily true since consumers may skip or reverse stages. Consumers buying their regular brand of orange juice go directly from need for orange juice to the purchase decision, skipping information search and evaluation of alternatives. The model of the buyer decision process in Figure 2.1 shows the range of considerations that arise when consumers are confronted with a highly involved new purchase and that the buyer decision process begins before the actual purchase and continues after the purchase.[11] Consequently, marketers need to focus attention on the process rather than just the decision. Information is an important part of the process. For information about products and services, women are significantly more likely than men to rely on television advertising and less likely to rely on newspapers and

Figure 2.1
The Buyer Decision Process

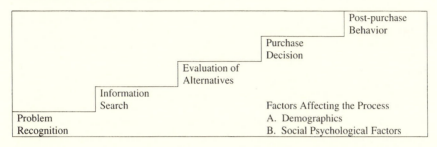

radio. There is also a strong correlation between education and primary source of information about products and services. As the level of education increases, there is more reliance on the print media, particularly magazines. The Internet has been a major influence in helping educated people make a decision about buying an automobile, a computer, or selecting an investment product. Consumers are strongly influenced by media they consider to be credible.

Problem Recognition

The buyer-decision process begins when a problem is identified or an unsatisfied need or desire is activated. A consumer might consider purchasing a car when his current one has to be repaired a few times in one month. When one experiences the use of a camcorder by a friend, this may arouse the desire to purchase a camcorder for one's own use. Because consumers may not always recognize that a problem or a need is present, a company uses a variety of strategies such as advertising, sales promotion, packaging, and sales personnel to stimulate consumer awareness of needs and desires. There is a distinct possibility that consumers may experience problem recognition rather slowly or quite quickly. Problem recognition is a critical stage in the buyer-decision process because unless the problem can be identified movement to the next stage, information search, will not progress. Awareness of an unfulfilled desire may revolve around emotional motives such as self-image, status, or appearance. Rational motives may include product performance characteristics, service, or delivery.

Many buyers are reluctant to pursue the buyer-decision process further because of the risks. There is less expertise with unfamiliar items than with the replacement of a known product. Whether the buyer will proceed further in the consumer decision process will occur only if the purchasing problem is perceived as feasible or worth solving.

Information Search

The consumer engages in internal memory scanning for relevant information on the product or store choice alternatives and external information from a variety of sources. A milder search state is referred to as heightened attention and at this level the potential buyer simply becomes more receptive to information about the product. A more intensive external information search can be derived from several sources such as personal, commercial, public, and experiential sources, which are defined as follows:

- Personal sources: family, friends, neighbors, acquaintances.
- Commercial sources: advertising, packaging, displays, dealers, salespeople.
- Public sources: mass media, consumer organizations.
- Experiential sources: product usage, inspection, handling.

The degree of influence on the decision-making process of these sources vary depending upon the product category and the buyer's characteristics. Methods of reducing uncertainty and risk would be applied depending upon the situation. Endorsements or testimonials may be used as a risk reducer, provided the buyer has confidence in the individual who renders the product endorsement. Some buyers will purchase only well-known brands of products because they rely on a brand's established reputation. Depending upon the type of product and its costs, buyers may rely upon private testing organizations' rating services. Consumers new to a market might desire to explore their options and try to avoid risky ones. Therefore, there is a focus on low-risk, well-known brand names; but eventually this focus will extend to lesser-known brands and, if the choice is rational, with an emphasis on utility.[12]

Evaluation of Alternatives

Once information has been gathered, the consumer must evaluate the sources by establishing evaluative criteria. When multiple criteria are involved, rather than a single criterion, they typically do not carry equal weight. Good nutrition may be more important than taste. Consumer motives affect the weighting of alternatives. For example, economic buying motives include product efficiency in operation, dependability, and quality or economy in use. Emotional and experiential buying motives may include emulation, pleasure, prestige, or romance. Product-buying motives include ease of installation or ease of making repairs. Patronage-buying motives include reliability of the seller, location of store, personal attention by salespeople, promptness in delivery, or variety for selection. Consequently, each product feature's performance would be evaluated and weighted as to importance to the buyer.

Purchase Decision

The consumer selects a product from a set of products that may solve the purchasing problem. The intended product to be purchased may not be the same as the item actually purchased because various factors that can intervene between the purchase intention and the purchase decision. These factors include the attitudes of others and unanticipated situational factors. Personal influence of friends might be especially important for individuals who lack confidence in their ability to evaluate the value of a product. A situational factor, such as the loss of employment, might halt the purchase of a new car. The purchase act includes deciding where to buy, agreeing to terms of sale, paying for the product or service, and taking delivery.

Postpurchase Behavior

After the purchase is made, the consumer's satisfaction or dissatisfaction with the product will influence subsequent behavior. The purchase of a dress may lead to the purchase of matching shoes. The purchase of an automobile may cause the consumer to reevaluate whether performance expectations have been satisfied. Should dissatisfaction be present, future purchase behavior may result in brand switching and negative word-of-mouth communication with friends and relatives.

Dissonance-reducing behaviors are necessary if the consumer feels conflict about whether the purchase decision was entirely wise. Providing reassuring information that supports the original decision can reduce dissonance. Dissatisfaction is frequently the result of cognitive dissonance, doubt that a correct decision was made, which can be reduced by follow-up telephone and service calls and extended warranties. On the other hand, the higher the satisfaction from the purchase, the greater will be the benefit of word-of-mouth referrals and repeat purchasing.

The consumer buying-decision process is also affected by demographic, social, and psychological factors. These factors are useful in developing lifestyle market segmentation profiles. A time-pressed consumer would move through the buyer decision process more rapidly than a retired individual. An affluent customer might move through the process more quickly in purchasing a new car than a middle-income consumer because of diminished financial risk.

THE ELECTRONICS INDUSTRY: A CASE STUDY

After making the purchase, a consumer will evaluate the product again. This postpurchase behavior often affects future purchases. A consumer who feels cognitive dissonance may attempt to return the product or may seek positive information to justify its choice. For example, the purchase of a personal computer leads to the acquisition of blank and preprogrammed diskettes. But dissatisfaction may result in brand switching, changes in retail patronage behavior, and negative comments made to friends.

Products sold by electronic store retailers such as Circuit City, Best Buy, and Radio Shack are prone to cognitive dissonance. Dissonance typically increases as the value of the item increases. To illustrate, purchasing a computer or a television set creates more dissonance than buying a radio.

Electronics retailers, with the help of the manufacturer, can take measures to minimize the amount of customer postpurchase dissatisfaction. Companies can follow up purchases with messages affirming the wisdom of their brand choice. Request for suggestions for improvements and strategic locations of available repair services can ease purchase risks. Instruction booklets can also ease purchase reservations. Finally, postpurchase communications demonstrating new product applications and providing for rapid redress of consumer grievances will reduce cognitive dissonance. Focus groups, consumer panels, and consumer surveys render important insights for better satisfying the customer. A strong alliance between manufacturers and retailers can reduce consumer postpurchase dissonance.

TYPES OF CONSUMER DECISION MAKING

Lifestyle market segmentation has gained in acceptability because lifestyles influence consumer decisions on how to spend leisure time and money. Environmental influences lead people to adopt certain lifestyles. Consumers adopt a living pattern that includes the goals they desire to achieve, such as to be successful in work or sports. Buyer behavior can also be based upon impulse.

Consumers make many purchasing decisions to satisfy their current and future requirements. The amount of time and effort expended for any specific purchase decision will depend on numerous factors such as the price, importance of the purchase, visibility of the product, and demographic, social, and psychological variables. The degree of involvement which expresses the perceived relevance and personal interest in a product or a brand will have an impact on the decision-making process. A large amount of time and effort in purchase involvement is referred to as extended problem solving while a very small amount of time and effort is referred to as routine purchasing.

Extended consumer decision making occurs when a buyer purchases expensive, complex items and has had little or no experience with the product. Purchases are generally made infrequently and considerable time is expended on information search about the product category and evaluation of alternative brands. Consumers do not have the time to engage in extensive decision making and consequently the major purchase decisions made by a consumer may be limited to selecting a university to attend, buying a home, an automobile, or considering a pension contribution plan.

Limited decision making is used for products that are purchased occasionally or when a buyer needs to acquire information about an unfamiliar brand in a familiar product category. For example, the introduction of a new fragrance line requires a moderate amount of time and an external search is involved.

Routinized purchase behavior is made on the basis of habit or even impulse. The impulse purchase is the most routine decision-making process prior to the purchase. Examples of routine purchases based upon habit might include beer or soft drinks. Since low involvement is an aspect of the purchase, paper towels might fall into the category of a routine purchase and the purchase decision might be simplified by purchasing an inexpensive brand.

THE CONSUMER ADOPTION PROCESS
FOR NEW PRODUCTS

Consumers differ in their readiness to try new products. The adoption process is the mental and behavioral process used by the individual before purchasing a product or service not previously used. The adoption process occurs when individuals go through the various stages of adoption—awareness, interest, evaluation, trial, and adoption. In the awareness stage, the consumer becomes cognizant of the innovation but lacks information about it. The interest stage reflects the stimulation needed for the consumer to seek information about the new product. The evaluation stage takes place when the consumer evaluates the new product in relation to established goals and financial resources. A decision is made whether to try the new product. The consumer tries the new product in the trial stage to help gauge the product's value. Sampling, if possible, in small quantities may be used. The adoption stage occurs when the consumer decides to make full and regular use of the new product. Sources of information are an important part of the adoption process and different sources are valued more highly at different stages. Promotion should be utilized to generate widespread awareness of the product. During the interest stage, information should be used to describe the benefits, advantages, and perhaps even some of the product limitations. Salespeople can provide consumers with a comparison of competitors' products in the evaluation stage. Free samples, displays, and product demonstrations aid buyers in the trial stage of the product.

The process by which new products spread through the social system is called the diffusion process and describes when different market segments will enter the market to buy the product. Some consumers will adopt a new product quickly after it has been introduced, while others will delay before accepting the new product and still others may never adopt it. Researchers have pinpointed five categories of consumers based upon a time dimension when they adopt a new product in the diffusion process. Innovators are the first group to adopt a new product followed over an indefinite time period by early adopters, early majority, late majority, and laggard consumer market segments. Table 2.1 shows the classification of adopter groups.

Product adoption of some products and services, such as a new dishwashing liquid may have minimal consequences, while the adoption of other innovations such as a laptop computer may lead to important behavioral and lifestyle changes. Examples of innovations having a major impact on society include the automobile and television, and more recently, the computer and the Internet. Frequently, innovations are resisted because consumers perceive them

Table 2.1
Classification of Adopter Groups

Adopter Category	Percentage of Population
Innovators	2.5
Early Adopters	13.5
Early Majority	34.0
Late Majority	34.0
Laggards	16.0

as incompatible with their needs or values. In essence, a new product spreads through the population and affects the total sales level of the product as it moves through the product life cycle.

Innovators

Innovators are a venturesome group who are eager to try new ideas and new products. This group tends to be younger than later adopters. They generally are better educated than the average consumer, are financially secure and have a high social status. They tend to have high incomes and a great deal of self-confidence in their judgment. They also rely more on impersonal sources of information rather than on salespeople or other word-of-mouth sources.

Early Adopters

Early adopters are greatly respected and are perceived as opinion leaders who help to determine which new products are acceptable and which should be rejected. This group tends to be a more integrated part of a local social system. Marketers who try to speed up the diffusion process try to work through early adopters since early adopters can be expected to influence their friends and acquaintances, thereby contributing to a new product's progress. Early adopters have many of the same characteristics as innovators—self-confidence, high incomes, and good educations—but are a part of a local social system. This group reads upscale magazines such as *The New Yorker* and *Esquire*. The early adopter is an important link to the mass market because this group popularizes the products accepted by the innovator group.

Early Majority

The early majority is made up of middle-class consumers who are more cautious in making purchasing decisions than early adopters. The early majority is influenced in their buying behavior by the early adopters. They exert considerable influence over the remaining groups of adopters. The early majority member is socially active, but seldom a leader or an opinion leader. This group will assume some risk but prefers to have this risk tempered by the early adopters. This group is considered slightly above average in social and economic standing. Its members rely greatly on advertisements, salespeople, and contact with early adopters. The key to entering a new market is the early adopter while the key to market share begins with the early majority.

Late Majority

Members of the early majority tend to be slightly more educated and better off financially than those in the late majority. The late majority tends to be older, more conservative, and more traditional. They tend to be a skeptical group. This group relies on either their peers or the early majority as sources of information. Advertising and personal selling are less effective than is word-of-mouth. Members of the late majority are skeptical about new product ideas and may adopt because of social pressure or because the purchase risk has been diminished. They constitute 34 percent of the market and are an important target market.

Laggards

Laggards are a tradition-bound group. They are suspicious of innovators and innovations. Laggards are older and resist changes to past fashions and traditions. This is especially evident when the product in question is clothing. Frequently, the laggards may adopt a clothing style when other groups have discarded the style.

The speed of adoption may be affected by the relative advantage of the new product. This relative advantage may be reflected in lower cost or superior quality. The degree to which the new product or idea may be sampled on some limited basis may also affect the adoption rate. Another factor would be whether the consumer could observe a change in a situation as a result of immediate use of a product such as an insect spray. Naturally, there are people who never adopt new products or ideas and these people are simply referred to as nonadopters. The adoption process is the decision-making activity of the individual whereas the diffusion process is the procedure in which the innovation is transmitted within the social system.[13]

MANAGING CHANGE

Although the traditional adoption process model of awareness, interest, evaluation, trial, and adoption has helped marketers to more fully understand the buyer-decision process for new products, it has several limitations. The model does not recognize that product evaluation is a continuing process. The product adoption and diffusion processes are two useful concepts to guide the planning and nature of policy changes. The basis for lifestyle market segmentation strategies may be provided by the characteristics of the various adopter groups.

New product introductions have been an integral part of managing change in the soft drink industry. Coca-Cola developed a new products group in 1989 that reformulated Fresca and introduced the sports drink Power Ade. Moreover, Caffeine-Free Coca-Cola Classic was introduced to address the health concerns of a specific market segment. Coca-Cola reformulated Cherry Coke and Diet Cherry Coke, again demonstrating flexibility in satisfying the need of a specific target market. Pepsi demonstrated a pronounced interest in the development of alternative drinks by developing All Sport, a new sports drink, and single servings of Ocean Spray juices in stores and vending machines, and by forming an alliance with Lipton to distribute tea. The agreement to distribute Ocean Spray was discontinued in 1996 as Pepsi wanted to give its own juice brands more attention.

The soft drink industry from the 1980s to the present has focused upon lifestyle product positioning. Pepsi concentrated on creating advertisements to make Pepsi a drink for middle-class consumers to serve guests. Coca-Cola developed Tab to satisfy the needs of women for a low-calorie drink. Diet Coke was introduced to meet the needs of the entire family and simultaneously satisfy health concerns. 7-Up shook up the cola industry with its Uncola campaign. In response, caffeine-free colas were launched. Alternative products such as bottled water, sport drinks, tea, and fruit juices have gained increased momentum. However, the core of the soft drink market still remains Coca-Cola Classic and Pepsi Cola. Dr. Pepper, 7-Up, bottled water (marketed especially by Perrier), and Gatorade (marketed by Quaker Oats), have made inroads into the soft drink market but the core cola market remains loyal.

Social and cultural patterns in the United States are changing rapidly. These changes are reflected in consumer attitudes and self-concepts and are at the core of cross-shopping behavior, the expenditures of an affluent society, the new role of women and the simplification lifestyle trends. The impact of an affluent society has a profound affect on present and future lifestyle trends. Multi-income families have become much more the norm and Wall Street has broadened its definition of the low-end of the affluent market. Bank of America and ETrade designate $100,000 as a minimum balance for special accounts and Fidelity and J.P. Morgan have designated $250,000 for private banking customers. Once this high-end market was the domain of clients with $1 million or more in liquid assets. Firms in other industries will also likely target this more broadened definition of the affluent market.[14] Niche marketing allows Neiman-Marcus to target the high-end of the affluent market with made-to-measure suits for $4,000 and Brooks Brothers to start at the low-end of this market by offering suits for as little as $800. The soup industry has responded to consumers' time constraints with the sale of dehydrated soups. As there has been a growth in the singles market and families with members on different time schedules, the soup industry has changed its packaging to serve single portions of soup. Campbell Soup has also taken into consideration changing lifestyles in introducing products. Campbell's launched their first chicken noodle soup in the 1930s. Subsequent product changes have been made to this product that include family-size, chunky chicken noodle, low sodium, homestyle, Healthy Request, the addition of Ramen noodles, low-fat, and microwave chicken noodle soups. All these changes are the result of a better understanding and definition of their customers.

The significance of the product adoption process is that not all consumers pass through the adoption process with the same speed. The speed of adoption depends upon whether the product is compatible with current lifestyles and if consumers with high discretionary incomes are willing to try the new product offering. Other important factors are the degree of functional, physical, financial, social, psychological, and time risks in purchasing the product. The decision-making process considers the advantages that the product has over competitive offerings on the market, the ease of product use, and the importance of the product to the user.

NOTES

1. Abhilasha Mehtn, "Using Self Concept To Assess Advertising Effectiveness," *Journal of Advertising Research* 39 (January 1999): 81–90.

2. Jennifer Aaker, "The Malleable Self: The Role of Self-Expression in Persuasion," *Journal of Marketing Research* 36 (February 1999): 45–58.

3. David Stauffer, "For Generation XERS, What Counts Isn't All Work or All Play," *Management Review* 86 (December 1997): 7.

4. John Burnett and Alan Bush, "Profiling the Yuppies," *Journal of Advertising Research* 26 (April–May 1986): 27–35.

5. Bill Stoneman, "Beyond Rocking the Ages: An Interview with J. Walker Smith," *American Demographics* (May 1998): 45–49; and Margot Hornblower, "Great X," *Time*, 9 June 1997, 58–59.

6. Ellen Newborne and Kathleen Kerwin, "Generation Y," *Business Week*, 15 February 1999, 80–86.

7. Michael E. Porter, *Competitive Advantage* (New York: The Free Press, 1985), 33–61.

8. John Kenneth Galbraith, *The Affluent Society* (Boston: Houghton Mifflin, 1958); and M. David Potter, *People of Plenty* (Chicago: University of

Chicago Press, 1954).

9. Debra Goldman, "Paradox of Pleasure," *American Demographics* 21 (May 1999): 50–53.

10. Robert Madrigal and Lynn R. Kahle, "Predicting Vacation Activity Preferences on the Basis of Value-System Segmentation," *Journal of Travel Research* 32 (Winter 1994): 22–28.

11. William P. Putsis, Jr. and Narssimha Srinivasen, "Buying or Just Browsing? The Duration of Purchase Deliberation," *Journal of Marketing Research* 31 (August 1994): 393–402.

12. Carrie M. Heilman, Douglass Bonoman, and Gordon P. Wright, "The Evolution of Brand Preferences and Choice Behaviors of Consumers New to a Market," *Journal of Marketing Research* 37 (May 2000): 139–155.

13. For a foundation of diffusion theory, see Everett Rogers, *Diffusion of Innovations*, 4th ed. (New York: The Free Press, 1995).

14. Jeff D. Opdyke and Carrick Mollenkamp, "Yes, You Are High Net Worth," *The Wall Street Journal*, 21 May 2002, D1.

CHAPTER 3

Purchasing Behavior

Consider how people decide to purchase a television set. One person shops in three or four stores, compares, and makes a choice, while another person relies on the ratings of television sets by *Consumer Reports* before making a decision. A third person reads the newspaper advertisements looking for a sale while another person walks into a local store and buys a television set without investigation. Consumer buyer behavior is difficult to predict.

More recently, Internet selling and niche retailing have had a profound impact on the way consumers buy. By purchasing books over the Internet, consumers have forced companies to change the way they sell. Amazon.com, founded in 1994, is the leading retailer of books in the United States. Amazon.com has a long-range vision to become the Wal-Mart of the Web. Besides books, Amazon.com sells CDs, videotapes, audiotapes, greeting cards, and toys. Even electronics stores such as Rex Stores, Circuit City, and Best Buy have established Web sites to respond to changing consumer purchasing behavior. Traditional retailers, in the drugstore sector such as Walgreens, in the home improvement sector such as Home Depot, and in the specialty-clothing sector such as Gap, all offer merchandise online. Some 38 percent of Americans shop online, compared to 25 percent of Britons, 24 percent of Canadians, and 20 percent of Japanese.

In the past decade, there have been changes in consumer buying behavior that have encouraged the growth of niche retailing. The retail industry is a good illustration of how purchasing patterns have changed and consumers have turned their attention to the discounters and niche retailers. Many consumers have made purchases from niche retailers that carry a broad selection of educational toys or toys that build on a child's creativity. For example, Zany Brainy offers an in-store computer center that stock more than 600 software titles. A movie theater provides children with not only movies but also live performances. Moreover, Imaginarium, another educational toy retailer, stocks about 3,000 products, 1,500 books, and has developed private label items. Niche retailers such as Zany Brainy and Imaginarium have found that new technologies are enabling them to market to their customers in a way the customers want to buy.

Toys "R" Us and KB Toys are among the large toy retailers that have survived the changes in the purchasing behavior of consumers. Consumers have responded positively to Internet selling despite concerns about online security, the depth and breadth of merchandise assortment, and delivery. Even with the Internet, many Americans tend to be conscientious comparison shoppers.

Niche retailers in the bookstore sector have established stores that target children and mystery readers. In the footwear sector, chains such as Footlocker aim at the sneaker and athletic market segment. In the furniture sector, Pier 1 Imports dominates a niche that desires exotic imported furniture and housewares. Williams Sonoma offers culinary and serving equipment for consumers interested in cooking. Niche retailing and Internet selling have caused manufacturers to reexamine and revise their distribution systems to better serve retailers and consumers. Britt wrote over fifty years ago that we do not understand very much about consumers' underlying motives to dress as they do, eat as they do, or engage in a myriad of other buying motives of daily living. Moreover, there does not seem to be a universal set of explanatory motives and every situation is different and requires separate analysis.[1]

Although marketers know much more about consumer motivation today, the buying process is complex and still remains a mystery. Buying is a strongly embedded element of culture in the United States and is a manifestation of personality and lifestyle. Changes in societal values, such as the Protestant Reformation, the rise of materialism, and the absence of a formal class structure, are external socioenvironmental factors reflected in consumer motivation. Universal motives and desires to be loved and admired, for peer approval, to be entertained, to be attractive, and to be in control of our lives still exist. Simple measures of like or dislike of possessions or belongings will not help marketers understand consumer purchasing behavior. There are new techniques that explain why consumers behave as they do and comprehend what consumers do not fully understand about themselves.[2] The techniques of motivation research include observation, focus groups, depth interviews, and metaphor analysis.

Factors that affect consumer purchasing behavior are personal relevance and individual values, goals, and needs. For example, if we learn that one of our friends has just returned from Italy or Greece, and we are interested in the history of past civilizations, this event could be relevant to our vacation plans. When we purchase certain types of clothing, this bears upon our self-concept and helps us to define ourselves. Therefore, it is more likely that products such as automobiles, dresses, and television sets would be more personally relevant than products such as detergents or facial soap. The job of marketers is to make the product or the service as personally relevant as possible. More opportunities exist to do this with products such as insurance, retirement plans, homes, and home decorating products.

Products are personally relevant to consumers because they are consistent with their values, goals, and needs. Marketers have identified the existence of a health-conscious food segment which has led to an introduction of low-calorie and low-fat brands. Some consumers desire to lose weight and others require a salt-free or fat-free diet. Affluent consumers are concerned with tax shelters while other consumers are saving for retirement, to finance the college education of children, or to purchase a starter home. Needs and goals are interdependent. Some people may not be aware of needs for social approval or for status. The purchase of a Volvo might be to satisfy conscious, utilitarian needs for safety, but subconscious needs for social approval and for satisfying ambitions may also be present.

The following are consumer purchasing characteristics:

- Motives
- Brand Decision Process
- Retail Patronage Considerations
- In-Home and Internet Shopping

Although motives are difficult to measure, marketers use them to segment markets. Economy, product durability, prestige, convenience, and other motives may affect various product purchases. Consumer brand decision factors help to evaluate product quality and also reflect psychological variables. Patronage considerations may involve price, location, merchandise variety, or services. In-home and Internet shopping reflects consumer convenience motivations. All these purchasing characteristics impact buying situations.

Since the increase in consumer wealth in the 1990s, there has been a shift in consumer purchasing behavior in the middle market for upscale products and services. Many consumers have survived the stock market's downturn and multi-income households are making their presence known more and more as families migrate toward the high-end of purchasing premium and luxury products. This change in purchasing behavior has been brought about by the baby boomers whose lifestyles changed as a result of empty-nest status. There are a growing number of baby boomers that believe middle-class status is a starting point not a goal. Thus, a store like Tiffany's has attracted less-affluent consumers, for example, by pricing diamond engagement rings from $850 to $850,000 while the average sells for between $7,000 and $8,000. Moreover, in the early 1980s many consumers viewed the purchase of home air conditioning systems, dishwashers, and home computers as luxuries; these goods are now perceived as necessities. In the early 1990s cell phones were viewed as luxuries and now consumers often have more than one cell phone for their personal use.

CHARACTERISTICS OF MOTIVES

Marketers cannot observe motivation. A motive is an internal state of the purchase. While consumer behavior is observable, motives are psychological constructs that can only be inferred. Buying motives for consumer products may be classified as economic, emotional, product, and retail patronage. Some of the motives may be rational while others are emotional. To illustrate, economic motives include product durability or economy in use. Emotional motives might include romance, pleasure, or prestige. Product purchase motives might involve ease for making repairs or ease of installation. Patronage motives relate to variety for selection or promptness in delivery. Motives relate to perception. Motives come from the consumer's real self, self-image, ideal self, and looking-glass self. The way consumers envision the situation to themselves helps to shape their reactions or responses to marketers' appeals.

Consumer goals and needs are constantly changing in response to environmental conditions, interaction with others, and physical conditions. As individuals realize their goals, new objectives may be established. New levels of aspiration may surface. For example, if an individual loses ten pounds of weight another objective to lose an additional fifteen pounds may be established. Moreover, marketers need to be attuned to changing needs and goals. Automobile manufacturers have recognized the consumer's need for prestige or status. This need may be less important as some consumers seek safety or family enjoyment as reasons for purchasing a new car. Since many families own more than one motor vehicle, ownership of a Volvo sedan or station wagon, a pickup truck, and an economical used car for an adolescent might represent diverse needs.

The reason consumers choose one brand over another may be vague and unknown to them. Why consumers choose one brand of refrigerator over another may be based on personal experience, an advertisement, a friend's comment, a salesperson's presentation, the location of the retailer for service or some other factor or combination thereof. Brand switching may occur as a result of changing needs, a dissatisfaction with the current brand used, or because a friend, relative, advertising campaign, an article in *Consumer Reports*, or other influence persuaded that consumer that a better benefit or value can be derived by switching brands.

Marketers, by identifying and appealing to consumers' motives, can generate a positive environment for the sale of their products. A study of men depicted their motives for purchasing specific magazines. The male population was divided into traditionalists (27%), searchers (22%), achievers (20%), fast trackers (17%), and young urban techies (14%). Traditionalists have a high regard for religion and family and enjoyed reading about cars and hunting. Searchers were likely either to be divorced or single and tended to watch a lot of science fiction or television. Achievers earned the most money, exhibited great confidence in every aspect of their lives, and tended to read business, news weeklies, and computer periodicals. These three groups tended to be middle aged and older. Fast trackers tended to be about age twenty-five and prized earning money and eventually believed they would be successful. The young urban techies averaged about age twenty-seven and were well-educated and politically progressive.[3] This study linked attitudes based upon market segmentation and results in understanding the lifestyles and motives of a market segment of males.

MOTIVATION THEORIES

Many of an individual's specific needs are dormant or latent much of the time. The arousal of any particular set of needs may be related to the individual's physiological condition or may emanate from the emotional or cognitive processes or may be a reaction to stimuli in the external environment. The diversity of motives among consumers makes it difficult to activate motives that are satisfying to groups of consumers. However, it is possible to identify groups with common motives and goals. Marketers have been more successful in developing strategies that involve product classes rather than spe-

---

cific choices within a product classification. A need must be aroused or stimulated before it becomes a motive. Some of the reasons that needs, and thus motives, are never fully satisfied are that new needs emerge as old needs are satisfied.

Physiological Cues

Most physiological cues are involuntary. Since marketers cannot cause physiological arousal, measures can be used to satisfy this state once it has been aroused. Bodily needs are rooted in an individual's physiological condition. A drop in blood-sugar level or stomach contractions may trigger hunger awareness. The secretion of sex hormones causes the sex need. Thirst may be triggered by the dryness of the mouth. Marketers can demonstrate associations with these physiological needs that show solutions such as soft drinks, iced tea, or bottled water. Food snacks can be shown to revitalize or energize the individual. Males and females can be shown kissing an individual of the opposite sex who has just used a specific brand of mouthwash or chewing gum.

Cognitive Arousal

Motives can be triggered by information stored in the individual's memory. A cognitive awareness of needs can result from perceptions, attitudes, and beliefs that may serve to arouse motives. The cognitive processes are viewed as directional inasmuch as they serve the individual in his or her attempts to achieve need satisfaction and rely on the ability to reason. This approach is especially useful in introducing new products to satisfy new consumer needs.

The cognitive and behavioristic philosophies are both concerned with the arousal of human motives but are in opposition to each other. The cognitive school of thought maintains that all behavior is aimed at goal achievement. Needs and past experiences are classified and developed into attitudes and beliefs that act as predispositions to behavior. These predispositions are directed to satisfying needs. In contrast, the behavioristic school of thought considers motivation to be a mechanical process. Behavior is envisioned as a response to a stimulus. Elements of rote memory are used. An example is the Pavlovian stimulus–response theory of motivation. Impulse purchasing can be partly explained by behavioristic learning.

A single purchasing situation does not involve just one specific need. The consumer is driven usually by a combination of needs. It would be another mistake to believe that identical behaviors have identical motivational environments. Therefore, the purchase of a

BMW by different consumers results in the same purchase but the environmental backgrounds of these consumers vary. Although consumers have different needs based upon their personalities, experiences, and environments, usually consumers assign a priority ranking to the satisfaction of these needs. A set of needs is frequently determined by specific cues in the environment. Consequently, television advertising, for example, could activate needs for a new car or dishwasher that were only close to the surface and perhaps even dormant. The cognitive approach is designed to educate through promotional campaigns and usually provides more information about the product than other techniques.

HIERARCHY OF MOTIVATION THEORY

This approach arranges motives in a hierarchy or scale according to their strength. Abraham Maslow, who did much of the work on motivation, suggested that human needs can be divided into five basic categories: physiological, safety, social, esteem, and self-actualization.[4] Figure 3.1 shows how each category occupies a different level in a five-level hierarchy with physiological needs at the bottom and self-actualization needs at the top. Physiological needs include hunger, thirst, and sex. Safety needs range from security to protection. Social needs cover affection and a sense of belonging. Esteem needs include recognition, status, and self-esteem. Self-actualization needs range from self-development to self-accomplishment. To illustrate, marketers could demonstrate by promotional campaigns a smoke detector that would target safety needs, perfume advertisements showing social success, and achievement through knowledge obtained by the use of a home computer.

According to Figure 3.1, after physiological and safety needs have been realized, social needs, esteem needs, and finally self-actualization needs take priority. Self-actualization is our highest need. There is overlap between each level since no need is ever

Figure 3.1
Hierarchy of Needs

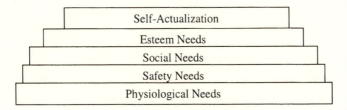

completely satisfied. For this reason, the lowest needs remain as prime motivators that influence consumer behavior.

Limitations of the Need Hierarchy

Maslow's hierarchy is a useful tool for understanding consumer motivation and it is readily adaptable to marketing strategy. However, this theory cannot be tested empirically and appears to involve more conscious motivation. Another criticism is that rising expectations are completely overlooked. Lower needs in the hierarchy are never completely satisfied and consequently are replaced by psychologically equivalent needs that are qualitatively or quantitatively more demanding. Moreover, the satisfaction of higher needs does not necessarily await the satisfaction of lower order needs. Maslow's theory is useful for a general understanding of motives. However, it has limited use in predicting specific outcomes of purchasing behavior.

MOTIVATION AND CONFLICT IN PURCHASING BEHAVIOR

Motives can conflict with each other and affect how consumers behave in purchasing situations. For example, should the individual make a down payment on a new car or use the money for a trip to Europe? Motive conflict can be viewed from a positive perspective in that although it may build tension, it may also facilitate goal attainment. Kurt Lewin, an authority on motive conflict, viewed motives as a positive and negative force once the individual is motivationally aroused.[5] The specific patterns of consumer behavior may vary widely depending upon the specific motives, the individual, and the purchasing situation. However, conflict is most likely when motives are of approximately equal strength. Lewin designated the short-term motivational situations: approach–approach, avoidance–avoidance, and approach–avoidance conflict.

Approach–Approach Conflict

This is a purchasing situation in which conflict exists between two desirable alternatives. The purchase choice may be between a car or a boat. Since both purchases will give some degree of pleasure this is the least painful of the conflict situations. Nonetheless, a certain amount of vacillation will occur between the alternatives because choosing one means losing the other. Some product offerings help to resolve the conflict, such as "fly now and pay later."

However, promotional literature might help to resolve the conflict between the purchase of a car or a boat.

Resolution of approach–approach conflict might also develop through a reassessment of goals. For example, it may be determined that a purchase of a car is more important at this time than the purchase of a boat. Another resolution of the conflict might occur if a decision is made to purchase relatively inexpensive models of both a car and a boat.

Avoidance–Avoidance Conflict

This purchase situation develops when there is conflict between two negative choices. For example, the choice may be the repair of a fifteen-year-old washing machine which would be quite expensive or the purchase of a new washing machine. Both choices involve the outlay of a large expenditure. This purchase situation may involve a considerable search for information. The purchase of a "do-it-yourself" repair kit is designed to turn the negative alternative into a positive one.

Approach–Avoidance Conflict

This purchase situation is probably the truest conflict and it develops when the consumer is both attracted and repelled in the same direction. For example, to purchase a home, a sizable amount of cash for a down payment may be needed. Resistance to the home purchase may be present unless the pressures can be reduced. Financial institutions may be able to make credit terms easier, thereby easing the avoidance aspects of such conflicts.

Prestige or status retail stores, such as Bloomingdale's or Neiman-Marcus, may offer private labels that identify the merchandise as expensive to others. The availability of credit cards, warranties, return privileges and more personalized selling contributes to the easing of large purchases at these upscale stores. Retail salespeople may try to summarize the features of each product to assist the customer in determining which alternative appears to be the better choice.

IMPLICATIONS FOR MARKETERS

Although much has been investigated about consumer purchasing behavior, it is frequently overlooked that consumer behavior consists of three distinct activities: shopping, buying, and consuming. John O'Shaughnessy focused upon consumer goals, wants, and beliefs to help explain why consumers buy.[6] Much of O'Shaughnessy's work was developed based upon different consumer motivation theories. However, little is known about consumer motives for the shopping function. Edward Tauber explored the determinants of shopping behavior.[7] The examination of why people buy and why people shop demonstrates the interdependence of needs and goals. Consumers are not always as aware of their needs as they are of their goals. For example, an individual may join a photography club to learn more about photography but may not be consciously aware of the need to meet new friends. The awareness of physiological needs is more apparent than psychological needs. When hungry or thirsty, appropriate measures are taken to satisfy those needs. However, the needs for social approval and self-esteem may not be as sharply identified.

Tauber has hypothesized that social shopping motives are social experiences outside the home, communication with others, peer group attraction, status and authority, and pleasure of bargaining. These variables would vary in intensity from individual to individual and environmental influence would also be an important factor. Tauber's study was not empirically tested. As a result, marketers still can only conjecture how to prioritize these social-shopping motives. Tauber maintained that there are also personal motives for shopping such as the following:

- Role playing—housewife or husband.
- Diversion—represents a break from routine.
- Self-gratification—reflects mood or emotions.
- Learning about new trends—may reflect symbols.
- Physical activity—an opportunity to get out of the house.
- Sensory stimulation—shopping is perceived as recreation.

Shopping motives can also be based upon impulse. The likelihood of going shopping on impulse has probably increased over the years as consumers' lives have become more complex. Moreover, the distance or time traveled to the mall, shopping center, or store is a convenience element that might trigger impulse shopping behavior. Time availability may also trigger impulse shopping either traveling to or from work. The list of personal and social shopping motives might suggest that social and recreational factors are an important part of shopping behavior and therefore a sense of drama or theater in the retail store would be viewed positively by consumers.

Purchasing motives are complex. There is a combination of rational, emotional, and patronage motives that comprise many purchases. Typical buyers for a product may have different motives than other purchasers. For example, both men and women of varying ages are buyers of the Ford Mustang, but the typical buyer is a middle-aged male, about forty-five, with an avid interest in motorcycling and power boating. The typical purchaser by inference would seem to enjoy showing off these material goods. The Ford Mustang sells best in Los Angeles, Dallas, and New York City and sells poorly in Lafayette, Indiana; Cheyenne, Wyoming; and Anchorage, Alaska.

Many markets have evolved first from niche marketing which targets individuals and responds to their special needs. For example, Intel directed their computer products to the hobbyist market a few years before Apple Computer abandoned this market because it was small. Apple built itself on the hobbyist market. Many of the early users of personal computers in education, small business, and the business professional market came from hobbyists or enthusiasts. Those personal-computer users had the motivation to master a complex product and to use it effectively to satisfy their wants and needs. This internal motivation of customers helped Apple Computer become successful.

Lance was among the first in the snack food industry to respond to the changing environment that emphasized consumer health concerns. Lance began to offer cholesterol-free, low-saturated fat, low-salt, and low-sugar snacks. Since 1988, Lance has been master of niche marketing. Niche marketing is profitable since the market niche learns about the target market consumer group so well that it can satisfy needs better than competitors who are casually selling to the niche. Consequently, in the beginning, Lance was able to charge a substantial markup over costs because of added value to the consumer. Lance had found an ideal market niche since it had growth potential. A fundamental principle in niching is specialization. Niching carries an important risk in that the market niche might be attacked. Moreover, high costs can be incurred in identifying and serving a niche segment.

Segmented markets that are close to fragmented markets are the wave of the future. Niching strategies will be more useful than most marketing strategies in targeting consumer markets. Consumers who comprise niche markets have clear and pronounced purchasing characteristics and motives. Changing demographics will have an impact on lifestyles. These lifestyle changes will bring with them substantial alternatives in consumer behavior and motivation. With an increasing aging population, more dual-income families and the expansion of nontraditional households, there will be new opportunities for marketers to serve these market niches.

BRAND DECISION PROCESS

Brands vary widely in consumer familiarity and acceptance. The consumer's familiarity with a brand moves from nonrecognition to insistence and is shown in Figure 3.2. Nonrecognition means that the consumer does not recognize the brand and the marketer must make the consumer aware of the brand. Brand recognition means that the consumer is aware of the brand but does not necessarily prefer it to competing brands. Consumers may need help in recalling the brand; this can be done by point-of-purchase materials in retail stores. If the consumer makes the purchase and is satisfied the probability of its being repurchased increases. Inexperienced consumers will purchase the most familiar brand and therefore brand recognition is desired by manufacturers. Brand awareness is a strategic asset and provides a sustainable competitive difference over time when one considers such brands as Kleenex, Band-Aid, and Crayola. Brand preference is the second stage of brand loyalty. Consumers will choose the brand over competitive offerings based on previous experience with it. Consumers might use another brand if that brand is on sale or if the preferred brand is out-of-stock or for the sake of variety. The marketer's goal is to achieve consumer preference and then brand insistence or brand loyalty. Whereas brand preference is a positive consumer reaction, brand rejection is a negative reaction. Brand rejection means that a customer will not purchase the brand unless its image or product attributes are changed. Brand insistence means that the customer will accept no alternatives and will search extensively for the product or service. Although brand insistence is the goal of most marketers, it is seldom realized. Since many consumers cannot recognize their favorite brands of beer and soft drinks in blind taste tests, brand preference is an important factor in the brand decision process.

The importance of brand loyalty cannot be underestimated. Tucker, in his classic article, concluded that some consumers would become

Figure 3.2
Achieving Brand Familiarity

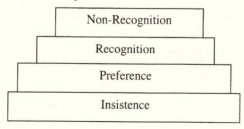

brand loyal even when there is no discriminable difference between brands other than the brand name itself. Tucker also concluded that consumers vary greatly in their susceptibility to brand loyalty.[8] Twedt, in his research study, found that product usage proved to be much more important than demographics for segmenting markets.[9] Both the Tucker and Twedt studies have been widely cited by researchers on brand loyalty. In a more recent study, the research indicated that patent expiration on twelve drugs had minimal impact on the drugs' market shares or price levels. This stability was attributed to brand loyalty to the pioneer product.[10] There are some brands that have demonstrated market leadership for over eighty years such as Campbell Soup, Sherwin-Williams paint, Life Savers candies, Gillette razors, and Wrigley's chewing gum. Consumer loyalty to these products reflects a decision when to buy, not what to buy.

The strategy of brand extension may be used if there is a high degree of brand insistence or brand loyalty. For example, General Foods has extended its Jell-O brand to Jell-O Pudding Pops. Brand extension is the strategy of using a brand name that has a high degree of customer loyalty for a new product entry. The new product begins at the recognition, preference, or insistence stage of the brand decision process because of the association of the established name. Consumers who rejected the existing product would be unlikely to try the new product but might under a different name. Some customers might not try the new product if the new product category is considered different from the original product category. Brand associations might reflect lifestyle such as the Pepsi Generation or symbols such as the Prudential rock or even product use such as Gatorade for sports activities and events.

Brand switching occurs not just because customers are dissatisfied with a present brand. A change in consumer lifestyle is another likely reason for change in consumer preference. The degree to which customers are loyal to their favorite brand varies significantly and therefore it is difficult to predict how successful brand switching campaigns will be on certain consumer segments. Established brands such as Gillette, Wrigley, and Rubbermaid are still doing well over the years but brands such as Budweiser and Hershey are facing more competition. Kellogg's is confronted with private labels or dealer brands eroding their brand share of established products such as Corn Flakes and Raisin Bran. Wal-Mart's private-label brand, Equate, is priced below Tylenol and Nyquil, thus gaining market share. Brands such as Fab, Gleem, Crystal Pepsi, Subaru, and Borden are in the process of brand elimination or simplification.

The improved quality of private-label products has narrowed the gap between manufacturer and private labels. Although the purchase process favors brand-name products, brand switching is a common phenomenon and brand loyalty is not strong. Brand strength parallels the economy and, consequently, consumers turn to less expensive store brands in economically uncertain times. However, manufacturers with national brands are in an advantageous position and can limit the encroachment of private labels if the competitive threat is taken seriously.[11] Marketers are not just producing products, instead there is a concerted effort to market aspirations, images, and lifestyles. The strategy is to establish a brand and to sell a lifestyle.[12]

RETAIL PATRONAGE CONSIDERATIONS

The reasons why consumers shop and make purchases at certain retail stores are referred to as patronage motives. The most important patronage motives are store prices and value, merchandise selection, purchasing convenience, location, store services, merchandise quality, consumer treatment by store, by store personnel, and store reputation and status. Consumers patronize some retail stores because of their proximity and in-store shopping convenience. Other stores are selected because of their wide selection of merchandise. Still other stores are chosen because they carry particular merchandise that is desired by consumers. A consumer's in-store shopping behavior is affected by such factors as sales personnel, displays, and merchandise breadth and depth. Retailers can develop their strategies in consideration of these factors. Retailers are able to tailor a retail offer or a portfolio of retail offers and even the design of the store to the lifestyles of specific market segments. Retailers such as the Gap and Laura Ashley appeal to a particular market segment. These retailers have also developed lifestyle brands which contribute to the desired lifestyle of the customer.

The retail store choice decision can be one of high involvement or low involvement. At times the decision may be highly important, and at other times, especially with convenience items, the decision may be of low involvement. For example, such products as automobiles, mattress and box springs, and a component stereo or home theater system have high relevance because of their high price, complex features, large differences among alternatives, and high-perceived risk of making a wrong decision. Toilet tissue, light bulbs, and aluminum foil tend to be low involvement decisions for most consumers. There is not much risk if one brand is used rather than another. The products do not challenge the individual's self-concept and brand substitutions are commonplace. At the extreme, brand loyalty may dominate store choice decisions since some customers may switch stores if Weight Watchers products or Paul Newman's salad dressing is not offered.

Store loyalty is also a basis for market segmentation.[13] The store-loyal consumer is a profitable market segment on whom retailers may seek to focus their efforts. Consumer loyalty is a dominant construct for examining repeat purchasing behavior to predict store loyal behavior. Thus, purchasing motivation, brand choice decision, store choice decisions, and lifestyle consumer characteristics are intertwined.

The concept of store image may be envisioned as a composite attitude that consumers in a particular market segment have about a retail store as it relates to their set of expectations. For many consumers opening a jewelry box from Tiffany's has a different set of emotional feelings than if the same jewelry came in a J.C. Penney box. The perceived personality of the retail store is a development of the perceptions, emotions, and attitudes of consumers toward the various characteristics of the store. Market position is the sum of images that consumers have about the retail institution. These impressions consist of the retailer's merchandise assortment, ambience, personal communications, and internal and external nonpersonal communications. These factors must be coordinated to create a favorable store image that will attract the patronage of consumers in defined target market segments and create a competitive differential advantage. Victoria's Secret conveys an aura of mystery that contributes to the store's atmosphere designed to attract its target market.

One of the most important aspects of markets is their heterogeneity. While some women customers want designer-original clothes others may want clothes from design collections while others may desire ready-to-wear clothes with a reputable brand name and still others may want inexpensive ready-to-wear clothes regardless of brand name. It is rather difficult for retailers to satisfy the diverse needs and wants of all of these customers. Therefore, retail organizations try to identify the market segments that—or should—patronize their stores. Retail organizations such as Neiman-Marcus or Saks Fifth Avenue serve a different type of clientele than retailers such as Kmart. This is not to say that some overlap of markets does not exist. For example, a customer of an exclusive store like Neiman-Marcus might purchase clothing there but purchase a toaster at Kmart.

It is difficult for retailers to satisfy the diverse needs and wants of all customers. Therefore, some retailers try to identify a specific market and concentrate their efforts on serving it well. This retail market segmentation reduces a waste of resources and marketing effort and stimulates consumers to buy by serving their specific demands. To illustrate, consumer reasons for shopping at outlet malls were revealed as economic encompassing price–value reasons, merchandise quality and selection, recreational, and time saving. The study endeavored to identify the reasons for the growth of factory outlets over the past decade for manufacturers.[14]

Department stores are aware of the need to specify their markets and to use research to determine which markets could most profitably be served. J. L. Hudson, a department store in Michigan, has traditionally appealed to an older customer but through research found that it needs to generate more business from the twenty-five to forty-four-year-old market. Another department store chain, J.C. Penney, has identified the three major segments it desires to serve: young juniors, who are highly fashion-conscious; contemporaries who spend more money than any other segment on quality clothing; and conservatives who want comfort and value.

Consumers engage in a decision process for store choice as well as for product and brand choices. For example, Sunkist has an association with healthy living activities as well as oranges and this image has helped in marketing other products such as soft drinks and fruit bars. These decisions may be complex or simplistic in nature. Demographic and lifestyle characteristics and other purchaser characteristics such as perceptions of store attributes lead to general opinions and activities related to shopping and search behavior.

BROOKS BROTHERS: A CASE STUDY

Brooks Brothers is a case study of patronage purchasing behavior patterns. These changing patterns started in the 1960s when the rest of the country grew its hair long and widened its lapels. Brooks Brothers stayed the same. During the 1980s, when casual dress became fashionable and men began demanding trimmer cut suits to offset their aerobicized physiques, Brooks Brothers did not change the way it did business.

Brooks Brothers was founded in 1818 and is one of America's oldest clothing stores. Theodore Roosevelt, Ulysses S. Grant, and Woodrow Wilson wore Brooks Brothers suits when taking their oaths of office. Authors such as Ernest Hemingway, F. Scott Fitzgerald, and Somerset Maugham depicted characters in their novels that wore Brooks Brothers suits. Among the male movie stars that have patronized Brooks Brothers have included Fred Astaire, Burt Lancaster, and Gary Cooper. Female movie stars such as Elizabeth Taylor, Katharine Hepburn, and Audrey Hepburn have purchased dressing gowns, slacks, and sweaters from Brooks Brothers.

Brooks Brothers in the late 1990s concentrated on improving its product lines and customer service. Brooks Brothers had missed out on the trend for apparel to be worn on casual days or dress-down days which even take place at banks and law firms. A transformation took place as khaki pants, casual shirts, and selections of brightly colored shirts and ties made the merchandise more appealing to fashionable male shoppers. Years ago Brooks Brothers was located in downtown shopping areas but now suburban upscale shopping malls include their stores. Brooks Brothers was doing a balancing act with a brand franchise that had some strong meaning to the professional person and upscale customer. Brooks Brothers needed to change their image to enlarge the market. After years of selling its famous button-down oxford shirts, purple gingham shirts and turquoise-striped ties were added to the product line. Once the average age of customers was fifty-five and now it is close to forty. Therefore, the merchandise has to appeal to a younger, more impulsive consumer who may shop in one of its stores. The salespeople are more receptive to the twenty-something customers. Aloofness has changed to a smile and a welcome. Employee-training programs are used to prepare a customer-friendly salesperson. Female salespeople have been hired to work with female customers shopping for themselves and the men in their families.

The challenge confronting Brooks Brothers is how to attract women and younger adults without losing loyal customers. Young men did not perceive the store catering to them with new styles and the new strategy alienated old customers who could no longer find the styles and quality that was once a reliable mainstay. Fabrics felt cheaper and classic products had been discontinued. Brooks Brothers forgot about the suit guy. Changing buyer behavior patterns is difficult and changing a store image is even more difficult. Brooks Brothers suits were the uniform for those in high managerial positions and of those who aspired to reach this level. For a particular social class, it was the veil of respectability. Even today Brooks Brothers makes great suits for presidents and ambassadors.

WHEEL OF RETAILING

The wheel of retailing model is based upon the premise that price-sensitive consumers are not store-loyal and that new institutions are able to implement lower operating costs than existing institutions. Retail innovators enter the market as low-status and low-margin institutions. These inconveniently located institutions save on rent, offer few services, and are inexpensively furnished. Gradually as these institutions mature, they offer increased services, acquire more elaborate facilities, feature higher prices, and carry merchandise lines that convey higher status.[15] Moreover, as existing retailers move up the wheel, store image is upgraded and the target market broadened.[16]

An emerging institution known as the "category killer" stores, such as Home Depot and Toys "R" Us, appeals to consumers who are interested in low prices and a large selection of products.

The wheel of retailing explanation for the evolution and eventual demise of some retailers has held true over the years. Moreover, the importance of some retailers for certain types of products has declined and other types of retailers have become more important. Drugstores have become more important as sellers of toys in the past twenty years as independent toy stores have gone out of business and discount stores have gained prominence. Competition today is not between products but between business models such as the Internet, which will change the relationship between consumers and retailers; it was Main Street in the 1950s, shopping centers and malls in the 1960s and 1970s, superstores in the 1980s and 1990s, and the Internet in the 2000s.

Price-sensitive consumers are frequently not store loyal and are willing to change their allegiance to retailers offering lower prices. These customers are willing to exchange store services and convenient locations for lower prices. Under the wheel of retailing hypothesis, these businesses gradually attempt to broaden their customer base as their prices and services increase. The wheel hypothesis does not account for innovation nor does it adequately explain the development of specialty stores, Internet e-commerce, or convenience store consumer shopping patterns.

RETAIL LIFE CYCLE MODEL

The retail life cycle is considered a natural evolutionary institutional process. The duration of the retail life cycle is indefinite. A retail institution could remain in a specific stage of the life cycle for some years. Innovation and early growth, the first stage of retail development, generally reflect a significant departure from accepted practices in product assortment, shopping convenience, location, or promotional methods. In contrast to the wheel of retailing hypothesis, retail innovation may encompass any major change from the traditional distribution practices. In this stage, costs are high and profits are usually small. During the second stage, known as accelerated development, profits and market share experience rapid rates of growth. New retailers that were not the original innovators enter the field. Conventional store outlets try to retaliate during this stage. More complex internal systems, larger staffs, and higher costs characterize the end of the accelerated development stage. The maturity stage shows a reduction in profits. Stores generally suffer from overcapacity and increased competition. Many retail organizations are able to prolong the maturity stage and avoid the decline stage that concludes the retail life cycle. Still the retail life cycle appears to be growing shorter.[17]

The jumbo size of the "category killer" store exemplifies a retail institution in the innovation stage. Adjustment and experimentation take place in this stage. A high level of investment is needed to sustain growth. An example of the innovation stage is when Barnes & Noble added the videodisc kiosk, an interactive computer terminal, to display products and related information on a video screen allowing the consumer to place an order in the store with a credit card without dealing with a salesperson.

The department store is currently in the maturity stage of the retail life cycle. Sales have declined over past years because of competition from specialty retailers, changing demographics, a rising standard of living, and time constraints. The final stage is the decline stage and has been experienced by independent drugstores as large chains such as CVS, Walgreens, and RiteAid have entered the market and discounters such as Wal-Mart and supermarket chains have added pharmacy departments.

From a strategic perspective, marketers and retailers make adaptations in their assortments, services, and products to best satisfy their target markets. It may be necessary for firms to reposition themselves at appropriate times to adequately serve their market segments. Many established brands and retail organizations have been slow to learn this lesson with unfortunate results.

IN-HOME SHOPPING

Nonstore retailing refers to making sales in consumers' homes. The major components of nonstore retailing include direct-to-home sales and mail-order sales. Such products as cosmetics, vacuum cleaners, dairy products, and encyclopedias have been successfully sold through direct-to-home selling methods. The party plan method requires a salesperson to make sales presentations in the home of a host or hostess. Tupperware and Wearever Aluminum products make extensive use of the party method. Toys, jewelry, and wearing apparel are among other products sold using this method. Large department stores such as J.C. Penney use decorator consultants who sell a comprehensive line of furnishings in the home.

Many firms combine both mail and telephone selling or use these methods separately. Mail order offers reduced costs to sellers and a large geographic area can be covered. Sears, Spiegel, and J.C. Penney offer a complete line of products in their general merchandise catalogs. The Franklin Mint, L. L. Bean, and the Book-of-the-Month Club offer specialty merchandise catalogs.

Since electronic sales are possible with Internet hookups, in-home retailing sales will increase in the future. Moreover, working wives, elderly shoppers, and those consumers who desire to save money through lower price offerings represent the best customers for this type of buying.

In-home purchasers have been characterized as more cosmopolitan, style and value conscious, convenience-oriented, and generally more demanding than those who make their purchases in retail stores. Additional lifestyle patterns reveal that their purchasing patterns are more flexible and risk taking is viewed positively. Marketers should stress information in their campaigns that reduces any risks associated with in-home shopping. Appeals should have a venturesome, self-assured, and cosmopolitan orientation.

INTERNET SHOPPING

Since 1995, the number of people roaming the Internet's virtual aisles increased about three times from 14 million to 42 million.[18] This expansion of shopping in cyberspace is viewed as an indication of how future shopping will take place. Price does not seem to be a competitive factor when shopping on the Internet. Internet retailers offer customers a wide selection, convenience, outstanding service, high-quality products, and in-depth information about product offerings. To illustrate, Amazon.com can offer 3 million book titles including highly specialized topics and titles. Charles Schwab offers the convenience of online brokerage service and Dell Computer makes its site super convenient and allows customers to compare prices. Garden Escape offers discussions with the site's "lawn doctor" and 1-800 Flowers, Inc. will send an e-mail reminder of a relative's birthday.

A study of Internet shopping behavior concluded that vast product selection, the capability of screening a large number of options, information reliability, and product comparisons were important consumer motives for shopping on the Internet.[19] Two fundamental advantages of interactive home shopping are the low cost of information search and that customers can complete transactions in a twenty-four-hour seven-day environment. This enhances sales effectiveness while reducing the time and errors associated with traditional retail selling. Another buyer motivation to shop on the Internet is brands can be easily compared. This facilitates the marketing of brands. Distribution of the brand might have been limited in some geographical territories but the Internet now facilitates brand selection and shopping.

There are a number of conditions that favor in-home and Internet shopping:

- Consumers are more concerned with self-identity through the purchase of goods and services and therefore desire a broader product assortment than most retail stores can display.
- A higher proportion of double-income families has less time to shop.
- There is a greater demand for specialty products and services that are not available to many customers.
- More consumers have the education to make use of home computers and the technology that facilitates in-home shopping.

Many affluent consumers prefer the Web sites of Amazon.com, Ebay, Land's End, L. L. Bean, J. Crew, and RedEnvelope. Although the reasons for purchasing from these Web sites differ, all buyers believed that these retailers made it easy for them to make a purchase. In fact, RedEnvelope matches gifts by occasion such as holiday and birthday and by lifestyle such as the gadget guru, the spa seeker, and the connoisseur. The saving of time is the paramount motivator for the affluent consumer to use the Web for purchases.[20]

MANAGING CHANGE

The change in consumer purchasing patterns is easily recognized in the automobile market. BMW is offering the Mini Cooper starting at $17,000 and Mercedes sells the C-Class Coupe starting at $25,000 to penetrate the low-end of the affluent market. Detroit automakers are profiting from the sale of SUVs that sell for more than $35,000. Ford is endeavoring to exploit luxury brands as Jaguar, Volvo, Land Rover, and Astin-Martin, and General Motors has invested nearly $5 billion to make far-reaching changes in Cadillac and Saab luxury brands. There is a risk that existing product brand images may become tarnished but the automakers are willing to assume that risk based upon changing purchasing behavior patterns.

Determining why people buy and why they make the purchase choices that they do is complex. Various product features such as status, prestige, economy, price, style, color, service, and warranties may appeal to different market segments. Purchase decisions extend from routine to major purchases that require deliberation and planning over extended time periods. Learning what motivates consumer-purchasing behavior is not easy. Basic fundamentals of motivation include the following:

- Motives are not permanent. Motives change throughout the life cycle.
- Aspirations tend to grow with achievement and decline with failure.
- Motivation is influenced by the performance of other members of a group to which a person belongs and by that of reference groups.
- Consumers are actively learning and acquiring new wants.

The adoption of direct selling to the consumer has benefited many firms. A lot of consumers prefer to shop at home. This trend might have been caused by a combination of factors such as increased education, more women in the workforce, spending leisure hours in other pursuits, or confidence that the seller is reputable and reliable. Moreover, the Internet has developed a new means of customer communication and will change operational strategies inasmuch as consumers will be given unprecedented control over the marketing process. Since retailers will be competing with Internet firms using this new method of marketing, it is expected that more loyalty programs will develop in the future. The consumer loyalty programs are expensive, however, slowing revenue growth in many merchandise categories will increase alliances with manufacturers to intensify consumer-loyalty activities.

Change is a pervasive dimension in purchasing behavior. The reasons behind fast and slow rates of change are necessary to comprehend in order to develop appropriate strategies. Some dimensions that are useful as guidelines in formulating strategies include the following:

1. Fast Rates of Change
   a. Rapid changes in consumer lifestyles, shopping patterns, and attitudes toward shopping.
   b. More intensive development of new services and products, and shorter product life cycles to satisfy changing consumer purchasing patterns.
   c. Less resistance to innovation because of rapid changes in technology.
2. Slow Rates of Change
   a. Lack of access by many marketers to capitalize on subsegments of markets.
   b. Increased economic concentration in industries leading to antitrust constraints and greater barriers to entry.
   c. More firms searching for collaborative agreements and strategic alliances to satisfy changing consumer purchasing behavior patterns.

An analysis of consumer purchasing behavior can help identify consumer market segments, namely target markets that can best be served by marketers. Information related to consumer lifestyles is then accumulated to determine how best to satisfy the most promising market segments. Lifestyle market segmentation is useful in defining markets. The process of studying lifestyle market segmentation dimensions can help keep marketers alert to changes in market conditions, competition, and environmental opportunities and threats.

NOTES

1. Stewart Henderson Britt, "The Strategy of Consumer Motivation," *Journal of Marketing* 14 (April 1950): 66–74.

2. Jerry W. Thomas, "Finding Unspoken Reasons for Consumer Choices," *Marketing News* 32, 8 June 1998, 2, 10.

3. David Whelan, "Men, Their Motives and Their Magazines," *American Demographics* 23 (October 2001): 18–21.

4. Abraham H. Maslow, "A Theory of Human Motivation," *Psychological Review* 50 (July 1943): 370–396.

5. Kurt Lewin, *A Dynamic Theory of Personality* (New York: McGraw-Hill, 1935).

6. John O'Shaughnessy, *Why People Buy* (New York: Oxford University Press, 1987).

7. Edward M. Tauber, "Why Do People Shop?" *Marketing Management* 4 (Fall 1995): 58–62.

8. William T. Tucker, "The Development of Brand Loyalty," *Journal of Marketing Research* 1 (August 1964): 32–35.

9. Dik W. Twedt, "How Important to Marketing Strategy Is the Heavy User?" *Journal of Marketing* 28 (January 1964): 71–72.

10. Meir Statman and Tyzon T. Tyebzie, "Trademarks, Patents, and Innovation in the Ethical Drug Industry," *Journal of Marketing* 50 (Summer 1986): 71–81.

11. John A. Quelch and David Harding, "Brands Versus Private Labels: Fighting to Win," *Harvard Business Review* 74 (January–February 1996): 99–109.

12. "Who's Wearing the Trousers?" *Economist* 360, 8 September 2001, 26–28.

13. Fred D. Reynolds and William R. Darden, "Developing an Image of the Store-Loyal Customer," *Journal of Retailing* 50 (Winter 1974–1975): 73–84.

14. Kiran W. Karande and Jaishanhar Ganesh, "Who Shops at Factory Outlets and Why? An Exploratory Study," *Journal of Marketing Theory and Practice* 8 (Fall 2000): 29–33.

15. Malcolm P. McNair, "Significant Trends and Developments in the Postwar Period," in *Competitive Distribution in a Free, High Level Economy and Its Implications for the University*, ed. A. B. Smith (Pittsburgh: University of Pittsburgh Press, 1958), 1–25.

16. Stanley C. Hollander, "The Wheel of Retailing," *Journal of Marketing* 15 (July 1960): 37–42.

17. William R. Davidson, Albert D. Bates, and Stephen J. Bass, "The Retail Life Cycle," *Harvard Business Review* 54 (November–December 1976): 89–96.

18. Heather Green and Seanna Browder, "Online Merchants: Cyberspace Winners: How They Did It," *Business Week*, 22 June 1998, 154–159.

19. Joseph Alba and John Lynch, "Interactive Home Shopping: Consumer, Retailer, and Manufacturer Incentives to Participate in Electronic Marketplace," *Journal of Marketing* 61 (July 1997): 38–53.

20. Peter Sealey, "How E-Commerce Will Trump Brand Management," *Harvard Business Review* 77 (July–August 1999): 171–176.

CHAPTER 4

Changing Values and Lifestyles

Individuals adopt lifestyles as the result of culture, social class, reference groups, and the family. Consumer lifestyles are derivatives of a personal value system and personality. Consequently, there is an overlap in meaning between core values, personality, and lifestyles. The identification of core values in the United States is a difficult undertaking. The United States is a "salad bowl" consisting of a variety of subcultures that respond to values and beliefs in their own patterns. It is a dynamic society subject to constant change in leadership and technology. And constant change makes it difficult to monitor the development of new values. There are times when Americans feel overwhelmed by change. The accelerated rate of change cited by Alvin Toffler in his trilogy *Future Shock, The Third Wave*, and *Powershift*, Peter Drucker in *The Age of Discontinuity*, and Jim Taylor et al. in *The 500 Year Delta*, presents challenges to business and marketing executives for the future.[1] For example, Generation Y or the Internet Generation has adapted behavioral patterns related to the advent of the personal computer and wireless communications. The term viral marketing has developed from these new behavioral patterns that encompasses word-of-mouth, advertising, direct mail, telemarketing, electronic mail, and the Internet. Viral marketing is a strategy that helps to develop close relationships with customers.

Consumers adapt to various lifestyles in part through a core of values that influence their subsequent behavior patterns. These values are developed based on their heritage and life experiences. For example, consumers who value fun and enjoyment may desire a specific brand of coffee for its rich taste whereas consumers who value a sense of accomplishment may desire a specific coffee brand as a mild stimulation to increase productivity and consumers who value warm relationships with others may desire a coffee break as an aspect of group companionship.[2] An understanding of consumer values is necessary, particularly if product consumption reflects consumer values.

Years ago an individual's occupation defined his or her lifestyle. Today, a person could be a dentist and a gourmet cook, a fitness zealot, a single living alone, and an environmentalist. Marketers could target each of these lifestyles since different goods and services are involved. For the gourmet cook, cooking utensils, wines, and specialized periodicals such as *Bon Apétit* are provided. The fitness zealot may be interested in purchasing athletic equipment and jogging outfits. The singles lifestyle may include an interest in ski resorts, equipment, and apparel. The environmentalist may be receptive to specialized travel vacation tours. The occupation of a dentist would embrace joining professional associations and the purchase of dental equipment. Occupation is still an important determinant of lifestyle but so are values and interests.

Personal values are considered an important market segmentation variable because they serve as determinants of attitudes and behavior and have manifested themselves in the formation of buying motives and brand attitudes. For example, one study found that the differences in value systems will influence activity preferences of tourists visiting a destination.[3] Personal value systems were better predictors of activity preference than demographic variations. Factors comprising items related to cultural activities, outdoor activities, sports activities, and roots such as visiting ancestral homelands and friends and relatives indicated that personal values were more useful than demographics in predicting tourist destination selection. Both automobile features and consumer values could be used simultaneously in market segmentation and developing positioning strategies for buyers purchasing American, German, and Japanese luxury cars.[4]

Recent years have witnessed consumers turning to component lifestyles whereby consumer attitude and behavior depend on specific situations rather than on overall lifestyle philosophy. A component lifestyle will allow consumers to take their children with them on holidays (family values), share such household tasks as food shopping (blurring of gender roles), or eat out on busy days (poverty of time).

Lifestyle fragmentation is most noticeable among affluent consumers as they increasingly emphasize style and taste. The affluent want to express their individuality. For example, cross-shopping is manifested as affluent consumers purchase pillows and sheets at Wal-Mart, suits at Brooks Brothers, and dresses at Ann Taylor. Consumers may possess sophisticated photographic equipment and low-priced home stereo components or systems. In the future, consumers may select goods and services that best express their growing sense of uniqueness. Successful marketing strategies recognize the product-specific and occasion-specific nature of the developing consumer environment.

The values of self-respect, security, warm relationships with others, sense of accomplishment, sense of belonging, self-fulfillment, being well-respected, and fun and enjoyment of life as value segments will vary in importance and priorities from decade to decade. Age, education, occupation, and gender will be variables as the assessment and significance of these values shift in importance. Marketers need to understand that consumers often purchase products for the benefit of value fulfillment and it is the function of marketers to help consumers realize their values.

Values are learned and are responsible for determining our self-concept. These values extend to social, religious, family life, entertainment, and other facets of life. Values are a mode of conduct which the individual believes is either correct or incorrect. To illustrate, values can be related to consumption expenditures with some people not purchasing products of American companies that sanction adverse working conditions for children abroad. Values can also reflect television-viewing habits. There has been pressure against violent and sexually explicit programming causing corporate advertisers to reevaluate their policies. In the final analysis, values influence purchase behavior. People who value time conservation prefer to do in-home shopping via Internet and catalogs and purchase from companies who make buying easy.

Although purchasing may be viewed rationally, many family purchases are inherently emotional and have an impact on the relationships between family members. For example, the decision to purchase a new toy for a child may be a symbol of love and commitment. Over time consumer values and lifestyles have been altered. To illustrate, wine consumption peaked in the mid-1980s and as consumers became more affluent the more expensive wines were purchased in the 1990s. Consumer tastes also reflect changing lifestyles as home furniture sales demonstrate a new formality featuring the Versailles look with crystal chandeliers and dining tables with pedestal bases. More affluent consumers prefer cherrywood

kitchen cabinets because the glazes make cabinets appear more fin-
ished and older than light oak.

MANAGERIAL IMPLICATIONS

Values can sometimes provide a deeper understanding of consumers and more information than demographics which is the foundation of SRI Consulting-Business Intelligence's Values and Life Styles.
The List of Values has greater predictive utility than does VALS in
consumer behavior trends. LOV allows marketers to obtain demographic predictions separately that identify the source of influence.
Moreover, LOV is easier to administer than VALS. Finally, it is easier
to preserve the exact phrase from a value study and incorporate it
into an advertisement. Thus LOV is better able to reduce communication errors than VALS.[5]

The LOV approach is not always the best market segmentation
technique but it permits marketers to better understand the precise
nature of a target market. Many consumer motives depend upon
values. Some people may contribute to a medical charity because of
a sense of belonging or because they want to protect their families.
Other consumers who value security may donate for self-protection.

The addition of value and motivational information to demographic data can increase market segmentation effectiveness. Marketers need to comprehend how and where a product, service, or
idea fits into the consumer's lifestyle and value orientation. Marketers must also ascertain how to position the product in each market
segment. Values can be important in this respect since product perception may be a result of these values. However, values do not necessarily predict all dimensions of buyer behavior. The use of
consumer values for segmentation purposes is best used for durable
goods such as automobiles, symbolic goods such as apparel, and
lifestyle activities such as vacation travel and books. The use of values for predicting buyer behavior is limited for certain commodities
and packaged goods. Moreover, demographics are not useful predictors since households with identical demographics frequently
react differently to meanings and values. Attitudes and opinions
generally change more quickly than values that are more durable
but subject to generational aging.[6]

The identification of consumer lifestyles is the beginning point
for developing a market segmentation strategy that will have an impact on all aspects of the marketing program. For example, the trend
that reflects more casual lifestyles demonstrates a desire to live a
less traditional, conservative, formalized lifestyle in terms of dress,
eating, entertainment, and other aspects of daily living. Many orga-

nizations have scheduled "dress down days" for employees. Even furniture sales reflect a more casual way of life, potentially reducing future long-term sales of formal living and dining room furniture. In contrast, there are growth prospects for indoor/outdoor furniture. Moreover, the trend for life simplification shows a desire to purchase furniture and home furnishings that are easy to care for, easy to repair, and require less maintenance. Consumers are also interested in environmentally safe products, energy-efficient products, and do-it-yourself projects. Time conservation is another aspect of life simplification and indicates a need for marketers to recognize that time is a critical resource and constraint in consumers' lives.

There are far-reaching managerial implications considering the increased concern over price and quality or quantity relationships. Consumers are increasingly elevating product and service expectations. Management must accommodate consumers' expectations through benchmarking and tightening product quality control. The extension of guarantees and warranties becomes more important.

The average consumer in the 1990s was employed at full-time jobs with good fringe benefits. They enjoyed shopping at the mall. The couple used their personal computer for e-mail and taped their favorite programs on their VCR. Purchases in discount stores and manufacturers' coupons represented good value. In the early 2000s, consumers lost their jobs and started their own businesses. They work out of a home office as they grow gray around the temples and their body joints stiffen. They have experimented with herbal remedies, spend more time in the bathroom Jacuzzi, and less time shopping at the mall. The computer and cellular phones are used to monitor their Individual Retirement Accounts. Purchases made through online shopping services have become more common.

QUALITY OF LIFE AND CHANGING VALUES

The quality of life of consumers in the United States goes beyond economic factors and includes an increasing concern with a sense of well-being. This reflects noneconomic factors such as crime rates and pollution. Consumer beliefs, feelings, states of happiness, and other behavioral measures are associated with consumer expectations. Generally, the quality of life is equated with a sense of satisfaction. This sense of satisfaction is derived from the elements of the good life: happiness, security, enjoyment, and accomplishment. Many of these elements tend to be subjective and therefore consumers may establish unrealistic standards. When this sense of well-being is brought to bear on business organizations, it translates into a belief that organizations should be more than economically efficient.

One of the more important quality of life issues has been ecology and public policy. Consumer values on this issue have changed over the years and are still evolving. A growing concern about the impact of environmental factors on product development labeling and other promotion strategies has emerged as a result of increased public awareness of new environmental needs. Consumer organizations have increasingly focused their attention on social and environmental problems. Moreover, attention by the mass media has served to make the general public aware that environmental safeguards are necessary.

The problems of ecology are holistic in nature and affect all consumers no matter where they live. The interfaces between marketing and ecology have become important as problems of air, water, and noise pollution, overburdened travel arteries, decaying cities, overpopulation, and poverty have received scrutiny.

Environmental groups have taken a stand against aerosol-spray cans because of their potential damage to the atmosphere's ozone layer, and they have been concerned with methods to produce and package goods that do not cause environmental damage. Nonreturnable or throwaway containers have been the subject of public referendums in some localities. The conservation of natural resources sometimes runs counter to economic growth policies. Finally, scarcities of oil and the potential depletion of other natural resources have caused many firms to invest heavily in research and development seeking other energy alternatives.

Public concern over ecological problems includes a variety of dimensions. Environmental parameters include such factors as population, economic development, and urbanization. Resources such as energy, solid waste, and recycling have been especially pertinent for marketers. Ecological factors such as climate and wildlife have taken on interesting dimensions. For example, consumers now have a tendency not to purchase animal furs. This has been the result of publicity showing the savage killing of seals and other animals. Control of air pollution, water pollution, radiation, pesticides, noise, and toxic substances has increased costs for some industries but has created opportunities for other industries. Finally, the concern for quality of life underlies environmentalists' policies on housing, transportation, aesthetics, occupational environment, and recreation.

Table 4.1 identifies the changing values and lifestyles that have evolved in the past few decades.

Trends such as the blurring of gender roles, health concerns, and time conservation are pervasive and are an inherent part of societal values affecting American lifestyles. Outcomes may change in subsequent years but values are permanent. Ordinarily, trends do not become values and such trends as changing morality and more ca-

Table 4.1
Changing Values and Lifestyles

Trends	Outcomes
More casual lifestyles	Dress down days in industry
Blurring of gender roles	Men grocery shopping and women repairing household items
Instant gratification	Services performed same day such as picture development and dry cleaning
Life simplification	Easy maintenance and repair
Health concerns	Nutrition, vitamin balance, diet foods, personal trainers
Desire for personalization	Unique products, antiques
Changing morality	Rental programs, sensual themes in advertising
Consumerism	Guarantees, warranties, labeling
Time conservation	In-home shopping by Internet and catalog, hand-held computer cellular phones

sual lifestyles will evolve over time. To illustrate, it took a long time before the Puritan ethic that forbade wastefulness passed from the scene and consumers were willing to throw away tissues and other products. The instant gratification trend is more a lifestyle change than a permanent value but products such as self-cleaning ovens and vinyl siding and windows are not only a part of self-gratification but part of life simplification as well. Shopping for furniture causes endless difficulties for customers in an age of instant gratification; therefore, the major challenge of the furniture industry is to solve the problems of long and delayed delivery services. Consumerism has taken on issues of prohibiting the killing of dolphins to the strict enforcement of food labeling. Moreover, there is an overlap between changing morality and consumerism as pressures mount for companies like Nike and Gap to abandon the sweatshops that employ children in Asia. These consumer pressures suggest that quality of life issues are considered not only in the United States but also in foreign countries.

Baby boomers seem to cherish life simplification and convenience. This change in values and lifestyles explains the attraction of prepared take-out foods and microwave ovens. There is also a growing demand for home delivery services for items such as furniture and groceries. Products that are reliable, durable, and easy to maintain are prized by this market segment.

MANAGERIAL IMPLICATIONS

Marketing has been able to play an important role in improving the quality of life. Marketers have been instrumental in encouraging companies to develop safer products such as childproof bottle caps and child automobile seats. Public service messages have been developed for energy conservation, driver safety, alcohol and drug abuse, and AIDS awareness and prevention. New ideas relating to good nutrition and exercise have been communicated to the public.

There are several approaches for improving the quality of life that reflect the changing values of society. These methods include passing legislation, developing appropriate technological innovations, and making undesirable behaviors more economically costly. The passage of legislation increasing tobacco taxes and specifying where tobacco products can be advertised illustrates efforts to increase the quality of life and health of consumers. Marketers have sponsored several campaigns including "Smokey the Bear" and "Keep America Beautiful."

The monitoring of ecological changes should measure how well resources are conserved, how well pollution is limited, and how well a balance can be developed between maintaining consumer needs and wants and maintaining basic environmental needs. The marketing of products beneficial to the physical environment will be even more important in the future. Products constructed from biodegradable packages are in greater demand as consumers seek ways of protecting the physical environment. The use of solar energy, water-conservation devices, organic gardening, and health foods have been obvious manifestations of the growing concern of consumers with the deteriorating quality of the natural environment.

CHANGING FAMILY VALUES AND LIFESTYLES

Cultural changes indicate a new American value pattern emerging that will affect marketers in many ways. First, increased affluence, education, and information resources will open new opportunities for travel, entertainment, sports and leisure-oriented products. Second, home activities will continue to activate the do-it-yourself market and such items as computers, swimming pools, and spas. Third, consumers will insist on safe and nonpolluting products and packaging. Fourth, there will be a continued shift toward self-fulfillment with its focus on inner rather than other-directed satisfaction and an increased demand for self-help books, hobby aids and equipment, and in-home decorating. Knowledge of consumer values will provide marketers with in-depth demographic and psychographic dimensions.

The impact of the 1970s on family structure in the United States was surprising to many. The population explosion faltered and there was zero population growth. Family mobility was evident as the Sunbelt states grew beyond expectations. The increase in the elderly population startled many business organizations. Government seemed unprepared for this growth. Moreover, average household size diminished drastically.

The 1980s witnessed the fading illusion of the ideal American family of the husband as the sole breadwinner and the wife as a full-time housewife taking care of the two (statistically, two-and-a-half) children. Marriage at a later age, fewer children, a higher divorce rate, and more working wives have all helped to change the concept of the traditional family. By the end of the 1980s, it became apparent that the family was changing and the household unit was considered a changing target market. Quite apparent was the movement of many women into the workforce. Women seemed to be opting for jobs not just as a stopgap until marriage but also for careers. The commitment to careers meant the postponement of marriage to a later age, smaller family size, and sometimes the decision not to have children at all. Family decision making in the selection of household goods and brand choice changed and how marketers adjust their strategies to these societal changes is complex.

In the 1990s the American family with two children and a two-car suburban lifestyle was a minority. The divorce rate made the extended family unit more commonplace. Purchasing-behavior changes over a lifetime reflect age, family life-cycle stages, and even psychological lifestyle-cycle stages. For example, where there are children with only one household head, the children exert a strong influence on brand choice. Life insurance firms might also find a market development opportunity present as the family headed by a woman might desire protection for children. In contrast, middle-aged divorced couples will find establishing two households expensive and probably purchase lower-priced furniture and used automobiles. There are limitations of using age alone as an indicator for stage in the family life cycle. There might be instances where an older man marries a much younger woman with children. This would be an exception and certainly not indicative of the vast majority of families.

All individuals occupy a role within groups, organizations, and institutions. Although family roles are changing, traditionally the father was both husband and breadwinner in the family. The father might have been a business executive, a little league coach, or even a student enrolled in a master's degree program. These roles assumed by father, wife, and children reflect purchasing behavior in varying situations within the family life cycle.

The most important reference group is the family. Spouses influence each other's choice in clothing, appliances, furniture, and other household items. Children influence parents' choices of stereo equipment and computers since, in many instances, they are more knowledgeable about these products. In turn, parents influence the college or occupational choice of their children. There are also many family group decisions such as a summer vacation or the purchase of a new home. Within the family, members may assume one or more roles such as the following:

- Information Gatherer—Collects product information and is knowledgeable about appropriate sources.
- Influencer—Establishes standards of brand comparisons.
- Decision Maker—Responsible for final selection.
- Purchasing Agent—Buys the product.
- Product User—Individual or entire family determines level of purchase satisfaction.

The marketer's challenge is to determine which family members (or member) are likely to have the most influence on the purchasing decision. In this way communications can be directed to the correct individual or individuals. The stage of the family life cycle or the family environmental situation may have an impact on purchasing behavior. For example, married couples who both work without children are more affluent. This couple is a good market for travel, entertainment, antiques, jewelry, motor vehicles, and durable goods. Once children arrive, discretionary income may decrease as expenditures on infant products, appliances, and furniture increases.

THE CHANGING SOCIAL SYSTEM

Three current trends have a profound impact on consumer behavior. The first trend involves the rise in double income families which constitutes a new social class. The second trend is the emerging role of the professional woman in society and the third is the changing role of men in the family.

1. Marketers are becoming increasingly aware that the double-income or dual-income family, where both husband and wife work full time, or the family unit where there are multiple people in the workforce is an important target market. The implications of this fact of economic life on buying patterns and marketing strategies will receive increased attention. The importance of this growing market cannot be underestimated. Multiworker families are a growing segment of American society. As the proportion of these families continues to increase, the impact on the economy of their higher family income and level of consumption will grow as well. Working husbands and wives will establish new patterns in making purchasing decisions in shopping behavior. Some of

the outcomes of increased discretionary purchasing power are that two-car families will become three-car families, one computer households will become two- and three-computer households, and cellular telephones will grow in popularity where every member of the family will have their own telephone. Although family size is smaller than twenty-five years ago, housing purchases will be directed to homes with more space. The dual-income family will usher in a new wave of prosperity.

2. The image of the woman employed as a secretary, typist, cashier, bookkeeper, or telephone operator is changing as more women attend college and hold professional positions. In the past, a woman who desired a professional career became a teacher, a nurse, or a social worker. Today, women are lawyers, judges, government officials, medical doctors, veterinarians, psychologists, college professors, editors, accountants, and pharmacists. In past decades, it was difficult for women to obtain these jobs. Consumption habits of these professional families can range from the purchase of joint life insurance policies to art objects to trips to exotic travel locations. These families shop at stores such as Bloomingdale's, Nordstrom, or Neiman-Marcus rather than Sears or J.C. Penney. They may also participate in self-improvement programs. The professional career woman will not have time to casually browse. Instead, she will desire special presentations aimed at her needs that are concise and to the point and are often delivered by the Internet.

3. "The times they are a-changing." More men are living alone than ever before. Increasing numbers of married men are doing the grocery shopping and at least some of the cooking. Male executives are spending more time shopping for clothes than they used to. Men of an earlier generation were by and large the sole providers for their families. The forty-hour work week was not really instituted until the 1930s. Men may have done some of the heavy work at home over the weekend; such as rolling up the rug or moving the piano, but cooking, shopping, and cleaning were women's work. Men would play with the children and perhaps baby-sit but they did not assume a caretaking role. Although most of these men were the sole family providers, many had wives who either worked part-time or were teachers, nurses, social workers, or executive secretaries. World War II served as the impetus for many women to enter the labor force. However, because women did not earn as much as men, their salaries were viewed as supplemental. Although they did not really believe in a full partnership, men believed that they should occasionally help out at home, even in the kitchen.

Who are the "new men" and what are their demographic characteristics? The number of men living alone nearly doubled between 1970 and 1990; approximately half are under forty-five years of age and nearly one-third are between the ages of twenty-five and thirty-four. The proportion of men still not married and in their early thirties has doubled in the last decade. Another 2 million men are family heads in households where no wife is present. Moreover, there seems to more acceptance of house husbanding among American men. Although younger, well-educated, moderately affluent men are more inclined to accept egalitarian roles, more blue-collar men are participating in household management.

These trends among men continued well into the 1990s. Younger men are more likely than previous generations to accept new values. Unlike the generation of men born around the turn of the century and during the 1920s, 1930s, and 1940s, these younger men, many of whom lived alone and married at an older age, may well carry over into marriage more interest in household operations.

Lifestyles of men are changing. There is a bit of "Mr. Mom" in most households. Just as many women find it difficult to balance the demands of job and home, increasing numbers of married men and single fathers are under similar pressures. Each new generation of men will participate more than the previous generation in household management and childcare activities.

MANAGEMENT IMPLICATIONS

No longer will men be content to "watch the car" while the rest of the family shops. Males, especially the baby-boomer generation, are eager to participate in shopping. What specific strategies appeal to male shoppers? Convenience of location means more to men who are shopping for groceries than do advertised specials or lower prices. Because saving time is important to male shoppers, quick checkout service needs to be emphasized. Another appeal is variety, especially in bakery and deli items and alcoholic beverages. Male shoppers tend to have greater brand loyalty than do female shoppers. Men are less prone to switch brands if satisfied. Advertisements should show men shopping and purchasing specific brands. Instantly redeemable coupons would be more effective for this market than having men save or accumulate coupons.

When shopping for clothing, men reported that women exerted a major influence on their purchase. The extent of the female influence probably will continue, but the male consumer has become more interested in fashion and is less inclined to delegate entirely his purchasing role to the female. Since men are marrying at a later age, their interest in cooking and shopping for food and making a good impression with apparel and accessories is likely to carry over into their married life. Retail stores and manufacturers would do well to promote their products in men's magazines. The male consumer is less willing to delegate to women the purchase of his own clothing. Correspondingly, the woman professional has less time to shop for such items, even for herself. Although women still may reign supreme in the kitchen and the supermarket, the male shopper is having increasing influence on family food expenditures. Men are increasingly shopping alone and thus relying on their own values and priorities.

The traditional roles of men and women are not as distinct as they once were. Products formerly marketed to men are now also being marketed to women. And products that traditionally were marketed only to women are also being marketed to men. Instead of appealing to the same old stereotypes, alert marketers must adapt quickly to the changing role of the male consumer.

THE CHANGING DECISION-MAKING ROLES WITHIN THE HOUSEHOLD

Wives are making buying decisions that once were made by the husband alone. This change reflects the gains made by women in education and the emergence of economically independent women who hold more responsible positions in the workforce. However, the role reversal works both ways. Men are now making decisions that once were made jointly or by the wife alone. Because of the blurring of gender roles, new trends are emerging in family decision making.

A number of research studies have been conducted to ascertain the shifting roles of men and women in family decision making where children are present and where children are not present. Where there are children, husbands tend to dominate decision making. But in families with no children, decision making is more likely to be shared. This seems to confirm that the larger the financial contribution to the family made by the wife, the more purchasing influence is exerted. Because the working wife has greater career commitment than women with children, women with no children have a greater influence in decision making.

Gender roles are shifting at an earlier age with both boys and girls enrolled in shop and cooking classes. Generational differences also influence gender roles. The cultural upbringing of each generation and family is an important factor that will determine the changing roles of men and women in the household.

Greater involvement by men in home and childcare will give them more influence over purchases of foods and household items. As more women use a car or a SUV for work, they will play a greater role in making decisions regarding the appearance and style of the vehicle and also in its ergonomics and technical performance. Since many children are raised in double-income and one-parent families, they often not only take care of the house but also do some of the shopping. As a result, children have learned to be discriminating consumers earlier. Hotels have recognized the growing importance of adolescent decision making by targeting teenagers with a variety of activities and enticements. For example, Club Med has added a teen program that includes in-line skating, free diving lessons, and golf at some locations, and at the Westin in St. John, U.S. Virgin Islands, the program includes games like potato-sack races, water volleyball for the entire family, and an archeological dig for teens only.

Family structure has changed inasmuch as the proportion of young adults at every age who are single has increased markedly. These singles maintain well-furnished apartments and they assume a role in purchasing behavior that was not present in previous generations. Such changes in consumer lifestyles have significant consumer behavior implications. The growth in single-parent households demonstrates a need for convenience items, day care centers, and appliances that young children can operate. Promotional messages directed at singles and single-parent families may differ significantly from those aimed at the more traditionally structured families.

Another change in decision making has been the trend in delayed marriages. Many men and women marry at older ages and bring a new sophistication and maturity to the decision-making process. These couples typically are in a better financial position to purchase high-quality furniture and spend more on housing and services.

DIRECT MARKETING AND CHANGING VALUES

Direct marketing will increase substantially in the future. The reasons most frequently cited include less time for women and, for that matter, the entire family to shop and increased emphasis on the standardization and branding of products. Internet shopping has also broadened the opportunities for direct marketers. The success of direct marketing is due to added purchasing convenience on the part of purchasing for the consumer.

Direct marketing is a form of retailing typically using direct mail, conventional or cable television, radio, or some other nonpersonal medium to contact the customer. The customer usually orders items by mail, telephone, or the Internet. Some major direct marketing firms are Sharper Image (expensive gifts and novelties), L. L. Bean (clothing), Discovery Toys (crafts and hobbies), Princess House (decorative accessories), and Herbalife (nutritional products).

Catalog marketing involves selling through catalogs either made available through stores or mailed directly to consumers. Over 12.4

billion copies of more than 8,500 different catalogs are mailed annually. The average household is sent more than forty catalogs per year. Another part of direct marketing is telemarketing which involves using the telephone to sell directly to consumers. Over $40 billion is spent each year using this type of selling. Television marketing and electronic shopping are relatively new ways of direct marketing while door-to-door retailing is centuries old. A form of electronic shopping is videotex. Videotex is a two-way system that links the seller's data banks by cable or telephone lines with customers. The videotex service comprises a computerized catalog offered by manufacturers, retailers, banks, and other business organizations.

There are more than 100 Web retailers and online retailing, or e-tailing, is growing faster than any other form of retailing. As more consumers shop the Internet, more retailers are establishing themselves in cyberspace. Books, clothing, and computer software are currently the most commonly purchased online products. Other products and services sold online include leisure travel, brokerage services, PC hardware, auto sales, drugstore products, furniture, music, shoes, and appliances.

Many of the leading firms in the retailing of apparel are using direct retailing strategies to supplement their in-store strategies. They include Banana Republic, Victoria's Secret, J.C. Penney, Bloomingdale's, L. L. Bean, and Spiegel. Spiegel is the second-largest catalog retailer in the United States after J.C. Penney. The company markets apparel, home furnishings, and other merchandise via its catalog and by computer. The company introduced a CD-ROM catalog in 1996 displaying more than 3,000 items. The CD-ROM catalog is the largest display of a single catalog retailer's merchandise in that format.

Consumers who purchase apparel by mail are generally more style-conscious and convenience-oriented. The affluent customer has been the traditional target market for direct retailers and this type of customer is also a target for Internet shopping. However, the increase in the affluent market segment—particularly among dual-income married couples—will most likely mean a continued increase in direct-retailing sales volume from both catalogs and Internet shopping. The rise in affluence may decrease price sensitivity for consumers who are willing to make purchases from direct retailers. As affluent consumers feel more time constraints, they want better quality goods and services on the Internet and in catalogs.

In the early days, the heart of the market for Montgomery Ward and Sears and Roebuck, two mail-order giants, was rural America. Farm families awaited the arrival of the catalogs. A money-back guarantee was offered if the customer was not satisfied and these mail-order firms became the most trusted names in retailing. The Sears catalog was to surpass Ward's and the Sears name was better known than the manufacturers' brands advertised in the catalog.

With urbanization, the importance of the rural market diminished. Although the catalog could reach all parts of the country, operating a mail-order business was especially difficult in periods of rising prices. Moreover, with the advent of the automobile, rural customers could make purchases from a variety of nearby stores. Another factor working against mail order was the growth of chain stores, some of which pursued a cost leadership strategy and achieved economies of scale through volume purchasing and were able to offer products at lower prices. Customers wanted to see, touch, and try on merchandise before buying. Sears is no longer in the catalog business and Ward has gone out of business.

A number of conditions are now present to support selling through the catalog:

- Consumers are more concerned with self-identity through the purchase of goods and therefore desire a broader product assortment than most retail stores can display.
- A higher proportion of dual-income families have less time to shop.
- There is a greater demand for specialty products and services that are not available to consumers locally.
- More consumers have home computers to facilitate in-home shopping.

Internet shopping has not only increased revenue for direct marketers but has also led to changes in lifestyles. Many consumers spend their free time on their home computers. Communication has been enhanced by fax and e-mail. Internet shopping is more convenient than going to a nearby mall.

SERVICE MARKETING AND CHANGING VALUES

When studying the yuppie market, an attempt was made to determine if yuppies' product preferences and purchase habits have an impact on the selection of services. A study found that yuppies have a greater concern for quality and services and will be more apt to travel to get these factors than the general population. Moreover, the study concluded that price is not an important factor for yuppies in selecting products and services if they are perceived as a quality offering.[7] Since the yuppie market has different values than the general population, it is necessary for marketers to offer services that will satisfy this market segment.

Intangibility makes service marketing difficult. A product is not necessarily exchanged but rather an act may be performed. Travel agencies and recreation facilities such as concert halls perform an act that does not relate to a physical product. Repair services such as the reweaving of Oriental rugs tend to increase the value of products while Hertz or Avis will rent goods. Services may range from necessities such as electric power and medical care to luxuries such as hotels and computer camps.

Marketers of services and ideas are confronted with the challenge of making those services and ideas available to target markets. For example, state universities locate branch campuses to serve growing populations in geographic areas. Hospitals with varying types of medical equipment must be conveniently located to serve local communities. Banks need to operate trust departments that may serve the needs of affluent customers.

There are marketers who combine the sale of goods and services. For example, an automobile tire is a product that may be sold with balancing. Services may be equipment-based, such as airlines or computer time-sharing, or people-based, such as appliance repairs or accounting tax services. Services can be offered in the following manner:

- Combination by acquisition—The service is added to the total product mix of the firm. Sears is now selling financial services because of its acquisition of Dean Witter.

- Combination through leased departments—Leased departments are independent organizations that rent or pay a percentage of sales volume to another organization. Many coin and stamp departments, cosmetic departments, and optical services operate as leased departments in department stores.

- Combination by tie-in agreement—These are contractual arrangements made by two separate firms. General Motor's automobile dealers can arrange to have their customers financed through the General Motors Acceptance Corporation. The extension of credit by MasterCard, Visa, American Express, and the Diners Club are variations of this plan.

The most important issue in the distribution of services is location because consumers increasingly value easy access to services. For example, banks are trying to locate their automated teller machines in fast-food establishments and supermarkets, which makes it difficult to control service quality and might even decrease service productivity. Airlines, car rental companies, and hotels use intermediaries such as travel agents to handle reservations.

An important strategic consideration of marketing services is matching supply and demand. For example, the public has become more nutrition-conscious and fast-food restaurants are broadening their menu offerings to include salad bars, potatoes, and even low-cholesterol foods. Finally, distribution can be modified to respond to changes in demand. Theaters may offer matinees over the week-end when demand is at its highest. Airlines have used differential pricing in high peak versus low peak tourist seasons. Hotels have used promotions and special price inducements to stimulate demand during weekends and off-season. The availability of services is closely related to product decisions. Services consist of assistance or instruction, convenience, and availability. Thus, marketing decisions on site location, pricing, and promotion are necessary decisions in marketing services.

LIFESTYLE MARKET SEGMENTATION AND HOTELS

The hotel industry for years was relatively complacent. The demand for hotel rooms generally exceeded the supply. During the 1980s, the hotel industry experienced a building boom and soon there was a decline in room occupancy. Management was confronted with the problem that hotels couldn't be easily remodeled to satisfy customers' changing needs and that a product differentiation strategy was needed to make one hotel different from others. Many hotels had similar facilities and offered comparable services.

To meet these challenges, a strategy of lifestyle market segmentation was employed. When Holiday Corporation learned that its mid-priced Holiday Inn hotels were confronted with competition from budget hotels and luxury chains, Holiday Inn responded by expanding into the high- and low-priced ends of the market. Embassy Suites, a chain of multiple-room suites, targeted mainly upscale business travelers and Hampton Inn hotels, a limited-service chain, targeted value-conscious business or pleasure travelers. Holiday Corporation also developed Homewood Suites, a chain of hotels designed for guests staying five or more nights. Other chains such as Days Inn and Motel 6 have targeted the budget end of the market and compete with Hampton Inn which accounts for a sizeable 20 percent of all hotel rooms in the United States. Some hotels host family reunions and pursue that market segment by advertising a reunion package for weekends. Residence Inn, a division of Marriott, specializes in providing accommodations on a long-term basis with stays up to six months or longer. All suites have full-service kitchens and the hotel offers a grocery shopping service.

Hotels carefully try to match the service offering with the desired target market. Emphasizing service-provider reliability can increase service tangibility. Efforts must be made to offer similar services to market segments with different demand patterns. Although hotels endeavor to standardize services, there is the danger that the personal touch may be lacking. For instance, creative pricing has been used effectively. Several chains offer lower rates for weekend night stays and charge nothing for children under eighteen accompanying their parents. Other chains offer bonuses for "frequent stayers," a promotion patterned after the airlines' frequent-flyer programs.

Each market segment requires different services. The business traveler desires efficient service, a desk in the room, a computer hookup, a fax machine, and nearby conference rooms. A tourist desires a comfortable room, recreational facilities, and connections for sightseeing. Transient tourists desire a convenient location, low prices, and fast-food service. An extended-stay resident desires a home away from home with kitchen facilities and apartment amenities. Convention participants desire large meeting rooms, exhibit space, preplanned sightseeing, and hospitality suites. To accommodate female business executives, some hotels offer rooms on security-closed floors. First-run movies can be seen in the room and hotel spas provide the latest exercise equipment and indoor swimming pools.

Because services are perishable, many hotels try to offset this limitation with visual images and tangible reminders of their services. Hotels provide packaged shampoos and soaps, shoe polishing cloths, sewing kits, and other amenities with their name and logos imprinted. The Waterford Hotel in Oklahoma City, Oklahoma stocks their bathrooms with fresh fruit and Perrier. Other hotels provide bathrooms with bathrobes, heated towel racks, dual-line telephones, and remote controls for radio and television.

A strong and clear hotel image can increase consumer confidence in its lodging and service accommodations. Because consumers' perception of a hotel can influence their reaction to its offerings, management is concerned with the hotel's image. Perception of a hotel's image is derived not only from functional attributes of price and convenience but also from the influence of architecture, interior design, colors, and promotion. Hotels have become more aware of the importance of lifestyle market segmentation.

RELATIONSHIP MARKETING AND
CHANGING VALUES AND LIFESTYLES

The philosophy that marketing strategies must be based upon an awareness of consumer needs and wants, market research, profitable sales, and a coordinated organizational effort is known as the marketing concept. A Pillsbury Company marketing executive, Robert Keith, can be given credit for popularization of the marketing concept in 1960. The marketing concept is a business philosophy that maintains that an organization should endeavor to satisfy the needs and wants of customers through a coordinated set of activities that allows the organization to achieve its goals at a profit.

One of the first companies to pioneer the use of the marketing concept was General Electric. John B. McKitterick, president of General Electric in 1957, expressed the marketing concept as a customer-oriented, integrated, profit-oriented philosophy of business. The marketing concept recognized that sales is just one element of marketing and that marketing includes a broad range of activities with the customer focus being paramount.

The development of the marketing concept as a business philosophy changed the nature of most businesses to adopting a customer orientation. Customers with similar needs were identified and strategies were planned and implemented to satisfy these market segments. This process of dividing a diverse market into groups of consumers with relatively similar characteristics has made it easier to reach customers who want the product. And, most important, the sale of the product must be profitable to the company.

Relationship marketing has emerged as firms seek to develop and maintain long-term ties with their suppliers, distributors, and customers. The variables of consumer overall satisfaction, trust, and commitment are an integral part of relationship marketing. Overall satisfaction by customers varies depending upon how many transactions are made with the firm over a period of time. The promotion of customer trust and commitment is deemed essential to the intensity of strength of the relationship. The advancement of relationship marketing maintains that there are attributes shared by all relationships. These features include better communications to share thoughts and feelings with one another and establish a bonding with consumers. This linkage leads to a sustained commitment. Qualities of caring give signals to consumers that the company desires a close relationship. This leads to a certain comfort or compatibility with company policies and personnel. Finally, even though a degree of conflict might be present, the element of trust stands out.[8]

Relationship marketing is a long-term strategy that recognizes the purchase transaction does not terminate when the sale is made. The relationship actually intensifies after the sale. This is true of financial services rendered by such mutual fund organizations as Fidelity, Vanguard, and T. Rowe Price or for the sale of annuities by insurance firms. Not all relationships between buyer and seller need to be at the same level or the same duration. Relationship management preserves an intangible asset referred to as goodwill and is not easy to accomplish. The automobile industry strives for ongoing ties with suppliers, intermediaries, and customers. A consumer hotline is established so that buyers cannot only address problems but can also have any matters resolved.

Although relationship marketing and the promotion and fostering of long-term customer relationships is a prized ideal and objective for businesses, there are elements that may diminish and curtail the effectiveness of relationship marketing. First, there are shortages of labor so that the hiring of qualified personnel may prove difficult. Second, unqualified personnel may give customers impressions of abruptness and not caring about their purchasing problems. Relationship marketing would have difficulty thriving with a lack of rapport between customers and company personnel. Home Depot has trained its personnel to spend whatever time it takes to help solve customers' home improvement problems. Afraid that consumers are losing their taste for fast food because of health concerns, McDonalds, Burger King, and other chains are offering healthy products such as salads, baked potatoes, or yogurt.

MANAGING CHANGE

Lifestyle trends include different and expanding roles for both men and women and increased consumer sophistication with new technology. Some consumers will experience a poverty of time and will desire convenience in shopping. Other consumers will have greater amounts of leisure time and will purchase more recreational goods and services. Consumers will be increasingly concerned with values such as self-respect, security, warm relationships with others, a sense of accomplishment, and fun and enjoyment in life.

VALS and LOV approaches reflect a population dominated by consumers in their twenties and thirties. As this population matures, values and lifestyles will change accordingly. Not only the aging of the baby boomers, but also the impact of a global economy, digital technology, and the increasing diversity of the population mix will contribute to future changes in values and lifestyles. Financial resources tend to increase as an individual ages. Moreover, increased education and improved health technology will contribute to a much more sophisticated consumer desirous of social and physical activity. These consumers will be open to new ideas and social change.

Tedlow's historical account of marketing in the United States demonstrates the development of market segmentation strategies.[9] Market segmentation with its goal of target marketing is one of the most important concepts in marketing. The need for more sharply focused target marketing has been aided by lifestyle marketing strategies due to modern technology.

Although there are few certainties for marketers, one is that conditions will change at an accelerated rate. Demographics, lifestyles, consumerism, new technology, and the regulatory environment are among the factors that will affect the long-run success of marketers. Marketers will be confronted with uncertain forecasts and must be flexible in developing and implementing their strategies.

The key steps in forecasting and planning are interpreting signals of change, assessing the marketing and managerial implications of change, and developing strategies to take advantage of those changes. As marketers grow more sophisticated in linking changing lifestyles with marketing planning, organizations will become more effective in identifying market opportunities. This has happened over the Internet with a strategy referred to as permission marketing. Permission marketing is an unfolding sales process in a series of stages. The marketer will not proceed to the next stage unless given explicit permission by the customer. Consequently, the customer becomes a participant in an interactive sales process.

Strategy development can be based upon goals or marketing compatibility. Goal development reflects the basic mission of the firm. In reality this basic mission can serve as a competitive weapon. For example, the USAA Insurance Company might maintain that quality service to its policyholders reflects their basic mission. USAA would consequently develop its marketing channels to include high-quality telecommunications equipment and well-trained service representatives.

Strategy development reflects not only part of the basic mission but the objectives that have been formulated to serve diverse market segments. For example, brokerage firms have problems with account executives leaving for other competing firms and taking their customers with them. Merrill Lynch developed the Cash Management Account which appealed to key customers who might be reluctant to follow a departing account executive. With this product, Merrill Lynch kept more control over their account executives. However, competing firms then developed similar products.

Bookstore retailers, with the development of superstores, have been able to offer much more than a mere assortment of merchandise. One of the fundamental distinctions between chain bookstores and the independents has been that the independents looked at their purpose as a place for the transfer of culture between the store and its customers while the chains combined fun and culture with coffee shops, book signings by noted authors, and browsing and reading space. Many of these superstores are as large as small-town department stores and contain benches for browsers, children's reading corners, a café selling cappuccino and snacks, and gift shops to enhance book lovers' collections. Shopping in a bookstore for consumers became a social activity. The children had puppet shows and the adults had lectures. The physical environment reflected a high visibility, upscale ambiance and usually a suburban location close to the target market. Social and cultural patterns in the United States are changing rapidly and many of these changes are reflected in reading behavior and have become an integral part of book marketing and retailing.

Strategy development is based upon market compatibility. Market compatibility relates the types of service offered to the type of intermediary and customer demands and expectations. Dry cleaning is generally offered by outlets that maintain convenient hours. Consumers will generally compare prices and other product features when purchasing automobile insurance. To a certain extent the automobile insurance agent is selling the intangibility of customer service. Specialty services such as travel or group tours will be sought out by customers in the specific locality where it is offered. This will be especially true if the contemplated vacation is overseas or in a distant location.

The development of strategies requires substantial investments in technology and database management. Firms will need to develop marketing programs that take into consideration the type of products and services their customers want, how the customers want to learn about these products and services and how the customers want to obtain these products and services.

Relationship marketing developed to promote customer trust. Consumers instead of viewing companies as allies perceive an adversarial relationship. The past two decades witnessed a meaningful relationship between buyer and seller, but with the turn of the twenty-first century, companies need to regain the trust that has recently diminished. Consumers believe that a confusing, stressful, insensitive, and manipulative business environment has developed; the Enron and WorldCom scandals are examples. These perceptions need to be addressed.[10]

NOTES

1. Alvin Toffler, *Future Shock* (New York: Random House, 1970); Alvin Toffler, *The Third Wave* (New York: Morrow, 1980); Alvin Toffler, *Powershift* (New York: Bantam Books, 1991); Peter Drucker, *The Age of Discontinuity: Guidelines to Our Changing Society* (New York: Harper and Row, 1969); Jim Taylor and Watts Wacker with Howard Means, *The 500-Year Delta* (New York: Harper Business, 1997).

2. Lynn R. Kahle, Basil Poulos, and Jay Sukhdial, "Changes in Social Values in the United States During the Past Decade," *Journal of Advertising Research* 28 (February–March 1988): 35–41.

3. Robert Madrigal and Lynn R. Kahle, "Predicting Vacation Activity Preferences on the Basis of Value-System Segmentation," *Journal of Travel Research* 32 (Winter 1994): 22–28.

4. Ajay S. Sukhdial and Goutom Chahraborty, "Measuring Values Can Sharpen Segmentation in the Luxury Auto Market," *Journal of Advertising Research* 35 (January–February 1995): 9–22.

5. Alan J. Bush and David J. Ortinau, "Service Marketing to Yuppies," *The Journal of Services Marketing* 2 (Spring 1988): 19–28.

6. Paul H. Ray, "Using Values to Study Customers," *American Demographics* 19 (February 1997): 34.

7. Ellen Garbarino and Mark S. Johnson, "The Different Roles of Satisfaction, Trust, and Commitment in Customer Relationships," *Journal of Marketing* 63 (April 1999): 70–78.

8. Barbara B. Stern, "Advertising Intimacy: Relationship Marketing and the Services Consumer," *Journal of Advertising* 26 (Winter 1997): 7–20.

9. Richard S. Tedlow, *New and Improved: The Story of Mass Marketing in America* (New York: Basic Books, 1990).

10. Susan Fournier, Susan Dobscha, and Davia Glen Mick, "Preventing the Premature Death of Relationship Marketing," *Harvard Business Review* 76 (January–February 1998): 42–51.

CHAPTER 5

Subcultural Segmentation and Targeting Changing Lifestyles of the Singles Market

Subcultural influences on consumer behavior are the values, customs, and traditions peculiar to a particular group. Subcultures or microcultures are not necessarily monolithic, even though there may be similarities, but instead often composed of various subsegments. Individuals may view the subsegment as only a slight influence while others find its influence a dominant force on their buyer behavior. Subcultures are delineated by geographic areas, religion, ethnic and cultural ties, and age.

Many cities have populations largely composed of nationality groups such as Cuban communities in Florida, Mexican-Americans in El Paso, Texas, Puerto Ricans in New York City, Asian-Americans in San Francisco, and African-Americans in Washington, D.C. Some individuals in these groups become acculturated while others retain their ethnic identity and might be reluctant to speak English.

Religious groups also provide important influences on consumer behavior. Many Seventh Day Adventists limit their purchases of meat and are targets for vegetable-based foods. The Jewish subculture desires products with kosher certification as do other subcultures who prefer to buy kosher chicken and hot dogs.

Age groups, such as singles, teens, and the elderly are also subcultures. Products intended for one subculture may sometimes flow into the general population or macroculture. For example, the growth of single-person households has led to single-size serving packages, smaller kitchen appliances, and frozen dinners. These products are also used by individual family members who eat at different times than the rest of the family.

Subcultural analysis allows marketers to focus on significant market segments. Marketing to the singles market or an ethnic group must avoid stereotyping and being condescending to that group. Analysis of the subgroup, its beliefs, values, and norms can help marketers develop appropriate strategies and seek out market opportunities. Although the singles market overlaps inasmuch as some singles are elderly, the focus can be directed to those people who are under the age of forty. Attention to this market is important because their distinctive lifestyles qualify them as a substantial subcultural group.

Table 5.1 identifies subcultural segmentation by category and typical segments so that marketing strategies can be designed for each segment. For example, a large number of Latin Americans and Cubans live in southern Florida and are a growing and affluent subculture. To reach this segment, *The Miami Herald* publishes a daily newspaper in English and Spanish, and emphasizes Hispanic, Cuban, and Latin American news. Another subcultural segmentation strategy is generational or cohort marketing which can also define lifestyles and social values. This strategy focuses upon a generation in terms of external events that occurred during their members' formative years. Generation X and Generation Y are part of the singles market. A subcultural group not included in Table 5.1 is the affluent group which emerged in the 1990s and has become a major target of marketers.

Each generation or cohort has its own purchasing behavior. In turn, each generational group forms its own reference groups which further delineates its purchasing patterns. These reference groups help to develop the socialization process in individuals and makes them aware of the behavior and lifestyles of other group members. A sec-

Table 5.1
Subcultural Segmentation

Category	Typical Segment
Age	Teenagers, Singles, Elderly
Religion	Jewish, Mormon, Muslim
Race	Caucasian, Black, Asian
Occupation	Professional, Clerical, Blue Collar
Nationality	Italian, Polish, Chinese
Region	Southern, Midwestern, Eastern
Sex	Male, Female
Social Class	Lower, Middle, Upper
Marital Status	Single, Divorced, Married
Affinity Group	Boy Scouts, Girl Scouts, Pet Owners

ond function of reference groups is a comparison function that allows for self-concept evaluation. Finally, a reference group can serve a normative function that directs compliance with societal norms. Societal-norms marketing is the art of persuading people to go along with the crowd.

Since 1970 the size of the singles market has more than doubled. Two fundamental reasons for this growth have been a divorce rate where more than 50 percent of all couples divorce and a large number of adults not marrying or postponing marriage until older. The singles market includes everyone from carefree youths in their early twenties to elderly individuals. They are widely scattered geographically although they cluster in large cities throughout the United States. The singles market has evolved from one in which there is dating with a search for a mate and marriage preparation to a market concerned with personal growth, the development of individual identity, and the accumulation of experiences.

When singles join a social group, they learn about how the group dresses, their athletic activities, and their recreational pursuits in addition to the group's values and norms. A new member of the social group consequently learns about the values, norms, and expected behavior patterns of the group. The process of socialization leads to stability for both the individual and the group. Moreover, reference groups provide a means of social comparison as the consumption of products is one form of social interaction. Symbolic meanings are conveyed to others when products are purchased and used. In the past, a high percentage of singles have purchased the Ford Mustang and in recent years there has been gravitation to the Volkswagen Jetta and the Honda Civic. It is important to note that the individual may be influenced by a variety of reference groups. Furthermore, the normative function produces conformity among individuals to the approved pattern of behavior of the reference group. Consumer behavior of singles and other subcultural groups is influenced by group norms. The individual's behavior is influenced by the behavior of others in the group. Compliance with group norms may depend upon whether the individual views the organization as just a membership group or subscribes to the values and norms of the group. Another dimension is that compliance to group norms may depend upon the type of decision.

The consumer may use extended, limited, or routine decision making. Extended consumer decision making occurs when considerable time is expended on information search and evaluation of alternatives. When purchases are made infrequently and the consumer has little experience with the product, extended decision making is likely to take place. Limited consumer decision making takes place when the product or service has been purchased previously but not regularly. Routine or habitual consumer decision making occurs when the product or service is purchased by habit. Generally, normative compliance should be considerably greater for a high-involvement publicly consumed product. The reference group may tend to influence consumption of mountain bikes, jewelry, or inline skates as opposed to a Jacuzzi tub or a body massager. The use of a reference group as an information source may serve to lower the individual's perceived risk when purchasing a specific product. Advertisers might use reference group appeals to gain and keep the attention of a specific target market. These appeals help to promote and differentiate their products.

A social organization or group consists of values, norms, roles, and status. Values are the goals that society deems as important. Norms are rules and procedures to be observed and followed in particular situations. Roles are patterns of behavior expected of people who occupy a position within a group. Status refers to the prestige accorded to the designated role within the group. The concepts of role and status define the customary patterns of group behavior. For one individual, a group might be considered primary. For another, the same group might be considered secondary. The critical distinctions between primary and secondary groups are the perceived importance of the groups to the individual and the frequency or consistency with which the individual interacts with them.

MARKET-ORIENTED GROUPS

There are specific groups that have a consumer-relevant impact on individual purchasing behavior. It is important to discern that singles, elderly persons, teens, and other members of subcultural groups may belong to the same market-oriented group. For example, the 2003 Honda Accord, once regarded highly for short trips to the supermarket now is expanding its target market to young single drivers who desire style and older empty-nesters who are rediscovering style. This impact on consumer behavior can be better understood by analyzing such market-oriented groups as surrogate groups, friendship groups, formal social groups, shopping, and work groups.

Friendship Groups

Although seeking and maintaining friendships is a basic drive of most people, the singles market especially values the opinions and preferences of friends. This influence is particularly true of those singles that have moved away from their family community. Friendship groups are typically characterized by a lack of clearly defined goals or objectives. After the individual's family, it is friends who are most likely to influence consumer purchasing behavior. For members of the singles market, friendships may be a sign of independence because they represent a breaking away from the family and the forming of social relations with the outside community.

Peer views and opinions can be an important force in influencing purchasing decisions. Singles are likely to rely on friends, after family, as prepurchase information sources in deliberating a buying decision. The friendship network offers security and support, especially in making purchasing decisions about products that are unfamiliar. Such groups strongly influence the single market's behavior by exerting pressure to conform. Marketers recognize the power of peer influence among members of the singles market. Products such as brand name clothing, fine jewelry, and alcoholic beverages profit from friendship depictions in their promotional strategies.

Formal Social Groups

An individual joins a formal social group to realize such goals as making new friends, advancing a career, broadening perspectives, or pursuing a special interest. Singles have a high propensity to join formal groups but certainly others such as ethnic group members, teenagers, and others also join formal organizations. Formal social groups can be classified as veterans, civic, political, ethnic, fraternal, economic, social, and religious organizations. Membership in these organizations makes use of interpersonal methods of communication. Word-of-mouth recommendations are an important purchasing influence.

Since members of a formal social group often consume certain products together, marketers should carefully monitor such groups. To illustrate, membership in a coin and stamp club is of interest to all those who sell supplies for these products and magazine publishers devoted to this special interest. There are some singles that are interested in skiing as a sports and social activity. Consequently, these singles patronize ski lodges and the membership of a ski club would be of interest to tour operators, travel agents, sporting-goods retailers, ski-magazine publishers, and the manufacturers of ski equipment and apparel.

Almost every reference group—whether it is aspirational, membership, or dissociative—influences the thoughts and behaviors of other people. Marketers are interested in learning which individuals in reference groups are opinion leaders. Opinion leaders are well-respected and tend to have expertise about a narrow range of products and therefore are perceived as very credible. The strategy of targeting opinion leaders with the expectation that information will be transmitted to others is known as the two-step flow hypothesis.

Surrogate Groups

Surrogate groups are ones with key individuals or businesses performing all or part of a consumer's information gathering, decision making, and transactional tasks. Examples include medical doctors and interior decorators. Many authorities believe that the selection of consumer goods by surrogates will be increasingly significant. This has already grown apparent in the singles market as travel agents and tour organizations put together cruises and vacations that are expressly designated for singles. Hotels and resort areas offer special premiums to travel agents to influence their clients. Specifically, hotels and resorts host conventions for single member organizations and have gained a favorable image with the singles market.

Many affluent singles and others use the services of medical doctors, travel agents, and interior decorators that order furniture and accessories for their clients. Moreover, many singles and others belong to buying clubs that negotiate discounts with participating manufacturers. Organizations such as Weight Watchers and Jenny Craig help guide members' purchases.

Suppliers devote much promotional effort to attracting surrogates. For example, pharmaceutical salespeople visit physicians, not patients. Textbook salespeople visit professors, not students. Welcome Wagon assists local firms to influence consumers who move to new communities and are unfamiliar with local retail institutions.

Consumers perceive surrogates as possessing expertise that makes their suggestions and opinions valuable in purchasing situations. Travel agents and interior decorators need to discern their clients' lifestyle patterns in order to offer a service that meets or exceeds client expectations. Book clubs have established organizations that target those consumers who have special interests such as history or world affairs, business, science, or just enjoy mysteries. These surrogate experts guide consumers in their selection of goods and services and as consumers grow more affluent, surrogate services such as financial planning will increasingly be used.

Work Groups

Although firms like Avon and Tupperware have formerly sold their products direct to women in their homes, now these firms encourage their sales representatives to contact working women at their places of employment. Business organizations have granted permission for these types of sales representatives to direct desired efforts to offices and plants during lunch hours. The business organizations gain because they desire their employees to stay on the premises.

The formal work group can influence purchasing behavior. The formal work group consists of those individuals who work as a team. The informal or friendship work groups are those individuals who have become friends as a result of working for the same organization. Both formal and informal work groups influence the types of products and brand choices of members of the group.

Shopping Groups

A special type of group is the in-home shopping group that emphasizes the party method. The party method is where one consumer acts as host and invites friends and acquaintances to a sales demonstration in their home. Tupperware, home accessories, clothing, and jewelry manufacturers have all used this method of marketing. In the past few years, organizations have sold health-food products through this selling approach.

Groups frequently include individuals known as group leaders or opinion leaders. These leaders might be the vice president of the local school P.T.A. or the secretary–treasurer of the local garden club. These group leaders might be friends who are admired because of their intelligence, athletic abilities, or special skills. If someone is planning to purchase a stereo system, that consumer may consult someone who has expertise in that area. The same individual may consult a different expert when purchasing fine wines or investment plans. Promoting to group or opinion leaders and then to the larger market is referred to as a two-step communication process. Home demonstrations meet consumers' new lifestyle needs for convenience and personal service. However, the growth of interactive telephone and Internet home shopping may diminish the impact of party-plan sales.

Reference groups can influence products and brands that individuals select. Intergenerational family influence can have an impact on brand preferences and loyalties, information search, media reliance, price sensitivity, and price–quality beliefs. The degree to which others observe the products in the consumption process would positively affect the degree of reference group influence. Peer group influence can be more important depending upon the product type.[1]

LIFESTYLE GENERATIONAL MARKETING

Lifestyle generational marketing is a relatively new marketing strategy that targets a market of each generation based upon the times in which it grows up—the music, movies, wars, and other events of that period. Lifestyle generational marketing targets various experiences in which that market shares during its formative years. A variate is cohort analysis that targets a major event such as the Great Depression or World War II. Cohort segmentation is a more focused concept of generation segmentation.[2] Some marketers may target baby boomers and others may prefer to target a World War II cohort. The theory is that each generation feels a bonding because they shared similar experiences and consequently marketers use and depict images and icons that were prominent during these periods.

1. The Great Depression cohort includes those individuals born between 1912 and 1921. This group has a propensity to be risk adverse and may be very conservative with money. They are likely to prefer low-risk investments and to avoid contracting debt. Saving would be a high priority. This market segment envisions retirement and leisure time as an outcome from hard work. Their favorite music is big band. Mail order organizations have targeted this group. These mail order businesses have found it more profitable to sell cassettes, compact discs, and old videos through the mail rather than through retail stores.

2. The World War II cohort comprises individuals born between 1922 and 1927. The formative years for this generation were the 1940s and their early experiences were of a nation at war. Nevertheless, their early childhood memories were shaped by economic strife and therefore they are also referred to as the Great Depression Generation. This generation, because of the war, rationing, and the economic depression, was raised with a spirit of self-denial. Like the Great Depression cohort, they were influenced by radio and motion pictures. Their favorite music is swing. Sports figures such as Joe DiMaggio were influential spokespersons for promoting products to this cohort.

3. Postwar cohort individuals were born between 1928 and 1945. This market segment was called the silent generation. Their teenage years presented memories of economic growth that followed the war years. The uncertainties of war and attack remained fresh in their minds as they endeavored to ease their lives by acquiring material possessions. This generation acquired a more balanced perspective toward spending and savings than either the Great Depression cohorts or the World War II cohorts. This market segment has fond memories of singers such as Frank Sinatra. This generation took Shirley Temple and the movie, *The Wizard of Oz* into their hearts.

4. The Baby Boomer I cohort consists of individuals born between 1946 and 1954. Early memories were of the Vietnam War, the assassinations of John F. Kennedy and Martin Luther King, Jr., and ventures into outer space. This market segment embraces the values of youthfulness and freedom. The hippie movement was present and

this generation has been referred to as the Woodstock generation. President William Clinton was the first member of this generation to be elected President of the United States. Elvis Presley influenced many fashion styles. This generation has frequently lived beyond their financial means and rather than subscribing to the Puritan ethic of previous generations, they prefer instant gratification and the desire to "buy now and pay later." Credit cards became an important means of payment for this cohort.

5. The Baby Boomer II cohort includes those individuals born between 1955 and 1965. Television made a marked impression on their lifestyle with programs such as *Father Knows Best* and *Leave It To Beaver*. On the other hand, the Watergate era took its toll on this group and a resulting loss of faith in the political system. This market segment tends to pursue personal goals and desires increased instant gratification. Many members of this generation wish to have a lifestyle as good as their parents and will incur debt to acquire material possessions. The Baby Boomer II cohort is very concerned about the environment and tends to purchase products that are environmentally friendly. They prefer rock-and-roll music and have a much more permissive view of sex than previous generations. This market segment is highly influenced by television and other types of media.

6. The Generation X cohort composes individuals born between 1965 and 1976 and is sometimes referred to as "baby busters." This is the first generation of latchkey children whose parents both work or are offspring of divorced or separated parents in approximately half the cases. Generation X may have sentiments of alienation and resentment due to difficulties in career placement caused by corporation downsizing and economic downturn. Therefore, some members of this generation may believe that they will be unable to match or surpass their parents' level of financial success.

There are feelings of high aspiration and low expectations that might translate itself into disillusionment. Music appreciation reflects anger such as rap and hard rock. Many members of this generational cohort continue to live, until their late twenties, with their parents. They are more likely to purchase items such as a new car or stereo than their counterparts. This generation has postponed marriage to an older age and has accumulated more savings before marriage than previous generations. Still, certain resentment pervades some members of Generation X as they make a statement against society with body piercing and tattoos.

Generation X represents an important market segment for music, movies, travel, beer and alcohol, fast food, and athletic shoes. They are also a significant market for PCs, CD-ROMs, online services, and video games. This generation spends a high percentage of their discretionary income on eating out and sometimes in trendy restaurants. Generation X is sometimes called the boomerang generation because they keep returning to their parents' home. Members of Generation X tend to be savvy but cynical consumers.

7. Generation Y individuals were born in the 1980s. Their generation is more at home with the computer and the Internet than other generations. Although many members of Generation X are sophisticated users of the Internet, it is Generation Y that has had formal instruction in its use. The software industry has directed most of its products to this generation. Titles such as Baby-Rom are designed to help infants learn from the computer.

Apparel manufacturers such as Ralph Lauren and Tommy Hilfiger are targeting the Generation Y group which prefers jeans, sports jerseys, and baseball caps to dress-up clothes. Their fashion choices have demonstrated a preference for hip-hop styles. Many members of this generation observe extreme fashions such as body piercing, tattoos, and hair dyed various colors. Generation Y prefers rap and grunge music. There is an interaction between music and clothing styles as Yers tend to emulate the dress styles adopted by popular recording artists. Hip-hop, a style of music popularized by African-Americans, reflects loose-fitting urban streetwear that includes baggy jeans and pants, sweatshirts, and hiking boots.

Changes in family structure, technology, the workforce, and demographics reflect attitude changes of this generation. Generation Y is much more diverse than the baby boomers. More than half of Generation Y has working mothers and one in three is not Caucasian. At least 25 percent of this generation lives in a single-parent household.[3] A much higher percentage of children under age seven have attended preschool than children did in 1970. These children have had early exposure to personal computers. As many as 10 to 15 percent of Generation Y children have been born into a household where a foreign language is spoken. Because Yers are a less homogenous market, marketers have found it profitable to reach them with a multiplicity of media types. Thus a broad spectrum of cable and satellite TV channels, and niche magazines such as *Sports Illustrated* have been used to target this generation. The cohort approach for understanding subcultural segmentation, whether through music, images, jokes, or values has been used by such marketers as Daimler Chrysler, VH1, Nike, and Levi Strauss.[4]

THE SINGLES MARKET

Young single adults comprise most of the singles market, although there are singles over the age of forty-five. Most marketers direct their appeals to a singles market who are typically in the beginning stages of their working lives after completing some form of job training, college, or career training. Many members of the singles market have left their parents' homes and are likely to spend their income on rent, home furnishings, automobiles, clothing and accessories, and travel and entertainment. Singles are interested in joining health clubs and participating in sports activities and are targets for products related to health club and sports activities. Special interest magazines are directed to young single men such as *Playboy* and to young single women such as *Glamour*. This target market has few financial burdens and are particularly influenced by fashion opinion leaders. Many purchases of goods and services are related to the mating game.

The increasing size, affluence and complexity of the singles market creates new opportunities and challenges for marketers. Single households account for almost one-quarter of all U.S. households. Single men allocate a greater proportion of their expenditures to food consumed away from home, alcohol, transportation, entertainment, tobacco, cash contributions, and to retirement investments than single women. Single women allocate a greater share of their expenditures to food consumed at home, housing, apparel, health care, personal care services, and reading material. Moreover, singles tend to prefer products that are low maintenance, affordable, and can be used safely. They prefer to live close to where they work and will move into housing such as lofts and condos that families with children usually avoid. Singles are good customers for restaurants and spend more on travel, convenience foods, and sporty automobiles. This market segment is attractive for purchasing fashionable apparel. The size of this market is estimated at approximately $600 billion and lifestyle market segmentation strategies are especially appropriate in reaching this market segment.

The singles market depicts a lifestyle that is unencumbered with responsibilities, has considerable mobility, and can make expenditures on goods and services that those with traditional family commitments would not generally make. Thus, the expenditure pattern of the singles market tends to vary from other markets. For example, their automobile preferences are different from the general population. The singles market has preferred the Ford Mustang but this preference is changing as the Volkswagen Jetta has grown in popularity. Moreover, a part of the market has desired the Honda Civic which is known as a "pocket rocket" when bolt-on performance parts and styling accessories are added. The Ford Motor Company is competing for this market with the Ford Focus which targets the under-thirties singles market.

There are several million unmarried people living together and some of these arrangements are temporary while others are permanent. Many of these unmarried arrangements are often in college towns but the majority are older couples living throughout the United States who prefer an unmarried lifestyle. Some insurance companies are structuring policies for unmarried couples and some banks have changed their policies about loans to unmarried couples for homes or other large purchases.

Club Med has been successful in targeting the singles market since 1955. However, as time passed, the singles market, once in their twenties with an image of "swinging singles," grew older. For many, the marriage age increased from the early twenties to the late twenties. Suddenly, Club Med was targeting an older singles market. This market was more affluent and more sophisticated. The Club's image of "swinging singles" was overpositioned and Club Med has had difficulty in changing this image. The majority of its guests by the late 1990s are married couples, causing some of their village resorts to have full-time childcare programs.

The singles market, which is highly concentrated in California and neighboring states, has made a marked impact on fashion styles and also lifestyle activities. An innovative pattern has emerged as the remaining singles in other regions of the country became emulators. However, many singles have clustered in the larger metropolitan areas and patronize downtown restaurants, hotels, health facilities, and other recreational institutions.

Today's singles are a much more educated group. College enrollments have increased steadily since the 1980s and the 1990s. These educational gains have developed in spite of increasing tuition and expenses. Part-time students and community colleges accounted for much of this growth. The age of the student population has increased as many have returned to complete degrees or seek additional education.

The singles market has grown in size. Among people aged twenty-five to thirty-four years old, 13.6 million have never been married and make up more than one-third of this age group.[5] Much that has been written about the singles market reflects the characteristics of the twenty-five to thirty-four age group. The southern and western states have the largest total singles population but it is the metropolitan areas where singles tend to cluster. Cities such as Los Angeles, San Francisco, Dallas–Fort Worth, Chicago, New York City, Philadelphia, and Miami are where singles live, work, and play. There is a concentration of 26 million central-city households composed of people who live alone and are single parents. This trend exists in both large and small metropolitan areas.[6]

The twenty-first century will witness a continuation of the central cities becoming centers for services, retail trade, and entertainment. The central city has an inherent vitality that often is lacking in the suburbs and therefore attracts singles. Naturally, cities such as New York, Chicago, and San Francisco present better opportunities for this market segment with their downtown coliseums and other recreational activities. If the downtown areas are attractively restored, the suburbs are unable to match picturesque settings such as Baltimore's Inner Harbor or the Civic Center in Hartford.

Medium and smaller size cities have been growing at a more rapid pace than the suburbs of the larger metropolitan areas in the 1990s. There has been exciting growth for such cities as Cincinnati, Milwaukee, San Antonio, Phoenix, Denver, and Houston. Marketers should explore the market potential of the Standard Metropolitan Statistical Areas such as Athens, Georgia; Charlottesville, Virginia; and State College, Pennsylvania. These smaller cities are not only college communities but are growing in other types of business organizations and are attractive places for singles to live and work.

The singles market is regarded as both a lifestyle and a demographic category that is subject to lifestyle market segmentation strategies. For example, within the singles classification, divorced men often purchase new wardrobes, join health clubs, find new apartments, and buy furnishings such as dishes, curtains, or Venetian blinds. The divorced male often needs to replace most of his household goods.

CHANGING ATTITUDES AND DEMAND PATTERNS

There have been significant changes in the attitudes and demand patterns of the singles market because of the entry of more women into the workplace and the phenomenal growth of the professional market for women. This major trend has spawned the child daycare business, increased consumption of microwavable foods, and office-oriented women's apparel. A large number of professional women under the age of forty have never been married or are separated or divorced. According to the U.S. Bureau of the Census, the number of adults living alone has more than doubled since the 1970s.[7] More adults have remained unmarried into their thirties than in previous generations.

Professional women have careers rather than just jobs. Time for shopping is limited and convenience is desired. Some retail stores are offering a personal shopping service that selects appropriate merchandise for customers who telephone in their needs and then come at their convenience to make a selection from the offered merchandise. A database of the customer's size, tastes, and apparel needs is maintained to facilitate data mining. Manufacturers increasingly need to presell the customer particularly by means of direct mail, national advertising, and coordinated promotions with retailers. The professional career woman will not have time to browse. Instead, the professional woman wants to make quick decisions and will desire special presentations aimed at her needs that are concise and relevant.

Many professional women purchase apparel by mail or on the Internet and as a group tend to be more style conscious and convenience oriented. The affluent customer has been the traditional target market for direct retailers. This type of customer is also a target for electronic shopping. The rise in affluence may decrease price sensitivity for consumers who are willing to make purchases from direct retailers. As affluent consumers often have more time constraints, they are more likely to desire better quality goods and services. Many professional women are concerned with self-identity through the purchase of goods and therefore want a broader product assortment that most retail stores can display. Moreover, professional women generally have personal computers to facilitate in-home shopping.

Another significant change in demand patterns has been targeting the educated market. Amazon.com has pioneered ordering books on the Internet. Moreover, by strategic placement of warehouses, getting the book to the purchaser has been accelerated. As Barnes and Noble and others use Internet selling, buyers are finding it easier to order out-of-print books, hard-to-find books, and books by small publishers. Amazon.com and others have rapidly moved into the sale of products such as toys, CDs, videotapes, and audiotapes through the Internet.

The field of Internet selling is beginning to significantly change buyer purchasing patterns as Rex Stores, Best Buy, Tandy, and Radio Shack began selling electronic products on their Web sites. Even home improvement stores such as Home Depot and furniture stores such as Ethan Allen now use Internet selling. Many have believed that appliances and furniture would be hard-to-sell merchandise over the Internet but demand patterns are changing as convenience and time constraints become more important influences in consumer decision making.

Single women and married women who are in the work force have similar time constraints and value convenience. However, married women with children have other obligations. There are categories of stay-at-home housewives and plan-to-work housewives and also married women who are just-a-job working women and career-oriented working women. Single women and also single moms with children comprise a large percentage of just-a-job working women and career working women. These working women spend much less time shopping than nonworking women do. Even in households where husbands are present, it is the husband who does much of the shopping for groceries. Many working women are likely to shop during evening hours and on weekends and to make purchases through direct-mail catalogs and the Internet. Demand patterns have changed as women purchase almost half the automobiles in the United States. Moreover, many women are making purchases in home improvement stores such as Home Depot and Lowe's where, in the past, women were not regarded as customers in home improvement stores. Sexual roles have blurred as many women are willing to participate in many home improvement projects in their households. These women may be either single or married or could be categorized as single moms with children. Home Depot and Lowe's are trying to gain the patronage of single women as they are currently the fastest growing group of first-time home buyers in the United States. Since 1970 the percentage of single women aged thirty to thirty-four has tripled and from 1980 this rate has almost doubled. As more women than ever before are enrolling in U.S. colleges and universities, the ranks of professional women will increase.

The decade of the 1990s and emerging trends into the new millennium indicate that among men there are significantly changing attitudes and demand patterns for fashion apparel. A decade ago, women performed 80 percent of the shopping tasks for men's clothing; whereas now half of the men do their own shopping.[8] For the first time, men's clothing sales are accelerating at a quicker pace than women's. Prices for luxury men's apparel have soared and men have become more fashion conscious.

CHANGING MOTIVES AND ASPIRATIONS

Each decade demonstrates how motives and aspirations can change. The middle class that enjoys six-figure incomes are mostly between the ages of thirty-five to fifty-five, live in major metropolitan areas, have a college education, and are interested in status symbols. Status symbols that represent success through the decades are as follows: 1900s, model T-Fords, pianos, radios, and hand-cranked victrolas; from 1910–1919, status symbols included fur hats, electric clocks, fountain pens, Cadillacs, Kodak cameras, and transatlantic travel; in the 1920s, fur coats, movie "talkies," gin, vacuum cleaners, and electric washing machines symbolized achievement; the Depression era of the 1930s featured status symbols that included baseball tickets, canned food, and indoor plumbing; the World War II era of the 1940s featured television, air travel, college degrees, and electric refrigerators; the 1950s and 1960s status symbols were color televisions, credit cards, visits to Disneyland, convertibles and

Porsches, stereo sound systems, 35mm cameras, and Andy Warhol lithographs; from the 1970s to the 1990s, designer jeans, VCRs, solar-heated homes, vacation homes, microwave ovens, the BMW, computers and flat-screen computer monitors, Internet stocks, cell phones, and sport utility vehicles; now, the symbols are Internet cell phones, Black Berry pagers, flat-screen digital televisions, and designer accessories for pets.[9]

Many of the status symbols of the more affluent in one decade have become mainstream items for the middle class and general population in subsequent decades. Social class influence reflects that people with similar life experiences are more likely to demonstrate similar lifestyles and behavioral patterns. These similar lifestyle and behavioral patterns are as meaningful for married people as for singles in the acquisition of goods and services. The norms and behavioral patterns of consumers in one social class can influence consumption patterns in other social classes. The trickle-down model is one explanation of social class interaction whereby trends that are initiated in the upper classes are later emulated by lower socioeconomic classes. This phenomenon occurs because those in lower classes may aspire to raise their social standing by emulating higher socioeconomic classes. Common examples of this behavior occur in the adoption of fashion and clothing styles.

Unlike the trickle-down explanation, the status-float model suggests that trends start in the lower and middle classes and then spread upward. To illustrate, Levi-Strauss introduced the rugged, tight-fitting blue jean that dates back to the 1848 California gold rush days. The blue jeans were first sold to miners who needed durable clothing in their work. The product gained widespread acceptance in the United States among lower and middle class teenagers since it symbolized rebellion against the establishment. The wearing of jeans spread to upper class youths as a symbol of rebellion against their parents' rigid rules. Jeans evolved with the introduction of designer labels such as Calvin Klein as fashion items in the 1970s. The status-float model has notably also operated with the blues and rap music originating in the lower socioeconomic classes.

Changing motivations and aspirations of the singles market are shown by breaking down that market by age category. The singles market under the age of thirty-five has completed more formal education than the general population. This educational broadening may account, in part, for more interest in travel than other groups. Because this group has more freedom in spending, more money is used for recreational activities, apparel, and casual clothes. Manufacturers of luggage, sports equipment, fashion jewelry, cosmetics, and low-priced home furnishings will find numerous market opportunities present in the single under-thirty-five market. Many nondurable goods and services such as convenience foods, laundry services, and restaurant meals are purchased. Convenience is often a more important attribute than price and is a salient evaluative criterion in the consumer decision process. Frozen foods, microwave ovens, and other convenient cooking appliances are in demand by this market. This market tends to patronize fast-food franchise outlets.

Those members of the singles market who have high earning potential tend to desire immediate satisfaction of wants rather than postponement of pleasure for the future. This group's lifestyle is rich in discretionary income. To satisfy this group there has been a proliferation of singles bars, ski lodges, and travel tours designed for the independent individual. This affluent singles group is an important one for manufacturers and retailers that offer quality home furnishings, quality clothing, alcoholic beverages, and more expensive health and personal care products. Those associated with the travel and insurance industries will also find lucrative opportunities in this market. The affluent singles have high levels of aspiration and envision themselves earning more in the future. They are busy acquiring more sophisticated tastes and preferences that will probably be even more expensive.[10]

BROADENING TARGET MARKETS

The evolution of marketing appeals motivating the purchase of a motorcycle depicts the changing motivations and aspirations of a consumer niche market. The association of black leather jackets, switchblades, and rowdy behavior patterns with motorcycles was a stigma that manufacturers had to remove in order sell motorcycles. Hollywood movies like Marlon Brando in *The Wild One* (1954) and Jack Nicholson and Peter Fonda in *Easy Rider* (1969) did much to tarnish the motorcyclists' image.

Originally sold to the singles market, Honda introduced the theme, "You meet the nicest people on a Honda." Honda advertising made use of such key words as "nice," "easy-going," "friend," and "frugal." Motorcycles were seen in advertisements parked at tennis courts. Fathers were shown riding with their children on a motorcycle. An "in" image was created in the minds of the appropriate target market. The Honda became fashionable and motorcycles were bought by that segment of the market that might have purchased other types of products.

Honda sells more motorcycles in the United States than any other manufacturer to a mid-price range consumer. Harley-Davidson dominates the upscale-user market. The typical Harley-Davidson purchaser is a middle-aged forty-six-year-old and has a household income of approximately $75,000. Target markets do not remain fixed. Although singles still purchase motorcycles, the demand for a Harley-Davidson upscale motorcycle has shifted to an older consumer and has become an accepted part of family transportation.

CONTRIBUTIONS OF BEHAVIORAL AND SOCIAL SCIENCES

Different disciplines are useful in explaining consumer behavior. These explanations suggest consumers may be influenced by a single dominant factor. This is not true. Consumer behavior is complex because a combination of factors—rather than a single factor—influence consumer behavior. Alfred Marshall, Ivan Pavlov, Sigmund Freud, and Thorstein Veblen are responsible for establishing the foundation on which behavioral scientists have built a framework for explaining consumer behavior.[11]

The Marshallian Economic Model

The Marshallian model of buyer behavior maintains that the consumer is a rational thinker and will act in his best interest. Therefore, if it costs $5 to eat out in a restaurant and only $3 to eat at home, the consumer will eat at home. This perspective ignores the pleasurable aspects and the utilities of eating out. Another view expressed by the model is that a price reduction of a product increases the value of the goods in buyers' minds and leads to increased sales. However, some individuals may believe that the quality of the product has declined or that ownership has lost its status value. The Marshallian model does offer a useful frame of reference for analyzing consumer behavior but economic factors alone do not explain variations in sales.

The Pavlovian Learning Model

The Pavlovian model proposes that learning is an associative process that contains four central concepts: drive, cue, response, and reinforcement. This is a behavioral model of learning based on classical conditioning principles. Pavlovian theory emphasizes the desirability of repetition in advertising and that strong cues are essential in markets characterized by strong brand loyalties that will lead to a person making the buying decision. Important phenomena such as perception, the subconscious, and interpersonal influence are not satisfactorily treated by Pavlov. However, marketers have been able to develop a substantial number of insights concerning brand habit and in how to use advertising cues that stimulate and arouse drives and associations.

The Freudian Psychoanalytic Model

The Freudian model emphasizes symbolic and unconscious motivations. Three parts of the human psyche, the id, ego, and super-ego constantly balance impulses to gratify immediate needs with adherence to social norms. The model has been expanded by others so that perspectives have been formulated on power, cultural mechanisms, and personality development. The model's most significant implication for marketers is that buyers are motivated by symbolic as well as economic–functional product concerns. Motivation researchers use projective techniques such as word association, sentence completion, metaphor construction, and role playing. The goal is to learn about consumer motivations that are not necessarily known to the consumer because these motives are beneath the surface of consciousness.

The Veblenian Social Model

The Veblenian model has made marketers aware of the importance of social influences on individual tastes and preferences. Essentially, the impact of present group memberships and aspired group memberships is stressed. Conspicuous consumption operates in the purchase of clothes, cars, and houses. Marketers have been able to expand on this theory through the use of methodologies from sociology, cultural anthropology, and social psychology. Culture, subcultures, social class, reference groups, and face-to-face groups influence consumers and their purchasing and consumption behavior. Marketers still need to define which of these social influences are most important in purchasing specific products.

The goal of marketers is to put all of these explanations of consumer behavior together and add the other behavioral theories in order to understand consumer behavior. Consumer behavior is at times contradictory and prevailing attitudes do not necessarily guarantee certain types of behavior.

CHANGING ECONOMIC CONDITIONS

As consumers' incomes have increased significantly in recent years, marketers can anticipate pronounced shifts in the relative demand for different categories of goods and services. Purchasing power is a more important factor than population in the purchase of a wide variety of products. Household income trends are especially important since the household is the primary economic unit of consumption. For example, the singles household market has doubled since 1980 and together with increased educational and income levels, this market offers lucrative potential to marketers. The singles market has shown a steady growth of interest in opera, ballet, theater, symphony orchestras, various sports activities, and travel.

Changing economic conditions are intertwined with the impact of psychology and especially consumer perceptions. To illustrate, an older generation was brought up believing that leather shoes were of much higher quality than sneakers. Leather shoes were purchased in specialty shoe stores or department stores. Sneakers were deemed inferior in quality and purchased in variety stores known as five-and-dime stores. Even leather shoes targeted to lower socioeconomic classes were considered to be of higher quality than sneakers. Motives of status and prestige were intertwined with the purchase of leather shoes regardless of price. Sneakers were to be worn over a brief period of time and discarded.

A younger generation was brought up believing that sneakers reflected quality. This generation wears sneakers not only for athletic events but also for walking and for fashionable styling effects. Employment opportunities and rising incomes have been present in the 1990s so that sneakers can be purchased for different functions. Prices of some brands of sneakers are higher than for leather shoes. Even the older generation in the United States are wearing sneakers for all types of events.

Purchasing power of consumers is a function of income, prices, savings, and the availability of credit in the marketplace. Easy credit and low inflation have increased the standard of living of many consumers. This has been particularly true of the singles market with few financial responsibilities.

Although the economic environment is probably the best-understood sector of the macroenvironment, many uncertainties still exist. The impact of declining birthrates from the baby boom years, a maturing population, a changing American family with more single moms, the increase of nonfamily households, geographic shifts in population, increasing educational attainment, consumer expenditures, and ecological perspectives must be monitored. However, assumptions are not always correct and the results of incorrect forecasting can be staggering. Marketers need to carefully evaluate and interpret economic implications in formulating, developing, and implementing strategic marketing plans. Moreover, there are pronounced differences of economic demand in various regions of the United States. For example, people in Seattle purchase more toothbrushes per capita than consumers in any other city in the United States, people in New Orleans use more ketchup, and people in Salt Lake City consume more candy bars.

The impact of all the changes is a fragmentation of the mass market into numerous submarkets or subsegments based not only upon lifestyle, but age, sex, education, geography, family structure, and other characteristics. For example, at Gap's Banana Republic stores, jeans sell for about $60. Its Old Navy stores sell jeans for about $25. Both chains are profitable. At Haagen-Daz the focus is on the need for self-indulgence when buying ice cream while at Baskin-Robbins the focus is on the availability of more flavors to satisfy varying consumer tastes.

POSITIONING STRATEGY

Positioning strategy is an important step in lifestyle market segmentation strategy formulation. The first step is to identify market segments. For example, the singles market could be targeted as a whole or targeted based upon lifestyle activities such as sports or travel. After choosing the market segments to target, the next step is to position the segments. The most frequently used positioning strategy is by product attributes or benefits. However, the product can be positioned by quality or price, by use, by product category, or by competitors. Positioning aids customers in evaluating competing products or brands so that they can select the one that offers them the most value. Rockport Shoes positions itself as "the leader of the walking fitness movement." Although the singles market is not targeted specifically, singles are obviously a part of this athletic shoe market and it is better to include as wide a market as possible. Another aspect of the same market was the positioning strategy by Reebok that depicted Nike's Air Jordan with the phrase "Pump Up and Air Out."

Identity and image need to be established in a positioning strategy. Nike succeeded in making the Nike swoosh one of the most recognized symbols in the world. For young people the Nike symbol is an attitude that reflects a particular lifestyle. Nike has gone through a transformation from hip to mainstream and this change has diminished the loyalty of twelve- to twenty-four-year-olds. Airwalk and other brands have gained market share. Airwalk started off as a technical skateboarder and snowboarder shoes and young people like the extreme sports image associated with the shoe.[12] Product positioning is a part of a natural progression when market segmentation is used. Segmentation allows the firm to aim a given brand at a portion of the total market. For example, Kellogg's Special K is positioned as a cereal that has a low-cholesterol appeal. Positioning a brand to avoid competition may be appropriate when that brand has unique characteristics that are important to buyers.

Measurement and analysis by the use of Likert scale surveys, perceptual mapping, focus groups, and other techniques should give credibility to positioning decisions and to the marketing-mix strategies that positioning generates. The following information is needed for positioning decisions:[13]

- How consumers perceive the product category in general.
- The product category features, benefits, and advantages considered most important.
- What companies and brands consumers perceive to be the product category leaders and why.
- The characteristics of the competition's brands and one's own brands.
- The limitations of the competition's brands and one's own brands.

Responses to these inquiries will help to determine the current and desired brand position. Product positioning will design the company's image and offer value in such a way that target customers understand and appreciate what the company stands for in contrast to its competitors. The positioning task identifies the possible competitive advantages to exploit and which advantage to select.

Al Ries and Jack Trout were early advocates of the positioning concept and envisioned positioning strategy primarily as a communication strategy rather than a total marketing mix strategy.[14] Ries and Trout focus on the psychology of positioning or repositioning a current brand in the consumer's mind. However, many marketers focus upon a total marketing mix approach that is based on the desired positioning strategy.

A firm differentiates itself from competitors by bundling competitive advantages. Michael Porter, a recognized authority on competitive strategy, refers to this bundling process as the value chain.[15] Porter maintained that every organization is a collection of activities directed to design, produce, market, deliver, and support its product. Value, in competitive terms, is the amount that consumers are willing to pay for the products and services provided. For example, service activities such as installation, repair, parts supply, and product adjustment would be useful in formulating competitive strategy. Differences in customer needs will necessitate tailoring the focus for competitive advantage. Value-chain analysis helps marketers separate the fundamental activities a firm performs in designing, producing, marketing, and distributing its product or service. A competitive advantage that can be used in positioning strategy can then be developed from these activities and implemented using the marketing mix.

MANAGING CHANGE

Singles in the twenty-five to thirty-nine age bracket are a large market segment. Compared to the general population singles tend to be the following:

- more affluent.
- more mobile.
- more experimental.
- more fashion and appearance conscious.
- more active in leisure activities.
- more sensitive to social status.

Singles share common beliefs, preferences, and behaviors. Therefore, the singles market when combined with other market segments that subscribe to voluntary simplicity can be targeted. In fact, this target market has contributed to L. L. Bean's growth. L. L. Bean is a firm whose mail-order catalog is aimed toward outdoor enthusiasts and the educated "preppie" type. During the 1960s, the recreation boom focused upon family camping and backpacking. Many young adults sought to return to nature and indulge in outdoor activities. Soon these young adults began to wear their outdoor apparel and footwear every day.

This lifestyle of voluntary simplicity developed in the 1960s and 1970s has continued well into the twenty-first century. Consumers who adopt this lifestyle seek material simplicity, strive for self-actualization, and adopt an ecological ethic. Voluntary simplicity is marked by a new balance between inner and outer development and growth. It is a throwback to frugality and puritanical self-reliance. Outdoor activities such as camping, rafting, and fishing reflect a part of this lifestyle. Ecological awareness becomes paramount and so does the interconnection between people and natural resources. This new consciousness is concerned with the reduction of environmental pollution and is receptive to new products, such as bottled water, which preserve and maintain the natural environment.

Customer satisfaction is fundamental to L. L. Bean. The company refunds the purchase price on merchandise sold if the customer is not totally satisfied. The L. L. Bean organization values word-of-mouth referrals. L. L. Bean personally tests every item sold either in the retail store or catalog. Over 2 million people a year visit Freeport, Maine, a small village of 6,000 people, to make purchases at the store. L. L. Bean has concentrated on customers first and has designed its product and service strategies to satisfy the needs of a carefully defined consumer market segment.

The affluent consumer constitutes a new subcultural segment. The lifestyle activities of the high end of the affluent market are ranked in importance as follows: socializing with children and grandchildren, entertaining close friends, planning investments, taking photographs, watching children or grandchildren play sports, and attending religious services. Many of the affluent eat at McDonald's or Burger King and limit spending. This same group is highly interested in visiting museums and, surprisingly, vacationing in Paris is low on their preferences.[16]

NOTES

1. Terry L. Childers and Akshley Rao, "The Influence of Familial and Peer-Based Reference Groups on Consumer Decisions," *Journal of Consumer Research* 19 (September 1992): 198–212.

2. Geoffrey Meredith and Charles Schewe, "The Power of Cohorts," *American Demographics* 16 (December 1994): 22–27, 31.

3. Ellen Newborne and Kathleen Kerwin, "Generation Y," *Business Week*, 15 February 1999, 80–86.

4. Michael M. Phillips, "Selling by Evoking What Defines a Generation," *The Wall Street Journal*, 13 August 1996, B1.

5. *Current Population Survey (CPS) Reports*, (March 1998 update), U.S. Department of Commerce.

6. Christy Fisher, "City Lights," *American Demographics* 19 (October 1997): 41–48.

7. A. F. Saluter, "Marital Status and Living Arrangements: March 1991," *Current Population Reports* 461, series P-20 (April 1992).

8. Sam Walker, "Fashions' Latest Victims: Men," *The Wall Street Journal*, 1 December 2000, W1, 16.

9. Jan Gertner, "What is Wealth?" *Money* 29 (December 2000): 94–107.

10. Basil G. Engles and Michael R. Solomon, "To Be and Not To Be: Lifestyle Imagery, Reference Groups, and the Clustering of America," *Journal of Advertising* 24 (Spring 1995): 13–34.

11. Adapted from Philip Kotler, "Behavioral Models for Analyzing Buyers," *Journal of Marketing* 29 (October 1965): 37–45.

12. Patricia Sellers and Lenore Schiff, "Four Reasons Nike's Not Cool," *Fortune*, 30 March 1998, 26–27.

13. Robert A. Kriegel, "Positioning Demystified," *Business Marketing* 7 (May 1986): 106–112.

14. Al Ries and Jack Trout, *Positioning: The Battle for Your Mind* (New York: Warner Books, 1982).

15. Michael E. Porter, *Competitive Advantage* (New York: The Free Press, 1985), 33–61.

16. Thomas J. Stanley, *The Millionaire Mind* (Kansas City, Missouri: Andrews McMeel, 2000).

CHAPTER 6

Targeting the Changing Lifestyles of Children, Tweens, Teens, and College Markets

The children, tweens, teens, and the college market represent enormous potential for marketers. Marketing to this segment has a great deal to do with the psychological development of children and their dependence on their parents. As children's ages increase, their influence and independence increases. According to the 2000 U.S. Census, 25.7 percent of the population, 72.3 million people, is under the age of eighteen. That represents a growth of 13.7 percent over 1990. The U.S. Census Bureau estimates that the number of babies born will reach 5.7 million by the year 2050. There are at least six recognized youth segments: ages 0–2, 3–5, 6–8, 9–12, 13–15, and 16–18 with age compression and ethnic factors having an impact on each of these segments. Age compression is a term that means children are growing up more quickly than they did a generation or even a decade ago. The tweens are between the ages of nine and twelve and are replacing Barbie and Lincoln Logs with video games, clothes, and cosmetics. Children no longer have to play dress-up since they can wear children's versions of their parents' clothes from stores like Gap and Laura Ashley. A decade ago girls were interested in Barbie until they were age nine or ten years and now they lose interest at age five or six. This acceleration process is a result of access to influences and information, the speed with which trends move, and working mothers who give children the opportunity of seeing what other children do in their homes.

Another significant change has been emerging interests of parents and grandparents in educating their children at a much earlier age than a decade ago. Zany Brainy targets the educational toy market with products such as video and audiotapes, computer software, crafts, and other learning products. Purchasing toys, apparel, and other items from the Internet for this segment is also growing because more homes have computers and many parents have an aversion to taking children to stores where they might be pressured to buy items that they do not want to purchase. A significant number of shoppers are opting for the more quiet environment of their own homes to do their shopping. Traditional toy retailers such as Toys "R" Us and FAO Schwarz have entered the world of Internet selling to compete with Wal-Mart, Barnes and Noble, Gap, and Amazon.com.

Determining what kids buy and why they make the purchase choices they do is complex. Product features such as status, economy, price, style, color, comfort, and service appeal to different market segments with specific sensitivities. Purchasing motives are not permanent and change throughout the child's growing up. Motivation is influenced by other children. Children are actively learning and acquiring new wants that will subsequently modify their lifestyle characteristics. Some believe children are divided more by taste and psychographic profile than by age. They have tremendous influence over purchasing power at home due to the changing dynamic of the family. They spend a lot more time at the store with their parents.

Young people like to belong and reference groups serve as an important frame of reference for individuals in their purchasing decisions. Reference groups are an especially important influence during the teenage and college years. The norms and standards of the reference group are used as a guide for the individual in developing their own behavior patterns.

Automatic groups are groups where the individual belongs as a result of social role assumption. This reference group relationship involves the individual's perception of societal expectations. For example, a boy compares his behavior with boys, teenagers and with other teens.

Membership groups are those groups to which the individual belongs such as social, educational, community, and religious organizations. The extent of influence would depend upon how important membership in the groups is to the particular individual. Lifestyle may be influenced to the extent that a young woman may wear a certain style of skirt or blouse because she belongs to a sorority. Alcoholic beverages may not be consumed because of membership in a church group.

Aspiration groups are those groups that a person desires to join either in the immediate present or the future. Occupational groups may be aspiration groups of a great many individuals. For example, some college students may carry their lunch in an attaché case as a way of identifying with business executives. Decisions may also be made in the hope of becoming a future member of a particular group. This is true for students who want to join a sorority or fraternity.

Dissociative reference groups are those which the individual seeks to avoid. These are groups whose thinking and behavior is avoided by the individual. For example, a college student may not desire to join a specific fraternity or sorority because they do not want to be associated with the values and behavior of that group.

Socialization is the process by which the individual learns and is affected by a larger society's values, beliefs, and behaviors. Socialization in childhood is learned through the play stage and later the organized-game stage. Socialization through the tween and teen years is acquired as the individual moves from nonresponsibility to responsibility and independent roles to an acceptable sexual orientation. A distinct teenage culture arises with certain forms of accepted language, clothing, fads, and other behavioral manifestations. Friendship groups provide social acceptance and guidance. During this stage of life there is likely to be a high degree of conformity to group norms.

Marketers can broaden their market for a product by associating their brand with a significant reference group or a respected individual. For example, Nike has associated their athletic footwear with Michael Jordan. An entire line of products can be based on a reference group. This can include jackets, hats, and shirts when designed with the name of a football or baseball team. Teenagers are especially conscious of reference groups.

Table 6.1 identifies trends in family relationships over the last twenty years. There is no longer a common American family. Couples have delayed marriage to achieve success in careers and are more financially secure and sophisticated in the consumer decision process than in the past. A high divorce rate usually means that children play a greater role in purchasing decisions. Since there are fewer children in marriages, more money can be spent on their clothing, toys, and other products, including education. Gender influence demonstrates changing sex roles that manifest themselves in the purchase of more unisex products. Age is also a factor in consumption. The most notable change in the past two decades has been age compression and the relationship between children and parents in the decades of delayed marriage, dual careers, and divorce.

Table 6.1
Changing Trends in Family Relationships

Family trends	Delayed marriage
	Dual careers
	Divorce
	Fewer children
Gender influence	Changing sex roles
	Differences in purchasing behavior
Age influence	Children—ages 1–8
	Tweens—ages 9–12
	Teens—ages 13–18
	College students—ages 18+

Environmental scanning—the collection and interpretation of information concerning social forces relating to the values of potential customers—can help to recognize market opportunities. To illustrate, the eyeglass industry has targeted a new market for toddlers. Eyeglasses designed with small Mickey Mouse icons at the temples are marketed to infants through children age nine. There is only one Barbie doll with glasses but a number of styles are designed for girls ages four to ten and Sesame Street has placed Elmo, rubber ducks, and musical notes on its frames for children age two to eight.

An important aspect of family relationships is that more than one individual can be involved with purchases. There are a variety of roles that may be performed in acquiring a product or service that are defined as follows:

- *Gatekeeper.* Those members of the household who collect, control, and screen information vital to the decision.
- *Influencer.* Those members of the family whose input influences the decision.
- *Decider.* The individual or persons who actually determine which product or service will be purchased.
- *Buyer.* The family member who actually purchases the product or service.
- *User.* The member or members of the family who consume the product.

Each role can be performed by different family members and therefore a marketer has to aim the marketing program to each party in the purchasing process. A common error is to assume that what works for one party will work for all. Parents are often the deciders and buyers of items consumed by children. When the perceived risk is high, joint decisions are likely.

Intergenerational brand equity research is only in its infancy, but it has been established as important for some brand and product categories, but not for others. The strongest linkage appears to be between mothers and daughters for soup, catsup, facial tissue, peanut butter, and mayonnaise brands. Coffee, candy bars, household cleaners, and canned vegetables provide the lowest impact to intergenerational influence. Marketers would do well to further explore this market segmentation base.[1]

MARKETING IMPLICATIONS
IN THE SHOE BUSINESS

Specialty store shoe retailers can improve their marketing to age groups by using cohort analysis. Whether it is the marketing of outdoor boots or athletic sneakers, market segmentation strategies are directed to some aspects of generational marketing and to shoppers with certain lifestyle characteristics. Cohorts are formed by significant external events that occur in adolescence or early adulthood such as economic booms and busts and social changes that redefine values, attitudes, and preferences. For example, there are the "financially scarred cohorts" who are concerned about financial factors and therefore want their shoes to last for a long time. These consumers value leather over sneakers and need to be convinced that sneakers can be of high quality. In contrast, there is Generation X which accepts cultural diversity and places their interests on individualism rather than a group. They will purchase shoes that help to achieve a given purpose such as running shoes or outdoor boots.

The focus today is on casual lifestyles and comfort. The growing maturity of the consumer has been a factor as well as price consciousness. There is also a concern about better service in the retail shoe business. Brand awareness is important but value shopping is also present. Many consumers patronize both specialty shoe stores and discount stores. Catalogs selling shoes have gained in popularity as consumers are increasingly pressed for time. The sales of outdoor boots will increase as consumers want to enjoy the natural environment. Shoe retailers will not just wait for customers, but will go to customers. For example, some retail shoe stores have developed a team-sports business by catering to school athletic programs.

Each market segment or target market may require its own marketing mix. Edison Brothers has accomplished this strategy with their 5-7-9, Bakers/Leeds, Wild Pair, and Shifty's stores that carry shoes as part of their merchandising mix. Edison operates specialty stores that target the youth market but not all their stores such as J. Riggings, JW/Jeans West/Coder, Oaktree, or REPP Ltd. stock shoes.

The tweens and teens are significant target markets for Edison Brothers because they respond to advertising. For example, Edison Brothers, with their 5-7-9 stores, serve girls ages eleven to fifteen. Shifty's serves teenage boys and girls and also carries an assortment of apparel and accessories including skate gear. The Wild Pairs stores provide cutting-edge footwear that appeals to stylish young men and women which includes London Underground, Robert Wayne, and Skechers. Bakers/Leeds sell "hip" affordable footwear for juniors and young women.

The difficulty in segmenting the youth market is that the market is a diverse group with a variety of motivations, pressures, and concerns. This is particularly true of teenagers. Teenagers may be socially driven. Expenditures can be made on shoes that enhance their drive for status. Moreover, socially driven teenagers can be brand conscious. Purchase motivation is reflected by their perception of brand images. Peer approval is paramount and often leads to the tendency to shop in upscale or prestigious retail stores.

Less precisely delineated segments of teenagers are the markets motivated by special interests. This group is energetic, adventurous, and has an appreciation of culture. They are interested in pursuing intellectual activities such as exploring rain forests and are interested in shoes manufactured with environmentally safe materials. Another market segment enjoys solitary activities. Walking or jogging may be of interest and they represent a market for specialized sneakers. The largest segment of the teenage market are those who are sports- and fitness-oriented. Sports activities such as skiing, skateboarding, bicycles, motorcycles, and mopeds are expensive and consequently teenagers and parents jointly make purchases. Teenage girls and boys can be reached by retailers and manufacturers through sponsorship of tournaments of specific sports. This approach can lead to future buying loyalty when the teenager becomes an adult.

THE CHILDREN'S MARKET

The child development process for buying behavior goes through five stages regardless of social class, family income, and education of parents, and whether there is more than one child in the household. The five-stage process is observing, making requests, making selections, making assisted purchases, and making independent purchases.[2] Children's interactions with the marketplace take place in the observing stage of the child development process. Children construct mental images of marketplace objects and symbols such as Ronald McDonald. Moreover, perceptions of sounds, sizes, shapes, and colors are developed. Making requests is the second stage and through pointing, gesturing, and statements desires are conveyed. At this point, children inform parents as to their wants. The third stage is making selections. Usually this takes place when the child learns to walk and can locate and retrieve products by themselves. Making assisted purchases is the fourth stage and occurs when the child participates in the exchange process. The median age is about five-and-a-half when the child pays for the product under the watchful guidance of the parents. The final stage in the child development process for purchasing and shopping is making purchases without parental assistance. The median age for transacting purchases alone is age eight when the child has acquired all of the skills to become an independent consumer from parents, peers, and television.

Aggregate spending by children, ages four to twelve, has approximately doubled during each decade from the 1960s to the 1980s and has tripled in the 1990s.[3] Entertainment-based licensed characters such as the Flintstones and Batman still make an impact on the kids' market. Hollywood movies and television shows generate must-have toys every holiday season. Specially designed products that include Dial for Kids (liquid and bar soap), Pert Plus for Kids (shampoo), Kid Fresh (flushable wipes), and Ozarka Spring Water for Kids are a big hit. The use of "kid-centric" marketing is the key to successfully reaching this segment. Products and services need to be especially designed to keep the kids coming back for more. Marketers have to reach kids where they live, learn, and play by advertising in kids' magazines, having a Web site just for kids, and offering special programs to schools on nutrition, travel, and history.

The primary source of funds for children are allowances, performance of household chores, gifts from parents, gifts from grandparents or other relatives, and work outside the home such as raking leaves or shoveling snow. Increases from these sources are due to children performing more household tasks for money. Essentially, dual working couples are saying that household responsibilities are shared and that money must be earned. Furthermore, money received from grandparents is more often spent on food and toys. Apparel spending is the fastest-growing category as children are influenced by their peers or may be assuming more responsibility for their own necessities. Young children tend to prefer to shop in convenience stores since they are accessible and offer a good merchandise assortment.

Children influence their parents' purchasing decisions both directly and indirectly. Direct influence occurs when the children actively participate with other family members in the purchase. This direct influence in decision making is due to changes in family lifestyle. For example, because families travel more together for leisure and recreation, children are playing a role in automobile selection. Marketers of minivans and sport utility vehicles have placed advertisements in magazines read by children. In contrast, indirect influence, which is sometimes referred to as passive influence, occurs when brands and products are purchased that parents know that their children prefer. For example, when grocery shopping Cap'n Crunch cereal may be purchased because of awareness of brand preference even though a child may not be present. The influence of children, both direct and indirect, is increasing as part of joint family decision making for products such as computers, entertainment centers, and furniture.

The market potential of children is growing. Kids ages four to twelve had $33 billion in income in 2000, of which 45 percent came from an allowance and 55 percent from gifts or part-time jobs. Parents are dressing young children in brands like DKNY, Eddie Bauer, and Tommy Hilfiger, and purchasing upscale luxuries such as beauty products and organic baby food. About 30 percent of apparel purchases for young children are gifts. Young children start becoming aware of what their parents buy between ages two and three, and most make specific brand requests to their parents. Children generally function as independent consumers in the first grade. Early exposure to marketing communications is expected to affect children's brand awareness and preference as they mature. Companies spend almost $1 billion each year on advertising on television to kids ages two to fourteen and more than another $1 billion on print advertising. McDonald's and Coca-Cola are already practicing what is referred to as cradle-to-grave marketing. Delta Airlines has initiated a Fantastic Flyer program for kids as a technique of generating future customers. Delta targets kids ages seven through fourteen with birthday greetings, special foods, and gifts during flights. The children of today will be customers of tomorrow. Firms such as M&M, Mars, and Target stores have developed programs to attract children as customers. Marketers have learned that young children have the ability to become adaptive decision makers during the preschool years in a limited fashion and that this skill develops rapidly thereafter.[4]

Changing Behavioral Patterns of the Children's Market

There are approximately 40 million children under age ten in the United States. Their purchasing patterns have changed over the years. Manufacturers and retailers are responding to these changes. Companies now aim their products at a computer-literate generation of children where children under the age of five are using computers. Change is a pervasive force where even Little League baseball has experienced significant declines in participation of about 20 percent since 1997. Instead, in the decade of the 1990s, hockey, lacrosse, skateboarding, and computer or video games have gained in popularity. Environmental scanning is necessary to identify these social and cultural trends.

A number of behavioral patterns are favorable for those firms targeting the children's market. There are more grandparents with fewer grandchildren and with more discretionary income. These grandparents enjoy indulging their grandchildren. There are more double-income families where there is more money to be spent on children for products such as furniture, toys, and apparel. Family sizes are smaller. This means that more is spent on children today than in the past. Internet shopping has helped to extend the buying season for products such as toys that once was centered around special holidays. Also, the development of all-weather malls and the Internet make shopping easier.

There are changes in purchasing patterns that pose other problems. Children are outgrowing toys earlier and are moving on to computers and electronic games. Toy spending seems to peak at age three and declines steadily for each age group. Spending seems to have moved toward more sophisticated and expensive electronic toys such as XBox and Gamecube consoles, and status toys such as Bob the Builder, Hogwarts Castle, Jam 'N Glam Barbie, and Monster, Inc. figures and "kid approved" fragrances. Bath and Body Works has developed a version of Chuckleberry and Silly Fruits scents for children.

There is a growing poverty of time available for shopping. Therefore, convenience that emphasizes a wide merchandise selection for children has helped discounters such as Wal-Mart, Kmart, and Target. Internet shopping has also changed the purchasing habits of consumers, and retailers selling apparel, toys, and juvenile furniture have designed Web-friendly sites.

Marketing strategies aimed at the children's market have varied in their success and failure. For example, the establishment of a target market for ice cream products can be quite elusive. Age, occupation, income, neighborhood residence, residence in metropolitan versus small-town geographical location, ethnic background, and other factors determine shopping behavior for purchasing various types of ice cream products and different flavors of ice cream. The use of a combination of demographic factors is much more useful than relying on a single factor for developing strategies of market segmentation and product differentiation. There appears to be a positive correlation between the size of the family unit and expenditures for ice cream on an annual basis. The decision process for buying ice cream demonstrates that children are highly influential when a father is not present and when the mother is the household head.

The breakfast cereal industry has been successful in targeting the children's market with appeals from sports personalities and from characters such as Tony the Tiger. Quaker Oats has appealed to the children's market with Cap'n Crunch while General Mills' Wheaties has stood the test of time. Branded products in the breakfast cereal industry have been positive enough to withstand the assault of private-label supermarket brands aimed at the children's market.

Campbell Soup is successful with their approach to this market. In the early 1990s, Campbell reached the children's market by introducing Souper Stars and Curley Noodles as part of the marketing mix for children. Advertisements depicted the Campbell's kids as astronauts for Souper Stars and fighter pilots for Curley Noodles. Souper Stars was introduced as a dry soup mix. Campbell also expanded its offerings to include children's Cup of Noodles and Campbell's Double Noodle Soup.

The candy industry has failed to take advantage of product-usage segmentation variables. Marketers tend to distinguish between two broad classes of variables: user-oriented and product-usage variables. User-oriented segmentation variables include characteristics such as sex, age, geographic location, and ethnic origin and psychographic and lifestyle variables such as motives, activities, interests, and opinions. Product-usage segmentation variables involve such factors as the amount of time, time of use, place of use, the user of the product, product benefits, and the occasion for consumption.

THE TWEEN MARKET

These kids are not babies and most are not yet teens. There are more than 20 million tweens between nine and twelve years old. The tweens are a marketer's dream. Tweens have more money to spend and more influence on parents' buying behavior. They make a lot of their own meals. They are into social interaction and peer pressure. The average tween spends about $5 per week which does not count what they get for gifts. Total tween spending is about $14 billion a year. A large number of these kids are the children of Generation X and are known for being better shoppers. They tend to be more knowledgeable of the Internet than their parents as well as more concerned about the brand of the product. The most common items on the tween shopping list are candy, games and toys, nail polish or perfume, soda, books, and fast food. Clothing ties with fast food on the shopping list but rises sharply over time as kids' interests change. In an effort to attract the tween market, Burger King experimented by distributing green ketchup made by the H. J. Heinz Company. Blue applesauce is another product currently being marketed to tweens. It is still too early to forecast whether colored food products will be successful. An important source of information for the tweens is the catalog. This age group does not get much mail and they like getting a catalog that is addressed to them.

A distinction can be made between tweens and teens in the following four areas: age compression, consumer socialization, latch-key environment, and mall congregation.

Age Compression

The tweens are the age group most affected by the social phenomenon known as age compression. Age compression means that the tweens are acting older and growing up faster than previous generations. Tweens are more accepting of new technology, styles, and trends. The Pokemon craze provides an illustration of a modern, media-fueled tween fad that has all the elements of a marketing success. Pokemon started in Japan as a Nintendo Game Boy video game in 1995 aimed at boys and girls involved in collecting and training pet masters. Sears, responding to the Pokemon craze, has established Pokemon boutiques.

Toys and apparel industries have been affected by age compression. Mattel is producing computers, computer accessories, and interactive software aimed at extending their famous toy lines. An alliance between Mattel and Hewlett Packard allowed these companies to build Barbie and Hot Wheels printers and imaging software. Tweens are more technology friendly and are familiar with e-mail, cell phones, and beepers.

Tweens have been raised on a diet of MTV and are susceptible to the images seen on television. A growing number of tweens, especially girls, have weight concerns while boys are concerned with body-building. Girls seem to form unrealistically thin body ideals. Early dieting and an awareness of fashion trends have taken place. The most read magazines are *Sports Illustrated for Kids, Nintendo Power, Teen Beat,* and *Super Teen.* Girls are interested in the make-up and clothes worn by such entertainers as Brandy and Brittney Spears. Beauty and lifestyle products for tweens are growing. CVS's new Girl Lab is a store within a store in 1,200 drugstores that carries beauty products, jewelry, and stationery items for tween and teenage customers.

Evidence of age compression is found in fashion. Dollhouse's holiday line of tween fashions includes dark denim jackets. Moreover, retailers that once offered childish smock dresses for ten-year-olds now carry sophisticated designs, such as beaded silk Capri pant suits, reflecting a more mature taste. Tweens learn about fashion trends by surfing the Web and reading magazines like *Cosmo Girl.* Designers such as Tommy Hilfiger, Ralph Lauren, and Steve Madden aim their advertisements to this market segment.

CONSUMER SOCIALIZATION

Consumer socialization is the process by which tweens acquire skills, knowledge, techniques, and attitudes relevant to their shopping behavior. This includes learning the value of money and saving versus spending. Shopping usually takes place with the mother. This type of coshopper has the highest economic motivation for consumption. It is suggested that retailers offer interactive merchandising that encourages children to handle products and show them to mother.[5] Once children begin to earn money outside the home by delivering newspapers or babysitting, they are less subject to parental control. Independence in purchasing is a function of social class as middle class children seem to have less independence in decision making than do children in lower and upper social classes. Middle class parents have a greater desire to supervise their children's activities. Finally, children of mothers who are in the workforce are more likely to be socialized faster since they are given more responsibilities.

Many children acquire their consumer behavior norms and motives through observation of their parents and older siblings. However, while tweens observe their parents, they are anxious to emulate the consumption behavior of teens and may look to them or friends for models of acceptable behavior. Because many mothers are in the workforce, more Internet shopping takes place than coshopping with children. Certain types of consumer socialization may be indirect such as the underlying motives that influence a male tween and a female tween to buy personal products.

LATCHKEY ENVIRONMENT

These children are home alone for part of each school day while their parents are at work. Products such as the computer, television, VCR, and DVD are in great use during this time period. Pokemon and Harry Potter products are of particular interest to this age group. Tweens are caught between childhood and adolescence as they are bombarded by media communication and Internet challenges.

Some authorities believe that in these days of divorced parents and extended families, brand name items make up a form of support that once was provided by the family unit. Many of these latchkey children help their working parents at home by washing dishes, preparing meals, or by using the microwave oven and other household appliances. Manufacturers such as Whirlpool, General Foods, Lipton, and Hasbro have made special efforts to target this group. Lipton, for example, distributes *Kidsmarts* magazine to over 100,000 households so that latchkey kids can use afterschool hours profitably. Lipton includes coupons for products that latchkey kids consume. Marketers appeal to the latchkey generation with the realization that brand loyalties established at a young age can have a lasting impact.

MALL CONGREGATION

The tweens congregate at the local tween mecca—the shopping mall. These kids are not necessarily spoiled or wealthy. They may have earned their own money or saved their allowances to purchase brand names that are meaningful to them and their peer group. The malls have become the center of fashion and music. Tweens are not only interested in toys but in items such as high-tech electronics.

Tweens are likely to have acquired friends from many different ethnic and racial backgrounds. This trend is far different than with previous generations that tended to have friends much like themselves. Tweens are computer savvy and accustomed to the information world and social contact based on e-mail. Tweens are a dream of the fashion world as they like everything from cargo pants to Limp Bizkit CDs. Tweens are highly influenced by the fashion cycle and the adoption process demonstrated by trickle-down, trickle-across, and trickle-up efforts. Manufacturers have introduced new labels from Dollhouse to megabrands like Nautica. Sears has introduced a tween shop named Girl Identity. The growth of Limited Too demonstrates that other retailers find it lucrative to appeal to the tween market.

Fashion Adoption Process

The fashion adoption process is a series of buying waves that develop as a given style is popularly accepted in one group and then moves to other groups until it finally falls out of fashion. There are three explanatory models of the fashion cycle:

1. Trickle down where a fashion cycle travels downward through several socioeconomic classes. For example, leather clothes at the turn of the twenty-first century are a fashion that trickled down from teens to tweens. Moreover, ear piercing and make-up cosmetics are now used by tweens trying to emulate teens.

2. Trickle across where the cycle travels horizontally and simultaneously in a number of social classes. For example, the style with different levels of quality and price is introduced at the same time in exclusive high-priced specialty boutiques, medium-price specialty and department stores and discount stores. However, the style or the look is basically the same. The trickle-across concept best demonstrates the adoption process for fashions which originate with name designers and then become mass marketed.

3. Trickle up where the process is initiated in lower socioeconomic classes and moves upward among higher-income and social groups. T-shirts for example, once the domain of blue-collar workers, are now designed by Yves St. Laurent, Calvin Klein, and others. Shoes like Skeeters also moved up the socioeconomic ladder.

Parents spend $176 billion annually on tweens. Tween closets contain brands such as Nike, Adidas, Tommy Hilfiger, Gap, and Cover Girl for girls, and Nike, Adidas, Tommy Hilfiger for boys. The boys also prefer Sony and Pepsi products. These brands can be found at every shopping mall. Enclosed shopping malls are attractive for tweens to congregate, browse, and shop.

THE TEENAGE MARKET

Teens today, referred to as the "N-Generation" or "cyber teens" are also growing up in an interactive world. The U.S. Census Bureau estimates that by 2010 the teen population will grow to 35 million. The typical teen spends an average of $89 a week and one in nine high school kids has a credit card cosigned by a parent. Internet marketing is particularly crucial when dealing with this group. As of 2002, 16 million thirteen to nineteen-year-olds had Internet access. Niche or indie labels which market to specific lifestyles such as skate, surf, punk, hip-hop, or rave have found success. Age compression, consumer socialization, and a latchkey environment have varying degrees of impact on teenagers. The years over age thirteen have the greatest impact and peer approval is more important to teenagers than to the tweens. Many teenagers drive their own automobiles and some are employed part-time or earn money by doing house-related activities. The degree of independence is the major distinction between tweens and teens.

The teenage years are marked by a search to develop a distinct identity and self-image which sometimes manifests itself in rebellion against parents and authority. Peer acceptance becomes paramount and purchasing behavior frequently reflects the motivation to join and belong to a group. Compared to a generation ago, teens born between 1981 and 1987 are a team-playing generation. However, these teens are sometimes more socially isolated than other generations since they shop and do their homework, research, and communicate with their friends on the Internet. This generation of teens desires to belong to some group much more than other generations. Teen cliques or "tribes" have their own distinctive markings ranging from hippie chic to body art or to buttoned-down prep clothing styles. A lot of anger is expressed in teen music. Teens are not necessarily alike. There are some teens that volunteer for community service, others seldom volunteer, and there are those who belong to a clique and those who live in a private adult-free world of the Web and video games. Most teens are peer driven and observe and learn from the media. This impacts their purchasing behavior. Teenagers consider shopping more of an experience than a routine. They buy to become more independent and to express themselves.

Teenagers travel more than their parents. As teens have earned more money than ever before, they have gained more financial independence than earlier generations. Teenagers wield increasing influence in household purchases. A host of brands that have prospered when the baby boomers were teens are now encountering some problems. Therefore, marketers of established brands need to rethink their marketing strategies.[6] Another manifestation of age compression is Avon's plans for expanding their market by targeting a cosmetic line to teenage girls and also recruiting them as sales representatives where in the past older women were targeted.

Teenage girls spend most of their money on apparel, cosmetics, jewelry, and fragrances. Teenage boys spend most of their money on movies, dating, entertainment, clothing, and automobiles. Gender purchasing influences that were once apparent in previous generations have become blurred as sex roles are changing. Girls and boys in previous generations took separate classes in shop and cooking. Today, both boys and girls attend the same classes. Thus, marketers will be able to focus appeals on unisex goods and services for teens. Male and female stereotypes will be less applicable. Increasingly, teenage boys may be asked to prepare dinner for parents who are in the workforce and teenage girls may be requested to repair or fix something in the house. Teenagers of both sexes will perform grocery shopping tasks for the household with both parents working or if the family is headed by a single parent. Today's teenagers spend more time grocery shopping for their families than teenagers did in previous generations.

In many respects the current teen generation has accepted new products. Some of the trends accepted by most teens have been alternative music, baggy clothes, baseball caps, MTV, sports, music videos, professional sports clothing, and eating healthy. Although teens eat fast food, there is a desire to eat healthy foods. If healthier french fries and other types of fast food with palatable tastes can be developed, teens would be a ready market. Even Wrigley, thriving on the strength of brands like Doublemint and Juicy Fruit, is experiencing changes in the demand patterns of teens. Teens are chewing less gum and have gravitated to a host of nongum products, especially mints such as Altoids, Mentos, and Tic-Tacs. Gum sales have declined about 5 percent in 1999 and mint sales grew approximately 10 percent.[7] Wrigley, in a effort to boost sales, has introduced Eclipse mint gum aimed at competitors such as Altoids and Dentyne Ice customers. Wrigley is also revamping old standbys like Juicy Fruit with youth-oriented ads and Internet tie-ins.

The teenage population is projected to reach 35 million in 2010 which will be the largest teen population in U.S. history. Retailers are utilizing a lifestyle marketing approach to gain their attention.[8] It is believed that teens will be more loyal to a brand that seems to reflect their lifestyle rather than just how teens dress. Consequently, retailers are revising their strategies to include music, sports, books, bedroom decorations, and anything else that will depict teen lifestyles. For example, the magalog of Abercrombie and Fitch offers everything from music reviews to travel in South Africa. Magalogs are a combination of magazines and catalogs that retailers like Target send to the teen market. American Eagle goes further by giving customers CDs if they spend enough. American Eagle Outfitters Inc. has staged a comeback in the past few years by establishing an image that appears to be more about lifestyle than about selling clothes. This lifestyle reflects an active outdoorsy image. American Eagle's magalog offers its branded snowboards and scooters as well as clothes. Items that are not typically sold by American Eagle such as an underwater camera and a compact guitar are also offered. The magalog is more a marketing tool than a selling tool.

Teenagers spend most of their money on themselves immediately. They are not inclined to postpone purchasing gratification, yet there is a trend among some teenagers toward savings and even owning financial instruments like stocks and bonds. Parents also pay for leisure-class goods that were previously paid for by teenagers. This can be attributed to smaller family size and higher disposable income. Should this trend continue, teenagers might concentrate their purchasing on luxury-class goods. This situation is also made possible by increased job opportunities for teenagers.

One of the tasks often delegated to teenagers is grocery shopping. Although they may be guided by shopping lists developed by parents, brand selection is frequently left to their own discretion. Teenagers have been shown to be more brand loyal than adults. For marketers of grocery items, this presents an opportunity for developing loyal consumers for the future. Finally, there is evidence that teenagers influence family consumer behavior. Although it is difficult to quantify this influence or discuss how accurately the influence is perceived, most marketers agree it exists to some degree and is gaining in importance. It would appear that adolescents are most successful in their influence attempts when they emulate adult strategies.[9]

PSYCHOGRAPHIC CHARACTERISTICS

Teenagers are no more alike than adults and are actually a diverse group with a variety of motivations, pressures, and concerns. Teenagers can be divided into four attitudinal market segments: Socially Driven, Diversely Motivated, Socioeconomically Introverted, and Sports-Oriented.

Socially Driven Market Segment

This market segment has a greater amount of disposable income than any other teen group. Expenditures are made on products such as clothing that enhance their drive for status. This group is brand conscious. The Socially Driven teenagers have little regard for price. Purchase motivation is reflected by their perception of brand images. The market segment prefers apparel, electronics, and automobiles that meet peer approval. Media campaigns appear in periodicals such as *Seventeen* and *Gentlemen's Quarterly*. Music tastes reflect popular groups and songs that have gained peer acceptance thus meeting their need for a trendy image and high status. Television is used carefully. Group involvement needs to be emphasized in advertising. Their consumption orientation and high disposable incomes easily define the Socially Driven. They tend to shop in upscale or prestigious retail stores that carry high-status-brand merchandise.

Diversely Motivated Market Segment

This group is the most cultured of the four market segments and has a wide range of interests. They are energetic and adventurous. This market segment is comfortable in a group or in a solitary situation. This group is a good target market for records, cassette tapes, compact discs, periodicals, books, and other cultural products. The Diversely Motivated are difficult to identify but it is known that a high percentage of their income is spent on music. It is likely that this group would be most likely to participate in high school bands and drama activities. Because of their variety of interests, activities such as chess and the more intellectually demanding games such as Trivial Pursuit may be of interest to this group.

The female Diversely Motivated teenager can be reached through general interest magazines such as *TV Guide* or *Teenage People*. Teenage boys can be reached through *Rolling Stone* which offers lifestyle perspectives that are a combination of counterculture and rock music. This group might include politically conscious teenagers who favor listening to the Irish rock band U2. Merchandise preferences of this market segment include tie-dye fabrics, Indian prints, leather sandals, and little or no make-up.

Socially Introverted Market Segment

This market segment prefers solitary activities. Electronic goods such as personal computers can be marketed to this group since it meets their need for isolation. This group may read a great deal and may especially enjoy reading the section in periodicals entitled "Letters to the Editor." Music listening may be through MTV since watching television could be a solitary activity and yet give members of this group an opportunity to belong to the teenage music culture. This group may also enjoy hobbies such as model airplane or boat building, photography, or coin and stamp collecting.

Sports-Oriented Market Segment

This market segment represents the largest market of the four teenager groups for sports and home video equipment. Sports and fitness are ranked highly by both boys and girls. This is a product category in which parents and teenagers increasingly share the costs of purchasing sports equipment. Sports activities such as skiing, skateboarding, bicycles, motorcycles, and mopeds are expensive. The Sports-Oriented teenager can be reached by advertisements in *Sports Illustrated*. Both teenage girls and boys can also be reached through sponsorship of tournaments for specific sports. The sport most kids play is basketball. It is the most popular organized youth team sport today in the United States with 10 million kids playing—4 million girls and 6 million boys. Soccer comes in second with 9.6 million participants.

Teenagers today are different from the teenagers of yesteryear. Current values are oriented toward consumption and financial success. Teenagers of the 1960s established a counterculture that rejected the traditional concepts of success as measured by the accumulation of material goods. Instead the focus was on social value issues and nonconformity with traditional societal norms. Peer pressures were strong. The popularity of denim jeans and the imitation of lifestyles established by folk heroes of that time established the groundwork for future activities.

Teenagers have specialized needs that are linked to their physiological and emotional growth. Hans Sebold, a well-known authority on adolescents, maintained that teenagers are searching for their new identity or life plan and therefore readily experiment with anything that encompasses these feelings. According to Sebold, much of rock music relates the epic story of adolescence. Teenagers find a sense of belonging to this music because of their search for identity.[10] This search for identity helps to explain teenage susceptibility to new trends and fads and with adequate income it promotes consumption values.

All teenage behavior is not goal oriented. Maslow's Hierarchy of Needs suggested that individuals are motivated by concrete needs and this is not always true in daily activities. Teenagers may spend a great deal of time just doing nothing where a specific goal is not suggested to the conscious mind.

Many of the changes in psychographic characteristics of teenagers can be attributed to the changing structure of U.S. households. Teenagers are given more responsibility for shopping since mom is in the workforce. Family size is smaller and more money can be expended on fewer children. Job opportunities for teenagers are abundant. The profile of today's teenager is one of affluence and the ability to satisfy consumption desires based upon current peer values.

THE COLLEGE MARKET

College students are still in the process of establishing many of their brand preferences and shopping patterns. The college market is diverse and can be segmented by type of college attended, public, private; level of college attended, junior, four-year, or comprehensive; location of college, urban or rural and area of country, eastern versus southern college. College students exert, in varying degrees, influence on the purchase decisions of their families. There are 15.6 million students in two- and four-year colleges and graduate schools in the United States with a combined purchasing power of $78 billion in 2001. Undergraduate college students have an average buying power of over $400 per month and graduate college students spend about $750 per month. Almost all these students have access to the Internet through a campus outlet. College students spend an average of $700 in college bookstores each year for books, food, CDs, and disposable cameras. These students generally pay for their purchases by check, credit card, cash, a bank debit card, or a campus debit card. About 10 percent of students will buy textbooks online while over one-third of students will make other purchases using the Internet. U.S. college spending online exceeded $5 billion in 2002. The size of the college population is expected to grow to 18 million in 2007. Minority students are anticipated to constitute about 80 percent of that increase and this will occur in five states—California, Texas, Florida, New York, and Arizona.[11] College campuses are now populated by more women, more minorities, and more non-traditional students than ever before.

Many college students are in the stage of the life cycle where they are willing to try different products and develop stronger brand commitments. Merchandise purchased includes CDs, DVDs and tapes, wireless communications, long-distance services, prepaid calling cards, discounted airline tickets, automotive products, clothes, food, cosmetics, and technology products. College students are also large purchasers of computers and software. Many of these are purchase "firsts" for this market segment such as first credit card and first long distance service in one's own name.

Credit is used by college students to purchase a wide assortment of goods and services. MasterCard has recognized that about 75 percent of college students maintain their first credit card for about fifteen years.[12] Because colleges have been concerned about student debt levels, credit card marketers have been restricted to either a certain number of days or areas on campus that can be used for student soliciting. This type of soliciting has not been extended to other marketers.[13]

Credit cards are an important tool for college students. In the past, credit was looked at as a sign of poor management of personal finances. This perception has changed and credit is an acceptable means of purchasing. One of the strongest values of the past was the Puritan ethic with its emphasis on hard work, economy, and thrift which has shifted to a new ideal of self-indulgence and pleasure. Another generation would have been shocked by the prevailing attitude of "buy now, pay later." In the past, it was believed that goods and services should not be purchased unless payment could be made immediately. Lifestyle trends are at the heart of the plastic wars.

Strategies to reach specific college markets and firm up images have been used successfully by the credit industry. The Platinum and Gold Cards issued by American Express are attempts to appeal to a status-conscious market. MasterCard and Visa have followed the American Express strategy. Affinity cards by various colleges are another effective strategy. MasterCard and Visa are obtaining a lion's share of this market.

Credit card organizations have used several strategies in the college market. One technique is to have parents cosign, thus signifying that they will be responsible for default. Another strategy is to limit the amount of debt to $250 to $500. Full payment must be made before the credit card can be used again. Also debit cards can be tied to the student's checking account.

The family is an important influence on the purchasing behavior of its members. Age plays an important role in the consumption behavior of family members. Teens and college students who need to establish an identity have an increasing influence on family purchasing decisions. Changes in family structure such as single parents with children and extended families are becoming increasingly important to marketers. These nontraditional family structures will change many of the lifestyle strategies aimed at the family and its members.

MANAGING CHANGE

When targeting children, tweens, teens, and the college market, environmental monitoring or scanning is necessary to pinpoint future trends. For example, Yankelovich, Inc. offers a syndicated research service to marketers designed to predict the forces shaping the lifestyles and behavior of kids ages six to seventeen in its Yankelovich Youth Monitor report. Environmental scanning or monitoring refers to an early warning system that assembles and analyzes information concerning external forces, events, and relationships and their impact on the present and future strategies of an organization. There are environmental factors such as inflation that cannot be controlled. However, environmental changes such as competitive conditions can be influenced to some extent. Consumer attitudes, opinions, and interests can also be greatly influenced. If prepared, the organization might be able to turn threats into opportunities, or at least cope better with a changing environment. For example, many young adults in their twenties and thirties are still living at home and are supported by their parents. This trend of dependency has been extended as students seek master's degrees and look at other career factors. Also, the average marriage age has been rising since 1970, extending codependency.

The tasks of marketers are to identify trends through environmental scanning and assess how these trends impact consumer wants and needs. Marketers need to identify how product characteristics are likely to satisfy their future customers. Finally, marketers must determine which opportunities will match the organization's objectives. Environmental scanning is used to identify the following changes:

- *Economic trends.* These changes develop from movements in the direction and magnitude of various fundamental elements. Among the major factors considered are gross national product, personal income, consumer and government spending, availability of capital, interest rates, employment versus unemployment, and savings and debt. For example, since there has been a proliferation of affluence, some hotels such as the Ritz-Carlton in Naples, Florida, and the Mark Hopkins in San Francisco, California, have established kids' lounges with video libraries, sandwiches, and cookies to attract a younger wealthy clientele group.

- *Social and cultural trends.* These changes are difficult to classify. Among these social and cultural patterns have been the emerging roles of women and minorities and changes in lifestyles reflecting the role of children in the family. There are also apparent declines in traditional values, increased education and its impact on work relationships and recreational pursuits, and a redistribution of wealth in society.

- *Political and legal trends.* These changes include regulatory policies, fiscal and monetary policies, environmental policies and consumer protection policies that affect markets. These policies are developed on national, state, and local levels. Policies that have affected children up to the age of eighteen, such as tobacco and alcohol use, have accelerated in recent years.

- *Demographic trends.* These changes reveal new or diminishing markets. The teenage market has contracted from the early 1990s but the college market exploded. Family size is smaller. The sunbelt states are growing at a rapid pace while the East and Midwest are stagnating. Population shifts reveal new Standard Metropolitan Statistical Areas for marketers to cultivate. Furniture retailers have anticipated the next baby boom and chains such as Pottery Barn Kids, Cargokids, and Bombay Kids have entered the market.

- *Ecology trends.* These changes deal with rising environmental issues and how better technology leads to different consumer behavior patterns. Matters such as the disposal of solid wastes and the recycling of materials have affected how companies package their products.

The era of the 1980s included a video-game explosion and skateboards. The 1990s brought about a growing awareness of environmental issues. McDonald's withdrew styrofoam packaging and replaced it with paper. Education in the 2000s is playing a more important role. Electronic learning aids are the products of the future. In addition, the trend toward a well-balanced diet will influence children's eating habits. Increasingly, teenagers are working and trying to improve their physical appearance. While sports have always been important among boys, girls have become more responsive to athletic activities. Allowances are larger than in previous years and children and teenagers have become more aware of brands. Brand choices of children and teens can greatly influence parent brand selection.[14]

NOTES

1. Elizabeth S. Moore, William L. Wilkie, and Richard J. Lutz, "Passing the Torch: Intergenerational Influence as a Source of Brand Equity," *Journal of Marketing* 66 (April 2002): 17–37.

2. James U. McNeal and Chyn-Hwa Yeb, "Born to Shop," *American Demographics* 15 (June 1993): 34–39.

3. James U. McNeal, "Tapping the Three Kids' Markets," *American Demographics* 20 (April 1998): 36–41.

4. Jennifer Gregan-Payton and Deborah Roedder-John, "Are Young Children Adaptive Decision Makers? A Study of Age," *Journal of Consumer Research* 21 (March 1995): 567–580.

5. Sanford Grossbart and Les Carlson, "Consumer Socialization and Frequency of Shopping with Children," *Journal of the Academy of Marketing Science* 19 (Summer 1991): 155–164.

6. Ellen Newborne and Kathleen Kerwin, "Generation Y," *Business Week*, 15 February 1999, 80–88.

7. Janet Ginsburg, "Not the Flavor of the Month," *Business Week*, 20 March 2000, 128.

8. Amy Barrett, "To Reach The Unreachable Teen," *Business Week*, 18 September 2000, 78–80.

9. Kay M. Palen and Robert E. Wilkes, "Adolescent–Parent Interaction in Family Decision Making," *Journal of Consumer Research* 24 (September 1997): 159–169.

10. Hans Sebold, *Adolescence: A Social Psychological Analysis* (Englewood Cliffs, N.J.: Prentice-Hall, 1984).

11. "U.S. College Population to Increase By 19% within 20 Years," *Education Market* 31, 12 June 2000, 5–6.

12. Carrie Goerne, "Corporate Sponsors Embark on Campus Tours," *Marketing News* 28 (September 1992): 12; and Terry Lefton, "Credit Cards Go to High School," *Adweek's Marketing Week* 11 (May 1992): 20.

13. Lisa Fickenscher, "Colleges Cold-Shouldering Campus Marketers," *American Banker* 164, 1 January 1999, 16.

14. Selina S. Guber and Jon Berry, *Marketing To and Through Kids* (New York: McGraw-Hill, 1993), 213.

CHAPTER 7

Targeting the Changing Lifestyles of the Senior Market

Although cultural values in the United States have emphasized a youth orientation, an increasing amount of attention is being given to the senior market. The growth rate of the senior market is expected to be twice that of the general population rate. The population of seniors over fifty is expected to rise to 30 percent of the population by 2030. The life expectancy has lengthened from sixty-eight in 1950 to eighty-three in 2002. This market presents an attractive potential for marketers for a wide variety of goods and services. Factors providing for a good financial situation for the senior market include built-in cost-of-living increases in Social Security, Medicare and Medicaid, long-term healthcare insurance, and improved pension plans. For this group, there is a high rate of mortgage-free home ownerships. Many seniors have been impacted by a decline in the stock market and regret retiring early. They are worried about their money running out before they reach seventy years old. Interest rates on investments are an important matter for the senior. More than 60 percent of the money in certificates of deposit are held by people over sixty years old. The number of older Americans with debt is growing. Recently, the average amount owed by people age sixty-five and older has tripled to $23,000 from $8,000. Bankruptcy filings by seniors were 82,200 in 2001 as compared to 23,890 in 1991. Seniors have become financially vulnerable. However, there are a large number of seniors who are recession-proof because they have stable, guaranteed incomes from their retirement packages, have little debt, and more discretionary income than other age groups.

Although the new senior citizen is healthier and may be more affluent than many seniors in the past, the senior market is being driven by information from television and the Internet, and the reality of their financial situation which may be dependent on the state of the economy. An increasing number of seniors are enrolling in programs offered by colleges and universities because they want to stay intellectually up to date. Travel, news shows, and documentaries expand their intellectual horizons. They also spend time reading product literature, guarantees, and warranties.

The senior market has a remarkable level of vitality and productivity. With seniors living longer, they typically have fifteen to twenty years of free time left after retirement. Seniors are joining and enjoying health spas and athletic clubs. Golf, tennis, bowling, aerobic exercises, walking, and swimming are frequent activities. Seniors also participate in literacy and volunteer programs. Over the years, experience and wisdom have been acquired and there is a desire to share this knowledge with others. Seniors vote at a higher rate than any other age group, are more interested in life activities, and are less self-absorbed than younger people.

Within this market segment, people in their nineties are the fastest growing segment of the senior population according to the U.S. Census Bureau. The 1990 census found that their numbers increased 38 percent between 1980 and 1990 to 1 million. By 2000, they increased 81 percent to 1.7 million people. There are some significant differences between the young–old (fifty-five to seventy years of age), the old (from seventy to eighty), and the old–old (over eighty). Consequently, subsegmentation is needed to describe the needs, motivations, and wants of each group as depicted in Table 7.1. There is not necessarily a classification scheme based upon age and some refer to some seniors as the young-again market (fifty to sixty-five) and others classify the youngest segment as the young–old (fifty-five to seventy), but factors such as health, education, and psychological outlook can be used as moderating variables. This current generation of seniors in many instances seem to act ten to fifteen years younger than the elderly did twenty years ago. The senior market, unlike other market age segments, encompasses ages from fifty to over ninety with an age spread of over forty years. Consumer behavior may vary widely within each submarket and therefore seniors should not be considered a homogenous market. There are differences based on regions of residence, educational level, household size, race, and family type on the various expenditures made by any of the age groups. Another consideration is the large number of baby boomers who will soon join this market segment in large numbers. These different age segments within the elderly market

Table 7.1
Segmenting the Elderly Market

Classification By Marketers	
Young–Old (55 to 70)	Young Again (50–65)
Old (70 to 80)	Gray Market (65+)[b]
Old–Old (80+)[a]	

Strategy Linkages
Healthy Hermits
Ailing Outgoers
Frail Recluses
Health Indulgers[c]

[a]Leon G. Schiffman and Leslie Lazar Kanuk, *Consumer Behavior*, 5th ed. (Englewood Cliffs, N.J.: Prentice-Hall, 1994), 464.

[b]Wayne D. Hoyer and Deborah J. MacInnis, *Consumer Behavior*, 2d ed. (Boston: Houghton-Mifflin, 2001), 366–368.

[c]George P. Moschis and Anil Mathers, "How They're Acting Their Age," *Marketing Management* 2 (September 1993): 40–50.

have been exposed to varying values concerning youthfulness, health, and spending. Some seniors in their fifties are forming new households after a divorce, and some in their sixties are still raising children. These situations suggest that lifestyle rather than chronological age is a useful approach for marketers for this segment in the future.

Table 7.1 lists the classification distinctions made by marketers and the strategic linkage to psychographics. Healthy hermits are in relatively good health but have few social contacts and few consumption needs. They deny their "old age" status and may have experienced the death of a spouse or have entered a time of social withdrawal. In contrast, ailing outgoers are in relatively poor physical condition and are socially active. This group is health conscious; their circumstances have not diminished their preoccupation with financial independence, security, and well-being. Some of these ailing outgoers may attend financial seminars sponsored by investment organizations. This group does not allow their physical limitations to stop their participation in activities. Frail recluses are inactive people with chronic ailments who tend to remain isolated and are likely to be conscious of physical and personal security. Healthy indulgers have more in common with the young–old or the young-again segments. This market segment is socially engaged, in relatively good health, and has strong needs for selective information.[1]

The young-again market segment is better off financially than the baby boomers and focuses on enjoying life. Cognitive age operates in targeting this market segment and other segments as well. Cognitive age is how the individual perceives one's self by how they feel and act, their interests, and their perception of their appearance. Cognitively younger, but chronologically older people, manifest higher self-confidence, are more interested in fashion, and have greater participation in cultural activities. The young-again market thinks more like baby boomers than seniors. In contrast, the gray market segment lived through the Great Depression and tends to save rather than to spend. Although birth-age constructs are not necessarily accurate indicators of lifestyle and behavior, they are convenient for describing the senior market. Marketers may find cognitive age is a much better predictor of spending behavior.

The lifestyle decisions of the young-again market and the healthy indulgers were influenced greatly by trends in marriage, divorce, and consumption patterns during the 1980s and the 1990s. These market segments monitor their diets and are good prospects for health clubs, spas, cosmetics, beauty parlors, and healthier foods. These groups are important target markets for financial products. This market segment does not cook at home as frequently as the seniors did in the past and indulges more in luxury travel, the theater, and purchases more fashionable clothing and jewelry. They are characterized by more discretionary behavior, more flexibility, and more complex ways of determining value than younger adults.[2] Moreover, this market segment is less price sensitive than younger adults and previous older generations.

Youth-obsessed marketers have turned seniors off with stereotypes of seniors as frail, inactive, and living on fixed incomes. Seniors, and particularly baby boomers-turned-seniors, make purchase decisions based on lifestyle, not age—and often an active lifestyle. As time goes forward, members of the senior market are expected to increasingly feel much younger than their chronological age. Successful marketers will need to close this gap between self-perception and reality in their marketing strategies. Yet despite their claims to youth, seniors do have less visual acuity and manual dexterity and this must be considered by marketers in packaging products. Packages that are difficult to open and labels with small print are especially irksome to the senior consumer.

Many industries have profited from the growth of the senior market. Among the winners will be financial services, travel, adult housing, media and entertainment, dietary supplements, and the healthcare industries. Each market segment—whether it is healthy hermits, ailing outgoers, frail recluses, or healthy indulgers—constitutes important submarkets for these products. The senior market's adjustment to retirement status is an important variable in analyzing senior submarkets. Life stage segmentation and buyer motivation are other potentially useful variables for segmenting the senior market. It is clear that a holistic approach is needed to link life stage segmentation with marketing strategies aimed at the elderly consumer market.

MARKET SIZE AND LOCATION

In the past decade, the population of seniors over age sixty-five increased 12.7 percent and those over eighty-five from 1.5 percent to 14.2 percent.[3] More than 885,000 of this group are making their homes with a partner to whom they are not married. Most of the future growth will be in the fifty to sixty-five age range as the baby boomers mature. People fifty and older represent 37 percent of the adult U.S. population, accounting for $2 trillion in income and 50 percent of all discretionary income. The largest increase in growth rates will be among those who are active and able to participate in social and recreational pursuits.

California, Florida, Illinois, Michigan, New Jersey, New York, Ohio, Pennsylvania, and Texas contain the largest numbers of the elderly. A high proportion of seniors live in the central cities of metropolitan areas. This is in contrast to the younger population which has established itself in suburban locations. Some of the seniors who formerly resided in the suburbs have returned to the central cities. Many seniors prefer the conveniences of larger metropolitan areas and have lived in them for some years and are now reluctant to make changes.

Florida has the highest percentage of seniors, making up over 20 percent of the state's population. States such as Arkansas, Connecticut, Iowa, Maine, Massachusetts, North Dakota, South Dakota, and West Virginia will have a high proportion of seniors. The Northeast has the largest percentage of people over age sixty-five.[4]

The senior population is expected to be skewed toward the younger age brackets. A unique characteristic of the mature market is the disproportionate number of females whose life expectancy is about six to seven years longer than that of men. This market segment represents a potential for housing community development. States with significant senior housing developments are Florida, Arizona, North Carolina, California, and New Jersey. Sunbelt states are expected to provide for seniors. New Jersey seems to be a surprise on this list. However, many seniors prefer to remain in nearby communities where they have raised their families, established careers, and have friends. Generally, eligibility for senior developments is over age fifty-five, and golf, tennis, outdoor or indoor pools, and sometimes auditoriums are provided where entertainment can be scheduled.

PURCHASING MOTIVES

The senior market does not like to be thought of as old. They often ignore products or services designed for older people. They prefer to be seen in a positive attractive way. Their purchasing rests on three fundamental bases. First, the product or service must perform as expected and be backed by guarantees. Second, the product should have social reinforcement expectations. Third, the product or service should satisfy consequential experience expectations. At the core of total customer satisfaction is the effective use of human resources and the development of consumer-friendly programs. For example, Giant Food has adhered to safety standards of age-labeling certain products they sell beyond those required by government agencies. Giant Food was the first large supermarket chain to offer unit pricing, open dating, and seafood labeling.

The most important reasons why seniors purchase goods and services are as follows:

- To replace goods or products that either need repair, are obsolete or to acquire new product features.
- To reinforce the lifestyles that are desired.
- To buy gifts for others.
- To serve as a basis for pleasing experiences.

Seniors are constantly trying to achieve life satisfaction goals. It is a period of life that is reflective as seniors search for meaning in their lives. Therefore, seniors are often influenced in their buyer behavior by perceptions of a product or service with potential to advance life satisfaction motives.

Seniors like to shop. This activity is a way of meeting friends and fosters social communication. Some seniors have become mall mavens, not only making purchases for themselves but for friends and family members. Moreover, seniors have the time to make product comparisons in order to obtain the best value for their money. Time is devoted to reading direct mail, package labels, and package inserts. Seniors are price and value sensitive. Shopping has a special meaning and, for seniors, has become a social activity as friends and couples shop together.

A high percentage of seniors own their homes and have no mortgages. This is a time of life when some seniors can upgrade their furnishings. Since this market segment is generally empty nesters, they have more discretionary income. When they were younger, automobiles were traded every five to seven years, now trade-ins are every three or four years. More women have worked in their forties and fifties and these two-income households beautify their homes with the latest furnishing styles. Seniors are receptive to new technology and purchase camcorders, VCRs, DVD recorders, large screen television sets, and the latest in stereo equipment.

THE FASHION MARKET AND SENIORS

The fashion industry in the 1980s and 1990s was directed at young women. Women over sixty-five spent about $14.7 billion in 1999 on apparel, which was almost the identical amount expended by the twenty-five to thirty-four-year-old female market.[5] Some marketers, including Banana Republic and Bloomingdale's, have already begun to cultivate the senior market. Many women perceive themselves as ten to fifteen years younger than their chronological age.

While Lane Bryant initially began to satisfy the needs of women by adding extra sizes in foundation garments, suits, blouses, sweaters, coats, sportswear, and bathing suits, this merchandise was designed for younger women. The Limited's 1982 acquisition of the chain brought about some changes in merchandise offerings and plus-size women's clothing became a hot retail category. Liz Claiborne has also developed plus-size fashions and their brand is distributed by Nordstrom, other upscale retailers, and their own stores. Many senior women have grown in size and now also demand stylish plus-size fashions. This was a departure from the plain basics that Lane Bryant sold. The new merchandising direction includes sheer, slinky knits, pinstripes, fashion-forward evening wear, and designer sportswear. Many seniors take cruises and will dress up on these trips. J.C. Penney also entered the field and has been successful with a specialty plus-size catalog. Bullock's, a Los Angeles based department store chain, launched a specialty chain for plus-size women known as Bullock's Woman. It is estimated the plus-size market will continue to grow as baby boomers mature.

Many fashions have come from Rome, Paris, New York, and Los Angeles. These cities are viewed as fashion centers. Fashions are believed to move from the West Coast to other areas of the country. This is especially true in regard to sports clothing and apparel for recreational and leisure activities. The gap between urban and rural areas has been closing with the development of better communications and transportation systems. Television, air travel, and, for some, the Internet have brought consumers closer. The risk associated with selling fashion apparel comes from the uncertainty of the consumer's degree of acceptance and the duration of this acceptance of the fashion. An important force driving the consumer is the continual search for newness. Guidance for marketers when planning strategy are the stages of the fashion cycle: introduction, accelerated development, and decline.

When purchasing fashion goods, the most important consumer patronage motives are price, merchandise selection, brands carried, purchasing convenience, store services, merchandise quality, customer treatment by store personnel, and store reputation. A store choice decision can be one of high-involvement or low-involvement. For example, a man's or a lady's suit to be worn for an important occasion may have a high relevance because of its price, large differences between alternatives, and the high perceived risk of making a wrong decision. In contrast, the purchase of a T-shirt might be regarded as a low-involvement decision. There is not much financial or social risk if one brand is purchased rather than another. Demographics and lifestyle characteristics as well as other purchase characteristics, such as perceptions of store attributes, lead to opinions and activities related to shopping and search behavior.

Research findings reveal that marketers could communicate successfully with the seniors market by appealing to family members and that adult children are instrumental in introducing seniors to new products. It is further suggested that stereotyped depiction of seniors in mass media may cause a degree of adverse reaction toward age-based marketing stimuli. Variables like socioeconomic status, race, and income have an important influence on the consumer socialization process.[6]

Greco pointed out in the late 1980s that apparel shoppers can be segmented on the basis of fashion consciousness rather than age alone and that age alone is a weak dimension for segmenting markets.[7] However, Macy's department stores did establish the Oasis Club for individuals over sixty years of age and offered members a 10 percent discount on certain days.

The fashion-conscious seniors are a viable market. The senior market does not like to be singled out or appealed to on the basis of age when fashion is considered. Therefore by appealing to older baby boomers, marketers can still attract fashion-conscious seniors. Women over fifty-five still have to shop and browse. Seniors who are fashion conscious feel ten to fifteen years younger than their chronological age. At the same time, it would be best to appeal to younger baby boomers by using them as models to demonstrate how these fashions can be worn. The limited use of silver-haired models may also be appropriate in some instances.

PSYCHOGRAPHIC CHARACTERISTICS

The way in which seniors adjust to their empty-nest status and their retirement can provide a useful classification system for differentiating market segments among them. These developments may lead to more appropriate strategies for marketers trying to serve these segments. Seniors perceive themselves as younger than their counterparts did some years ago. Consequently, marketers should look beyond chronological age to consumers' perceived or cognitive reference ages when segmenting this market. The key to understanding seniors is to forget age and focus on consumer interests and activities. Health status, time, and affluence are useful guides in determining consumer behavior of seniors. Travel, dining out, hobbies, and viewing sports and theater events assume a more important role in consumer satisfaction than the ownership of things or possessions. Intangible or aesthetic experiences, such as enjoying the beauty of a waterfall, are more important than the possession of merchandise. Seniors are more interested in a product's functional and social value.

The senior market has in many instances a different set of activities, interests, and opinions from those of younger consumers. A few of these behavior patterns may involve seasonal migration to warmer climates, less physical activity, more leisure activities, earlier bedtimes, and, if appropriate, less night driving over long distances. Some seniors deny the cultural stereotype that people possess about growing old by the type of clothes they wear, the automobiles they drive, and the activities in which they get involved. Many seniors have a fear of isolation and seek out company. Shopping is an activity that fills a vacuum. Often it does not matter what seniors are shopping for—the point is to shop for anything.

French and Fox reported the way in which seniors adjust to their empty-nest status and their subsequent retirement status. A useful classification system for differentiating market segments among them was developed into three broad categories: healthy adjustment, fair adjustment, and poor adjustment.[8]

The following are the subcategories found within the healthy adjustment market segment:

- *Reorganizers.* Successful in retirement living. Attempt to remain active. Substitute new activities for those abandoned in preretirement. Enjoy life by seeking new experiences and making new friends.
- *Focused group.* Adopt a mature approach to retirement. Target a small number of activities for participation. These activities bring satisfaction.
- *Disengaged, contented.* Activities are at a low level. Prefer not to participate fully in past personal associations or activities.

The reorganizers and focused groups comprise about 40 percent of seniors and are considered to have adjusted well to retirement. Both groups possess a positive image of themselves.

These categories are found within the fair adjustment market segment:

- *Constricted.* Preoccupied with their health. View old age and new experiences as threatening. Structure a narrow range of activities in order to avoid disequilibrium. Try to pursue a habitual pattern.
- *Holding-on.* An achievement-oriented group. Have driven themselves hard all their lives and now are defensive about their age and retirement image. As a defensive measure, they try to keep as busy as possible. Tend to be self-sufficient.
- *Succourance Seekers.* Prefer a passive life, but are moderately active. Maintain strong dependence needs and desire emotional support from others. Retirement for this group is a safe refuge after their work years and they are socially active.

The fair adjustment group account for about 25 percent of consumers. Maintenance of physical well-being plays an important role in this group. Members of this group have difficulty adjusting to old age.

Finally, the following are part of the poor adjustment market segment:

- *Angry Victims.* Consists of highly suspicious people who have experienced a series of disappointments in earlier life. They view past experiences as failures and tend to blame others rather than themselves. This group tends to be highly rigid in their perspectives.
- *Apathetic.* Have limited their social interaction and retreated to their rocking chairs. Believe that life is oppressive and that they are helpless to change circumstances. There is little effort on their part to participate in outside activities.
- *Self-Blamers.* Depressed and show little initiative. Perceived past failures cause them to be highly critical of themselves. Tend to live in the past.

This group may be difficult to reach as a target market. They have a low level of self-esteem. Limited spending power may be a variable.

Seniors can be segmented in terms of motivation and adjustment orientation. One research study classified this market into Self-Reliants, Quiet Introverts, Family Oriented, Active Retirees, Young and Secures, and Solitaries segments. The study was an attempt to define segments within the senior market based on lifestyle variations. The few demographic differences among the market segments supported the importance of using lifestyle variables to segment this large heterogeneous market. The segment descriptions and marketing implications of the study based on lifestyle variations by Sorce, Tyler, and Loomis follows.[9]

1. *Self-Reliants.* This group constituted 25 percent of the sample; its members had the highest factor score on the self-reliance scale. This group was low in security-mindedness, moderate in social venturesomeness, moderate in physical activity, and moderate in family orientation.

Marketers should target this segment for do-it-yourself products but not for new products or products designed for leisure activities that are physically demanding. Promotion activities should stress independence and provide extensive amounts of information because this group is actively involved in decision making. Prestige pricing should not be used and direct mail should only be used to facilitate rebuying.

2. *Quiet Introverts.* This group constituted 19 percent of the sample. The term Quiet Introverts was used to describe this market segment because its members are the least socially venturesome of the cluster and the least physically active. They are low on self-reliance and security-mindedness, but moderate in family orientation. This segment is not interested in volunteer work or taking educational courses and spends much less time in planning for retirement compared to the other market segments.

Marketers find it very difficult to target this group. They do not respond to the purchase of new products. Their attitudes appear to be negative and they may be suspicious of new ideas and promotional programs. Since this group is not receptive to change, further testing may not reveal feelings of high brand loyalty.

3. *Family-Orienteds.* This segment constituted only 10 percent of the sample. They scored low in social venturesomeness, were moderately concerned about security, were high in physical activity but were the least self-reliant. The life of this group revolves around their family and they tend to ignore the outside community. This market segment, like the Quiet Introverts, has little interest in taking educational courses or purchasing new products.

Marketers would do well to consider using prestige pricing strategies since this group is low in risk-taking and may believe in the price–quality relationship. Extended service contracts and warranties would reduce post-purchase dissonance. This group would be very receptive to promotional themes that emphasize the family shopping together and the integration of seniors with their families.

4. *Active Retirees.* This group comprised 20 percent of the sample. Active Retirees are socially venturesome and physically active. They are the most security-minded but moderately self-reliant and family

oriented. They are more likely to be female, to live alone, and to have the lowest income of any of the elderly segments. The Active Retirees are interested in volunteer work.

Marketers might be able to cultivate this group as opinion leaders because of their high levels of social venturesomeness and moderate interest in new products. Products and services that provide social and physical activity are desired by the group. Promotional programs should stress the physical vitality of seniors. Discount pricing should be used because of their need for financial security.

5. *Young and Secures.* A large number of this group was aged sixty to sixty-four and had low levels of security concerns. They were high in social venturesomeness but moderate in physical activity and self-reliance. The Young and Secures are very interested in taking educational courses, volunteering for worthwhile activities, and purchasing new products. They are likely to use the services of a financial planner.

Because this market segment of seniors is high in risk taking, new products may be targeted to it. Promotional programs should show seniors as socially active and as trendsetters. Direct-marketing techniques would work well with this group. Because of their desire to purchase superior products, a prestige pricing strategy would also attract this market segment.

6. *Solitaires.* They were the least family-oriented. They were moderately high in social venturesomeness, self-reliance, physical activity, and security-mindedness. This group was most likely to live alone and was composed of females. In other respects, they were similar to the Young and Secures in their buying attitudes and purchasing behavior. Unlike the Young and Secures, they are interested in travel to avoid harsh winter climates.

A psychographic survey was conducted in the mid-1990s by Moschis and depicts the demographic characteristics of gerontographic groups, the consumption-related needs of seniors, and provided information about their buyer behavior.[10] The study divided seniors into four groups: healthy hermits, ailing outgoers, frail recluses, and healthy indulgers. Sections devoted to needs and responses to marketing strategies helped to contrast seniors from the 1980s to the 1990s.

- *Healthy Hermits.* More than half are over the age of sixty-five and almost 60 percent were females. This group is more isolated than the other groups and about one-third have a college education. Healthy hermits along with the healthy indulgers had the highest income among all groups. Geographic location was proportionate in all areas. This group has a positive attitude toward new technology, is likely to pay cash for purchases, and is less concerned with financial security than the other groups. Healthy hermits are more independent and the least worried about safety and also have the most negative feelings toward age-based marketing strategies. Product discounts are popular with this group.

- *Ailing Outgoers.* More than half were between the ages of fifty-five and sixty-five and females were overrepresented. This group tends to live with others but has a relatively low level of education compared with other groups. The ailing outgoers and healthy hermits are the groups least likely to be married. Unlike other gerontographic groups, they tend to still be employed but have a low level of household income. This group is not concentrated in any geographic area and has a high interest in television viewing, radio listening, and magazine readership. Ailing outgoers have a wide variety of consumption-related concerns, especially about remaining financially independent, personal safety, and their ability to go shopping. They are receptive to promotional techniques but are likely to change their minds after buying a product if they are dissatisfied with the product or the promotional techniques used. Although cash is preferred for payment, credit is used and balances are slowly paid off.

- *Frail Recluses.* This group is older on the average than the other groups, and there is a disproportionately high number of older men. They are likely to live with other people. They have the lowest level of education among the five groups and tend to be married. Geographic concentration is in the north–central and southern states. Frail recluses were the heaviest viewers of television and report heavy newspaper readership. This group is primarily concerned with physical well-being and safety and is least likely to be concerned with travel and entertainment. Frail recluses are least likely to adopt new products and are more likely to have difficulty opening packages and containers.

- *Healthy Indulgers.* This group, along with the healthy hermits, is among the youngest gerontographic groups. A high proportion of this group live with others and females are highly representative. More than one-third have a college education. Many healthy indulgers are still in the workplace and report the highest annual income figures compared to the other groups. There is a concentration in the eastern states and a high proportion in the western states. Healthy indulgers are heavy consumers of information and are concerned with financial matters and oriented toward leisure activities. This group responds positively to buying new products and to retail store displays. Cognitive dissonance may occur after purchases are made. This group contains the heaviest users of credit.

MARKETING STRATEGIES

When marketers develop strategies they aim the product at an appropriate market segment. Consequently, they attempt to characterize the product as possessing the attributes most desired by the target market. When market segmentation strategies are used, product positioning is crucial. Decisions are directed to maintaining and shaping a product image in consumers' minds. Viable market segments for food products would be healthy indulgers and ailing outgoers. A good product positioning strategy would be to emphasize the product's nutritional value to the healthy indulgers and its taste to the ailing outgoers. Marketing strategies for apparel and footwear would emphasize social acceptance and approval to the healthy indulgers and product performance and social acceptance to the ailing outgoers. Since the ailing outgoers are the most viable segment for pharmaceutical products, positioning strategies could emphasize ease of product use, special promotions such as rebates and coupons, and peer approval. The segment offering the best market potential for travel and leisure services would be healthy indulgers and positioning strategies should stress convenience and price. Healthy indulgers appear to desire a variety of financial services and positioning strategies should emphasize convenience and personal relationships.

Mistakes can be made in targeting the senior market. For example, in response to the growth of the senior market, Gerber placed a picture of a senior citizen on their baby food jars and managed to gain supermarket cooperation to establish a separate aisle for senior citizen food. The senior's response was poor. This market did not desire to be singled out in such a way. The idea of special food in baby jars was abhorrent to this market.

There is difficulty in using lifestyle measures that will apply to a wide range of products for seniors. Moreover, contradiction may develop in attempting to fit seniors into artificial categories. For example, seniors may be perceived as relatively wealthy since they have more money than younger people. But seniors may have higher medical and insurance costs. In addition, seniors' financial net worth is often tied up in assets such as a house. Age and demographic variables could be misleading. However, lifestyle variables would seem to be the best measure available for segmenting this market. Seniors go through various passages in their lives such as empty nest, retirement, ill health, and loss of spouse. Consequently, their lifestyles are changeable. The seniors of today have developed a different kind of lifestyle than their parents did at the same age as attitudes, values, and priorities have changed considerably.

Studies demonstrate how lifestyles of seniors can be applied to the travel industry. Lifestyle segments of travelers aged fifty and over have been described as High Rollers, Retirement Years, Elderly-Aged-Homebound, and Very-Elderly-Dependent Years. Research on the

travel market reveals that the attitudes of the elderly toward pleasure travel remained consistent over a ten-year period from 1990 to
2000. Programs directed to the elderly need to be updated but not
necessarily changed.[11]

High Rollers (Aged 50 to 64)

They have a higher average income than any other age group, work
full-time, and have the highest per capita income in the United States.
Approximately 38 percent of their income is used for discretionary
spending. These empty nesters own two homes. One is their permanent residence. The other is a home near the shore or mountains. This
market segment purchases large cars, expensive apparel, and jewelry.
They participate in physical fitness activities and monitor their nutritional intake. The Higher Rollers feel young and desire to participate in varied activities. They are relatively unconcerned with costs
when on vacation. Whenever possible, they stay at four-star hotels. They
spend more on vacations and rely more on travel agents than any other
segment of the population. They travel when it is convenient for
them, even at peak season, and desire luxury accommodations.

The Elderly Traveler (Aged 65 to 74)

This market segment is less likely to possess as much discretionary income as the High Rollers but they spend more time traveling.
They are much more careful when making financial expenditures.
This group prefers to travel in a group. The incidence of widowhood is high. This group travels during off-peak periods in all seasons. Elderly Travelers are very flexible with time considerations.
Even though this market segment has less income than the High
Rollers more is designated for travel. Members of this segment may
combine travel with education through the offerings of Elderhostels.
Retirement communities attract this group. Their health is good and
they wish to remain active. Many may move into smaller homes,
remain where they are, move closer to family, or purchase condo-
miniums to reduce maintenance tasks. Social activities such as entertaining at home, eating out, and gatherings with friends are
important to this group.[12]

The Old–Old Market (Aged 75 to 84)

The incidence of widowhood is great. Travel is more in the form
of day trips rather than long and extended tours. This group remains

close to home and family. This market segment prefers products that will enable them to maintain themselves in their current homes and communities. Shared housing, home equity conversion plans, home chore services, and home healthcare services are of interest to this group. Members of this group may prefer retirement communities that offer lifelong care services. Group travel is important for the old–old market.

The Dependent Years (Aged 85 plus)

This group is not a market for travel. New services such as adult day care centers have been established for this group. Medical care is the largest expense of this group. The demand for nursing home and resident hotel facilities will be great in the future for this market segment.

The psychographics describing the market for travel and the more general descriptors of the senior market demonstrate how each can be useful to marketers. Psychographics are useful in identifying and profiling these segments. Analysis of the seniors market provides additional reality dimensions concerning how products and services could be used to enhance activities in daily living.

TARGETING THE AFFLUENT SENIOR MARKET

Members of this market are in relatively good health and possess a high amount of discretionary income and will explore new ways of socialization through active pursuits such as travel within the United States and abroad. Enrollment in college classes either to obtain qualifications or to learn for learning's sake are a popular pursuit.[13] Elderhostels for seniors play an important role in fostering social activities. Cruising to the Caribbean or to far-away places allows seniors with walking problems or other limitations to enjoy themselves. Many travel organizations have designed tours for seniors. Grand Circle is one of the largest organizations that specialize in serving the senior market. This market segment is more comfortable with electronics and knows that technology will help them live better. This market makes use of e-mail, cell phones, and other devices to stay in touch with their family, friends, and financial planner, and is one of the fastest growing segments using the Internet.

In contrast to younger consumers, the affluent seniors market will not need to spend major portions of their money on mortgages or save for retirement. Thus, they will have higher per capita discretionary income. This increased standard of living has permitted seniors to travel more domestically and internationally. Greater awareness of the positive impact of exercise has contributed to greater participation in health clubs and in a number of activities such as walking and golf. The affluent seniors market uses credit mainly for convenience whereas younger buyers tend to use credit to finance consumption.

Retirement status would seem to be a good predictor of activity levels. The newly retired suddenly have more time for exercise, shopping, entertaining, and travel. The affluent market would tend to increase buying of luxury items. Consequently, consumer behavior is motivated by purchases that will sustain their inner growth. Culture-oriented travel, gifts for family and friends, subscriptions to periodicals, hobbies such as photography, stamp collecting, woodworking, entertainment such as concerts, plays, and movies provide pleasure. For others, a splurge in restaurant dining may give satisfaction. Retirement is a time to explore new activities. This means that life satisfaction aspirations are influenced by psychological dimensions that have dramatically altered their spending motivations. For example, aggregate expenditures for recreation increased for seniors from 1984 to 1997.[14] The upscale seniors market is now in the stage of life that can enjoy activities for which previously there was insufficient time.

The affluent senior male is a heavy reader of both newspapers and magazines. Specifically, affluent males are more likely to read the news, business, travel, and magazine sections of both *The Wall Street Journal* and *USA Today*. In contrast, affluent females are more likely to read news, food, travel, and lifestyle sections. Affluent males and females demonstrated a heavier readership pattern than the moderate income seniors for *Business Week, Newsweek, New Yorker, Time, U.S. News & World Report, Forbes, Fortune, Money*, and *National Geographic*.[15] Significant differences were not evident when broadcast media was examined. The attitudes of the affluent seniors were negative toward advertising. Thus, a creative approach toward communications messages is necessary.

The best method for segmenting the seniors market would be income when targeting buying habits.[16] To illustrate, when selecting a retirement community, the affluent market is more likely to consider location in relation to the residence of their friends while the lower-income group is more concerned with personal security in the community. When deciding upon financial institutions, the affluent are concerned with personalized services and convenience while the lower-income group is more concerned with billing and payment procedures; similar reasons are expressed for patronage of department stores. Moreover, upscale seniors prefer to purchase vacation and travel packages by telephone whereas lower-income seniors rather visit the travel agency's facilities and pay cash.

Female seniors endeavor to participate regularly in their grand-children's lives. They are good prospects for gifts. Moreover, female consumers try to experience new interests and would also be a good market for travel, second homes, smaller primary homes, and furnishings and appliances. The travel industry would do well to cultivate this market for cruises and lengthy vacations. The children's products industry would do well to develop this market potential for apparel, toys, games, and children's sports equipment. Many retirees indulge in recreational activities such as walking, bowling, tennis, golf, and swimming, and purchase appropriate clothing, equipment, and accessories. In addition, many women feel that being attractive is paramount and therefore wearing the right clothes, observing a regular grooming routine, and the purchase of the right cosmetics and accessories are vital for their self-image.[17]

CHANGING LIFESTYLE CHALLENGES OF SENIORS

The following is a list of ways in which senior lifestyles are changing:

- More affluent and healthier than in previous generations.
- Feel and act younger than their counterparts of a few decades ago.
- Increased interest in exercise, health clubs, and spas.
- Increased interest in travel and educational activities.
- More money to spend on grandchildren.
- Fashion conscious.
- Better educated and more sophisticated as buyers.
- A larger affluent market segment.

The elderly market has significantly changed in the past two decades and manufacturers and retailers need to respond with new strategies. In marketing to seniors, it is important to recognize that they are not a homogeneous group. The over-fifty-five group consists of subsets based more on lifestyle and activity than age. Companies that have depended on targeting young adult consumers will now find the senior market controlling more than 75 percent of the wealth in the United States. In response to this new affluent retirement market, the Miami-based homebuilder Lennar Corporation has made their clubhouses more upscale by adding restaurants, concierge services, computer labs, and gyms. Moreover, a whole new $30 billion industry has evolved that targets grandparents and grandchildren. This industry features new ways to bond with grandchildren at summer camps and on travel tours. For example, Grandkids and

Me Camp offers canoeing, hiking, and dog sledding, and Archaeological Tours offers vacations led by an archaeologist with visits to pyramids, the Sphinx, and a Nile cruise.

RELATIONSHIP MARKETING AND SHOPPING BEHAVIOR

Relationship marketing is the process of creating strong customer loyalty.[18] This strategy includes a long-term, follow-up program to ensure customer satisfaction and retention. Insights from research studies on shopping behavior can be advantageous in developing relationship marketing with the senior market. For example, many elderly consumers live without social support. Interaction with sales clerks, service personnel, and fellow shoppers is an integral part of retail patronage behavior and presents retailers with many new relationship marketing opportunities.[19]

The aging baby boomer population promises to have different wants and needs than the present generation of seniors; therefore, research is needed to help explain and predict the changing demands placed upon the market. Since most of the research on seniors is exploratory with limited samples, findings must be interpreted with caution. The senior market may not make purchases in a hurry and many resist hard-sell efforts. Seniors would seem to be less pressured by peer approval than younger buyers—although reference groups may still serve an informational function—and therefore promotional communications need to be modified. Seniors have the time and inclination to read which is not characteristic of younger markets.

There are opportunities to develop relationship marketing programs among the seniors in numerous markets. For example, a lifestyle trend of some seniors is to seek self-fulfillment. The lifestyle of self includes the psychological as well as the physical. This lifestyle suggests an individualistic orientation. Those who subscribe to this philosophy want to purchase many diverse services as they seek to enjoy life and find adventure. Books on travel and adventure are paramount. Readers may find self-expression vicariously by attending book and poetry readings and participating in discussion groups. New book superstores with coffee shops have developed programs attractive to middle-age and seniors who have outgrown the cocktail scene.

Another changing buying pattern appears to be positive for both the apparel and toy industries. There are more grandparents with fewer grandchildren and more discretionary income. These grandparents often enjoy indulging their grandchildren. Since family size is smaller, much more money is spent on children today than on children of earlier generations. These factors have helped to extend the sales of toys beyond the traditional holidays.

The Medicine Shoppe, a specialty chain of neighborhood pharmacies, dispenses counseling and health information to senior citizens. Health screenings are an integral strategy in establishing and maintaining the Medicine Shoppe's store image. Prescriptions generate more than 90 percent of its sales volume. Medicine Shoppe's focus permits greater efficiency and provides a high level of service. Customers who wait more than fifteen minutes for a prescription to be filled are given a $2 credit. The chain selects sites situated in small strip malls and freestanding locations in established neighborhoods, particularly those populated by senior citizens. Medicine Shoppe supports the Senior Olympics. Many seniors need to renew prescriptions and therefore offer an opportunity for astute marketers to promote sound relationship marketing fundamentals.

There are a number of insights that can be developed from research on the seniors market. First, seniors as a group are active shoppers. Mature fashion-conscious apparel shoppers are often more similar to middle-age fashion-conscious shoppers than to their nonfashion-conscious elderly cohorts. Fashion-conscious consumers often see themselves as ten to fifteen years younger than their chronological age. They tend to be less price conscious than other adults. Shopping trips are used for exercise and recreation and to meet friends and acquaintances. Most seniors have no problems finding adequate transportation to and from retail stores.

Second, seniors are more likely than younger consumers to shop together and to engage in joint decision making for a wide range of products. They have not responded to any great extent to innovations in grocery shopping such as unit pricing, open-code dating, or ordering on the Internet. Recent studies suggest that the elderly do not want special services or amenities.

Third, it has not been clearly established that seniors rely on different sources of information than younger consumers. It would seem, however, that the use of radio and television is less important and print media would be more appropriate to target this group. Radio and television advertising—because of the speed of transmission—may not be readily absorbed. Since seniors like to shop together, word-of-mouth might be an important source of prepurchase information for some products.

Fourth, the mature market (age fifty to sixty-four) and active elderly (age sixty-five to seventy-four) would seem to be both very important and lucrative markets for marketers. People from fifty to sixty-four tend to be in the market for financial services, luxury items, travel recreational opportunities, and possibly a second home. Those sixty-five to seventy-four want more estate planning help, adult education, insurance, and service-oriented social events. Both markets are affluent and enjoy life by seeking new experiences and social interaction. Those who are retired tend to devote their time to fewer activities. Promotional campaigns might show products and services that are physically enjoyable; emphasis should be on service and product reliability with credible testimonials. Because the retired have more time, an extended information search and evaluation of alternatives is possible.

Seniors who are retired tend to be careful shoppers. Inflation greatly limits the buying power of consumers on relatively fixed incomes. They also have the experience and patience to find good value. They may be willing, if given sufficient incentive, to shift their purchasing to retailers' off-peak times.

More forward-looking marketers realize the market potential of seniors. They spend more on jewelry, sports cars, and cosmetics than other age groups. There are more than 60 million grandparents who spend more than $700 a year per grandchild. This age group controls 77 percent of the assets in this country, buys over 70 percent of all prescription drugs and accounts for over 80 percent of all leisure travel. For the fashion industry, women over fifty-five account for $20 billion in apparel sales each year. Approximately 25 percent of the U.S. national budget is earmarked for programs aimed directly or indirectly at seniors. Since seniors are able to exert political pressure, this market's viability and power seems to be assured. To be successful in reaching this market, companies have to get to know this segment and have to use situational appeals in their promotion materials that reflect the way these age groups live.

MANAGING CHANGE

Once a relevant change has been identified by environmental scanning, it is still necessary to keep abreast of further developments. Fundamental to understanding the changes in economic, social, cultural, technological, demographic, and ecology factors is the identification of the change agent. The change agent can be recognized as the groups, individuals, or organizations that develop change. For example, the American Association of Retired Persons (AARP) with its large membership can shape attitudes on product warranties, pending consumer legislation, and credit.

It is extremely difficult to connect changing technology with changing consumer lifestyles. The computer has confined many people to their homes and desks for hours. Air conditioning has had an impact on home living, theaters, and restaurants. Frozen foods have simplified meal preparation and television has influenced entertainment, shopping, and product awareness.

Conflict and tension are caused by different components within the marketing environment, for example, the competitive introduction of improved products by competitors or a shrinking market. Since the younger market for breakfast cereals has contracted, firms now focus their resources on the adult market. The appeal of good nutrition is relevant to the senior market.

The impact of culture cannot be overemphasized on shaping lifestyles. The traditional orientation of economic and materialistic values once permeated society, but now the current orientation is quality of life. Once, postponed gratification was a dominant value and this has been transformed to instant gratification. Culture is a fundamental determinate of how people live and what is purchased.

Environmental trends that affect the senior market include the following:

- The number of individuals over age sixty will increase substantially. Moreover, persons age eighty-five and over will also increase.
- More retirees will remain in the workforce or re-enter the business world.
- Family assistance or caregiving to elderly parents will become increasingly more challenging.
- Senior citizens will become more knowledgeable and assertive consumers.
- The American Association of Retired Persons and other organizations will have a larger impact on the political and legislative scene.
- Marketers will continue to increase their efforts to target a viable, mature market that feels and acts younger and participates in athletic and community activities.

The senior citizen market constitutes a moving target. The aging population will have a profound impact on families and their adult children. Moreover, business organizations, government, and society will be influenced by an aging population. The shopping behavior and consumption habits of seniors will affect food manufacturers, health care providers, financial institutions, travel service agencies, real estate communities, and retailers whose objectives are to reach this large consumer market.

NOTES

1. George P. Moschis and Anil Mathur, "How They're Acting Their Age," *Marketing Management* 2 (September 1993): 40–50.

2. Mary L. Joyce, "The Graying of America," *American Behavioral Scientist* 38 (November 1994): 38–47.

3. U.S. Census Bureau, *Population Estimates for States by Age, Sex, Race, and Hispanic Origin*, 1 July 1998, ST-98-40.

4. Ibid.

5. Ruth La Ferla, "Over 60: Fashion's Last Generation," *The New York Times*, 3 December 2000, Sec. 9, pp. 1, 11.

6. George P. Moschis, Anil Mathur, and Ruth Belk Smith, "Older Consumers' Orientation Toward Age-Based Marketing Stimuli," *Journal of the Academy of Marketing Science* 21 (Summer 1993): 195–205.

7. Alan J. Greco and Christie H. Paksoy, "Profiling The Mature Fashion-Conscious Apparel Shopper," *Akron Business and Economic Review* 20 (Summer 1989): 7–23; and Alan J. Greco, "The Fashion-Conscious Elderly: A Viable, But Neglected Market Segment," *The Journal of Consumer Marketing* 3 (Fall 1986): 71–75.

8. Warren A. French and Richard Fox, "Segmenting the Senior Citizen Market," *The Journal of Consumer Marketing* 2 (Winter 1985): 66–74.

9. Patricia Sorce, Philip R. Tyler, and Lynette M. Loomis, "Lifestyles of Older Americans," *The Journal of Consumer Marketing* 6 (Summer 1989): 53–63.

10. George P. Moschis, *Gerontographics: Life Stage Segmentation for Marketing Strategy Development* (Westport, Conn.: Quorum Books, 1996).

11. Stowe Shoemaker, "Segmenting the Market: 10 Years Later," *Journal of Travel Research* 39 (August 2000): 11–26.

12. Jeffrey P. Rosenfeld, "Demographics on Vacation," *American Demographic* (January 1986): 38–41; and Gloria Kostner, "The Gray Market on Vacation," *American Demographics* (October 1986): 35–38.

13. Barrie Gunter, *Understanding the Older Consumer: The Grey Market* (London: Routledge, 1998).

14. Geoffrey D. Paulin, "Expenditure Patterns of Older Americans, 1984–1997," *Monthly Labor Review* 123 (May 2000): 3–18.

15. J. J. Burnett, "Examining the Media Habits of the Affluent Elderly," *Journal of Advertising Research* 31 (October–November 1991): 33–45.

16. George P. Moschis, Evelyn Lee, Anil Mathur, and Jennifer Strautman, *The Maturing Marketplace: Buying Habits of Baby Boomers and Their Parents* (Westport, Conn.: Quorum Books, 2000).

17. Janice E. Leeming and Cynthia F. Tripp, *Segmenting the Women's Market* (Chicago: Probus, 1994).

18. Rajendra K. Srivastava, Tasadduq A. Shervani, and Liam Fahey, "Marketing, Business Processes, and Shareholder Value: An Organizationally Embedded View of Marketing Activities and the Discipline of Marketing," *Journal of Marketing* 63 (October 1999): 168–180.

19. Yong-Soon Kank and Nancy M. Ridgeway, "The Importance of Consumer Market Interaction as a Form of Social Support for Elderly Consumers," *Journal of Public Policy and Marketing* 15 (Spring 1996): 108–117.

CHAPTER 8

Culture and Targeting the
Changing Lifestyles
of the Black and Hispanic Markets

Cultural factors can exert the deepest influence on consumer purchase behavior. These factors are a complex set of values, ideas, attitudes, and other meaningful symbols that shape human behavior
and are transmitted from one generation to another. The roles, goals,
perceptions, consumption patterns, and consumption aspirations of
a society reflect the impact of culture on individuals and groups
and subsequently on their buying behavior. To illustrate, the Whirlpool Corporation in order to increase its market share hired an anthropologist to gain insight into consumers' often unexpressed
needs.[1] One of the findings was that, in busy families, women were
not the only ones doing the laundry. As a result color-coded washer
and dryer controls were developed to make it easier for men and
even children to operate the appliances.

There were many knowledgeable people who predicted that the
great wave of immigrants of 100 years ago would never be assimilated and adapt to the culture of the United States. Now there are
similar predictions about the Hispanic groups. These predictions
will be proven wrong. Almost one in five children born in the United
States today is of Latin American descent. Nearly 35 percent of the
U.S. Hispanic population is under the age of eighteen.

Social stratification takes the form of social class whose members
share similar values, interests, and buyer behavior patterns. Social
class is as important a concept in understanding black buyer behav-

ior patterns as it is in the case of white buyer behavior patterns or any other ethnic group or subculture. The black middle class has expanded in the past few decades and its lifestyle is similar to that of its white counterparts. Although the black middle class has grown appreciably in recent decades, there are still restrictions due to prejudice and discrimination to retard the acculturation process. The emergence of the black middle class seems to date from the 1960s with the Civil Rights Movement.

Marketing managers need an intimate knowledge of the total culture and specific subcultures that operate within the marketing environment. Culture helps define attitudes. Knowledge of diverse cultures enables marketers not only to comprehend and predict buyer behavior but also to assess what actions are or are not possible. Tailoring products to specific consumers can have a major impact on a company's business. Undoubtedly certain behavior patterns are characteristic in specific markets whether it is the Hispanic market or any other market. Marketers need to pinpoint these behavior patterns and become aware of any habits that conflict with current marketing strategies and policies. Strong cultural values may relate to the sale of the product and need to be identified. For example, varying cultural values are associated with the purchase of such products as tea, liquor, and tobacco. Product strategy as well as distribution and promotion strategies should not be formulated without understanding the cultural environment. For example, those Hispanics who have either recently immigrated or have difficulty mastering English feel lost in giant supermarkets and are afraid to ask questions. Therefore, much of their shopping is done in bodegas which are small neighborhood stores where only Spanish is spoken. In New York City, bodegas account for 30 percent of the grocery volume among Spanish-speaking residents. However, families shop together at J.C. Penney, Sears, Kmart, and other large stores. Marketers need to determine the information sources on which members of a particular culture rely. To communicate effectively with specific markets, promotional messages must be evaluated and specific appeals, terminology and illustrations tested against acceptable or unacceptable cultural values. This framework operates effectively when considered within three dimensions: temporal, spatial, and interdisciplinary.

TEMPORAL DIMENSIONS

This dimension indicates a relationship between cultural change, its effects on marketing strategy, and the various time and periods which it encompasses. For example, both the Hispanic and black markets reflect a youth-oriented culture. The population of these subcultures are younger than their white counterparts. However, as time progresses these markets will age and marketing strategies will need to be adjusted. Thus, the temporal dimension not only suggests the need to monitor cultural change over time but also reflects the development of a marketing strategy to meet the needs of a changing population.

SPATIAL DIMENSIONS

One of the easiest ways to appreciate the impact of cultural values upon marketing strategies is to contrast the cultures of various countries of the world. Since the Hispanic market is composed of people from Mexico, Cuba, Puerto Rico, other countries, and those born in the United States, there are distinct differences not only in culture but also in purchasing behavior. As a result of culture, people tend to resist change in whatever was learned early in life and more readily change whatever was learned late in life. Consequently, eating habits tend to be retained in later life. Hispanics are known to be heavy consumers of beans. For example, the children of Cuban Americans may retain their preference for black beans, the children of Puerto Rican Americans may retain their preference for red beans, and the children of Mexican Americans may retain their preference for refried beans. Eating habits are hard to overcome and may be the last to change in the assimilation process. There are major differences between U.S. and foreign-born Hispanics. The foreign-born Hispanics have larger and younger families, less education and income, prefer brands and products they used in their country of origin, prefer Spanish-speaking media, prefer to buy fresh produce when available, and focus on family get-togethers.

INTERDISCIPLINARY DIMENSIONS

The interdisciplinary dimension is the extent to which ideas, concepts, and issues are drawn from the behavioral sciences. The relevance of concepts in one field may provide a basis for the exploration of many different interrelationships. The anthropologist envisions people as members of society with its own culture which influences their decisions. The psychologist envisions people as having certain goals which motivate them to perform specific acts. The sociologist envisions people as members of a group which influences their decisions. To a certain extent, marketers should consider the impact of cultural change on people from all of these different perspectives.

The emphasis for future research on how cultural change affects marketing strategy should focus on the changes in a nation's culture that are the basis for market segmentation or long-range planning. The growing tendency to target subcultural market segments should lead to greater efforts to delineate markets. Further, the impact of immigration and the growth of distinct subcultural groups is of vital concern to marketing strategy development. Marketers need to study the various temporal, spatial, and interdisciplinary dimensions to better serve submarkets. To illustrate, consider women's clothing. The manner in which female apparel is purchased and worn is not based solely on functional or utilitarian values. Such cultural considerations as beauty, femininity, grace, charm, image, status, and sex appeal are all variables for purchasing motives. Moreover, social class membership may still be another important variable.

CULTURAL CHANGES AND CHANGING LIFESTYLES

Cultural patterns in the United States are changing rapidly and marketers consequently must adjust their marketing strategies to these cultural forces. Before 1920 cigarette smoking was the prerogative of the man, and women who smoked were not considered respectable. When this cultural orientation changed, marketers were able to sell cigarettes through food stores to female shoppers. Eventually, both female and male buyers of cigarettes patronized food stores for the product. As more became known about the hazards of smoking, many gave up this habit and a new generation declined smoking with some exceptions. Today, smoking appears to be a phenomenon of social class membership and educational attainment. For whatever reason, lower socioeconomic groups have more of a propensity to smoke than higher socioeconomic groups, and young female teenagers seem to have a higher incidence of adopting this habit.

Definite cultural forces have broken down the distinctions between the roles of men and women. Moreover, the role of the black woman in the African-American family has been modified. In many instances, the black woman has surpassed the black man as a wage earner and tends to dominate the black family. As more women participate in the workforce, interest in fast-food preparation has grown. In particular, working women with children no longer wish to spend long hours in the kitchen. This change has caused the increase in frozen food sales in supermarkets and the growth in the number of fast-food operations.

The cultural values and attitudes of consumers are changing. These shifts contribute to changes in lifestyles and in purchasing behavior, expectations, and product choices. A lifestyle is a particular set of attitudes, interests, and opinions and an identifiable pattern or mode of living.

Marketers can be slow to grasp the importance of changing consumer lifestyles. For example, instead of parents having three or four children, many parents have limited their families' size. On the other hand, many minority families of lower socioeconomic status are composed of larger family size. These families tend to shop in discount-oriented stores, in flea markets, or patronize garage sales.

One of the old values of the past was that an individual should not purchase anything unless immediate payment could be made. Easy credit, however, has changed this value. The average household can easily obtain credit cards from department stores such as Sears and J.C. Penney or from banks or oil companies.

There are a number of exciting trends changing family lifestyle habits. Camera manufacturers have satisfied consumers with instant photographs and digital cameras. People do not want to wait. Instant gratification has become an important theme. The trend toward instant foods and also fast-food restaurants reflects this theme. The microwave oven was an immediate sales success. The value of delayed gratification from another era has changed. Cultural forces and lifestyles are changing so rapidly that it is difficult for marketers to adjust marketing strategies to the needs of the market. An important change in the past two decades has been the emergence of ethnic pride that reflects changes in dress patterns.

There have been important cultural change perceptions in the roles of both men and women in the past decades. Females are now participating more in sports activities and this presents new opportunities for marketing female athletic equipment and clothing. Females are also traveling alone, purchasing automobiles by themselves, and insisting upon better security in hotels. Men are using a number of products previously not considered masculine such as hair dryers, hair sprays, and hair-coloring products. Even the color of men's clothing has become brighter and more adventuresome. Both women and men are opposed to the wearing of animal furs and animal rights have become a consideration in purchasing behavior.

SOCIAL AND CULTURAL DISTINCTIONS

It is difficult to describe the many cultural patterns that exist between black and Hispanic markets when neither market is monolithic. There are disparities between educated and affluent Hispanics and blacks and those that are operating just above the poverty levels and are uneducated. Nevertheless there are some ethnic distinctions worthy of mention. The following are some of the important distinctions between black and Hispanic markets:

- Language
- Family
- Education
- Small business ownership
- Affluent geographical concentration

Since many Hispanics are recent immigrants to the United States, a high percentage speak only Spanish. Some live in virtual isolation: reading Spanish-language newspapers, listening to foreign-language radio and television programs, and speaking only Spanish to family, friends, and neighbors. The children of these immigrants typically identify strongly with their heritage but have acculturated and are able to communicate in both English and Spanish. In contrast, the language spoken in most black families is English.

Purchasing behavior is dominated by the female in the black family. Extended family members in Hispanic households shop together and influence purchasing behavior. Family ties are stronger in the Hispanic household. Younger blacks generally under the age of thirty-five tend to be referred to as African-Americans but an older generation tend to prefer the term "black." Marketers would do well to use a bipolar approach since both younger generations have different preferences than older generations that would be revealed in purchasing behavior.

Blacks owned about 28 percent and Hispanics about 45 percent of minority business establishments. Approximately 43 percent of blacks and 29 percent of Hispanics were awarded postsecondary degrees in 1996. There were 259,000 black and 193,000 Hispanic households earning more than $100,000. The more affluent Hispanic markets are situated in Los Angeles, Houston, New York, Miami, San Francisco Bay Area, and Chicago. The affluent black markets are New York, Philadelphia, Washington, D.C., Baltimore, Atlanta, Chicago, Detroit, and Dallas–Fort Worth.[2]

SIZE, LOCATION, AND MARKET CONDUCT OF THE HISPANIC MARKET

The designation of Hispanic or Latino appears to be used interchangeably. Currently, Hispanic children make up the second largest ethnic group in the United States. The average Hispanic family has 4.2 children, as opposed to 2.4 for the general American population. Michael Barone, a leading authority on ethnic groups prefers the term Latino rather than Hispanic and maintains that the reference of Hispanic is imprecise.[3] The Census Bureau uses Hispanic as an umbrella term to encompass those new immigrants coming from different Spanish-speaking countries.

Since Hispanics are relatively recent immigrants, they have less formal education than either their black or white counterparts. Hispanic families spend a greater proportion for food eaten at home than either black or white families. Fewer Hispanic families live in rural areas compared to black or white families and more contain children than white families.

Hispanics are the second largest and fastest growing minority in the United States. By 2005, Hispanics will make up 13.3 percent or 38.2 million of the total U.S. population up from 11.7 percent in 1999. Asians and Pacific Islanders will comprise 4.6 percent of the population compared with 4.1 percent or 11 million people. The Bureau of the Census projects that by 2010 Hispanics will account for over 14 percent of the population and will outnumber African-American consumers. The Hispanic population is largely Mexican origin (61%), Puerto Rican (15%), or Cuban (7%).[4] There are significant cultural differences between Mexicans, Puerto Ricans, Cubans, Dominicans, and other Hispanic groups. They have clustered in certain cities: Miami for Cubans; Los Angeles, San Antonio, and Houston for Mexicans; New York for Puerto Ricans and Dominicans; and Chicago which offers a mix of all. There has also been a population shift of Hispanics to such states as North Carolina, Nevada, Kansas, Indiana, and Minnesota. Hispanics are growing increasingly affluent. The growth of Hispanic household disposable income has increased from $223 billion in 1990 to over $490 billion by 2000 and this amount is projected to more than double by 2007. Hispanics spend over $400 billion a year on goods and services. Since Hispanics have distinctive food-purchasing patterns, marketers are trying to learn more about food preferences and to satisfy a much greater potential demand in the future. Cuban immigrants have more formal education before coming to the United States than either Mexican or Puerto Rican immigrants. Occupations are predominately blue-collar.

According to the U.S. Bureau of the Census, Cuban Americans are the oldest, with a median age of thirty-nine, the most affluent, and the most highly educated with 20 percent of those age twenty-five or older having attended college. Mexican Americans are the youngest Hispanic submarket with a median age of twenty-four. As of the 2000 census, only about 6 percent have completed college. Hispanics in the United States are younger with a median age of twenty-six compared to age thirty-three of the remainder of the population and earn several thousand dollars less. A Hispanic family averages 4.2 people as compared with 2.4 for the average U.S. family.

Language is an important consideration in the formulation of a marketing mix aimed at Hispanics. Many manufacturers are renaming and repackaging existing brands to take advantage of Spanish language differences in the Hispanic market. There are three language group considerations. The first group is the acculturated Hispanics who speak mostly English and has a high level of assimilation. The second group is bicultural who is equally adept in either English or Spanish and the third group is comprised of those who speak mostly Spanish. The rate of acculturation may be slower than with other immigrant groups since many Hispanics have a distinct identity. Moreover, there is a strong orientation toward the family so dinnertime is often a social event for the entire extended family including aunts, uncles, cousins, and grandparents.

The Hispanic market has been long underdeveloped but marketers are increasingly realizing that the Hispanic market can no longer be neglected. Findings of purchasing patterns strongly suggest that during the immigrants' adjustment process to life in the United States social class was a more important indicator for behavioral changes than ethnicity.[5]

Since the fastest growing ethnic market in the United States is the Hispanic market, marketers need to adjust their marketing programs to this group. Hispanics spend more on infant formula, disposable diapers, and other baby necessities than the general market. Hispanics tend to spend more per shopping trip than non-Hispanic households and they take fewer trips to the store. Brand loyalty is particularly strong among households that prefer to or only speak Spanish. When developing promotional strategy it is interesting to note that the Hispanic market is more responsive to direct mail than the mass market because it has had less exposure to it than the mass market. Generally, their response rate to a direct mail piece is twice as high as the mass market. The Hispanic market is easier to reach through direct mail since approximately 60 percent of this target market resides in California, Texas, Florida, New York City, and Chicago.

Marketers are making a mistake in adopting marketing strategies that have been successful with non-Hispanics to Hispanics. A better approach would be to aim advertising strategies, for example, at a particular ethnic group for specific types of products.[6] Hispanics would appear to be more receptive to advertising on television and radio. Hispanics tend to be less responsive to newspaper and magazine advertising than their white counterparts. Hispanics place greater importance on purchasing prestige brands at well-known stores. Hispanic women prefer to pay cash rather than use credit cards.

Hispanic influence continues to grow as Spanish-language announcements are incorporated in service messages, Latin American music is included on mainstream radio, and Hispanic actors and actresses emerge on television and in movies.

HISPANIC STRATEGY DEVELOPMENT

Marketers are confronted with a challenging task since ethnic markets are substantially increasing in size and the marketing implications of multiculturalism have become more important. Lack of research is a major barrier to new product development in the Hispanic market. It is vital to recognize that there is not a single Hispanic market any more than there is a homogeneous white market. Consequently, there are many niches within ethnic markets that require niche strategies. For example, Goya Foods targets the nonacculturated Hispanic food preferences such as nopalitos (sliced cactus) and tostores (fried green plantains).

Marketers use different approaches to segment the Hispanic market. One approach is to offer one product or campaign as if this were a homogeneous market. Another approach is to segment according to country of origin. Other firms use lifestyle and psychographic variables. A fourth approach is to use Hispanic music and celebrities in advertisements. Although language may be a common base, these subcultural markets are indigenous to their country of origin. Marketers are aware that what might work in New York may not succeed in either Miami or Los Angeles. Strategy development may need to use a number of combination approaches to be successful.

Hispanics have not integrated as quickly as earlier immigrant groups. Because of their frequent contact with their homelands and their local concentration, Hispanics tend to cling to their language and culture. Although the average Hispanic has resided in the United States for nearly thirteen years, only about half are fluent in English. More than 60 percent of Hispanics speak Spanish at home and about half speak Spanish at social functions. However, younger Hispanics are most fluent in English and are better able to communicate in English than older Hispanics.

Television and radio are both important media for communicating with the Hispanic market. There are a number of Spanish television stations in the United States. Spanish television generally costs advertisers much less than general-market television advertising. Since Mexican stations have been added to cable networks, the marketer is increasingly able to reach the Hispanic market by using this medium. Moreover, there are at least 150 U.S. radio stations that offer some Spanish language programming. Radio ownership is high and so is frequent listening which is higher than the general population. Both Spanish language television and radio audiences are composed of less acculturated Hispanics. Advertisers targeting Hispanics have developed advertisements emphasizing their unique cultural values, such as highlighting shopping as a family activity. The Spanish language should be used to target Hispanic consumers since Hispanics prefer Spanish language broadcast media. Bank of America has allocated $30 million to Spanish advertising in 2003.

According to studies, such as the Yankelovich/Cheskin Hispanic Monitor, which compares the lifestyle and behavior of American Hispanics sixteen years of age and older to whites and African-Americans, Hispanics and Anglo consumers differ in terms of a variety of key buyer-behavior variables. New product adoption may be inhibited by language difficulties. Hispanics are less confident shoppers than Anglo consumers and tend not to be impulse buyers. Hispanic consumers tend to be more careful shoppers and more price-oriented.

There would appear to be considerable differences in brand preferences as reflected in brand share between Hispanic and non-Hispanic consumers for some food products. For example, Hispanics have a higher preference for Libby's canned fruit, fruit-flavored Hawaiian Punch, Breyer's ice cream, Oscar Mayer hot dogs, and Parkay margarine. Moreover, multiculturalism is creating new tastes. The growth of Mexican food offerings in restaurants is the tip of the iceberg. To illustrate, from 1993 to 1994, the sales of shelf-stable Mexican food have increased more than 6 percent. The sales of frozen Mexican food increased by more than 5 percent. Furthermore, the sales of salsa (Mexican sauces) soared more than 12 percent. Tortilla sales have been steadily growing by about 12 percent every year for the last fifteen years. Supermarkets account for this increase due to immigration factors and changing consumer perception of ethnic foods. Mexican food restaurant chains are also growing appreciably and Taco Bell has purchased Chevy's Mexican Restaurants which experienced sales gains over the years. Taco Cabana and Azteca Mexican Restaurants are also experiencing phenomenal growth rates.

The task for food marketers is to not only identify food preferences of the Hispanic market but to learn if a broad spectrum of Americans would also enjoy consuming the same types of food. For example, Gerber expanded distribution and marketing of its Tropical product line nationwide in the 1990s. Originally, their line of baby foods and juices was targeted to Hispanic markets in a limited number of geographic areas such as Miami, New York, Dallas, Arizona, and Southern California. Their product line was accepted by non-Hispanics and among the more popular baby food flavors were guava, papaya, peach, mango, and tropical fruit. Hispanics have been a good market for food, beverage, and household-care products. Hispanic consumers tend to be brand-conscious and believe the price–quality relationship. Generic brand products have not sold well to this market segment. This market segment exhibits a high degree of brand loyalty and therefore it is important for firms to cultivate this market before competitors.

Food marketers should be aware that the Hispanic market is highly individualistic in its product and brand preferences which are frequently reflective of cultural distinctions. This market is a very significant one for food purchases. Hispanics, partly because of their larger-than-average size families, spend more per week on food purchases than do other groups. Hispanics families also visit fast-food restaurants more than non-Hispanic consumers. Many Hispanics view shopping as a social event. They want to spend hours browsing and chatting to friends. They also like to eat while they shop and listen to music that reminds them of home. Stores with festive colors and designs make them feel more comfortable.

The main impediments in developing the Hispanic market for marketers are language and culture. The new immigrants tend to cluster together and endeavor to preserve both their language and culture. But as first and second generations of Hispanics emerge, knowledge of English increases as they adapt to U.S. culture. Many Hispanics see themselves as bicultural. Another variable is the age of the new immigrants. The younger the new immigrants are, the more rapid the acculturation process.

For some product categories, these differences in brand preferences between Hispanic and non-Hispanic consumers will have little or no impact on consumption patterns. Since the growth of interracial marriages, less emphasis of religion by some, and the adoption of English language usage, the assimilation process has operated well. Those forces have helped to blend the "melting pot" and to reduce differences among people.

Some marketers believe that reaching the Hispanic consumer requires targeting separate Hispanic markets. For example, Anheuser-Busch targeted advertising to the Puerto Rican community set in a disco and featured salsa rhythms. Commercials for Mexican-origin consumers were set in a rodeo to mariachi music. Advertisements to the Cuban market segment were set on a private ship because Cubans are the most affluent Hispanic group. Other manufacturers may use the same advertisement to the entire Hispanic market believing that country of origin would not be that significant in purchasing their product. Still another dimension of segmenting the

Hispanic market may be in terms of their degree of acculturation to the dominant America cultural values and customs. This acculturation may well reflect their degree of comfort with the English language and the length of time residing in the United States.

The diversity of the Hispanic population creates challenges for those endeavoring to target this market. One effective linkage to the Hispanic market is the church which is not only a place of worship but is also a center for social activities, charitable events, and holiday celebrations. Approximately 70 percent of Hispanics are Roman Catholic. Another unifying element among Hispanics is soccer since many of them grew up playing this sport. The world famous Pele, a prominent soccer player, became a celebrity spokesman. Art and music are the cross-cultural ties among Hispanics.

Product Strategies

McDonald's in the early 1990s added chicken fajitas to its menu for Cinco de Mayo, Mexico's major spring holiday. This item sold exceedingly well and was mainstreamed to non-Hispanics. In contrast, Pepsi used a different strategy by importing Mirinda, its popular Mexican soft drink line, into California. Mirinda comprises orange, apple, strawberry, and grapefruit flavors.

Hispanics are more brand loyal than other market segments and therefore it is difficult to get them to switch brands. Moreover, Hispanic Americans are willing to spend extra to purchase quality products for their family. In-store promotions that allow Hispanics to sample products would seem to be a more effective strategy than price reductions.

The same product can be sold differently to Hispanic and white consumers. Sears recognized the importance of the extended family in selecting baby furniture. For example, in the Hispanic advertisement, a teenage daughter and grandparents are shown shopping with the expectant couple. However, in the English advertisement only the husband and wife are shown selecting the baby furniture.

Promotion Strategies

Anheuser-Busch, Campbell Soup, and Coca-Cola are important sponsors of the nine-day Carnival Miami. These companies and others donate their products and in return gain brand recognition and product exposure. Coors has sponsored a two-year tour of Hispanic art throughout the United States and Pepsi Cola and Coca-Cola have sponsored Hispanic music awards.

Pearle Vision Centers advertise in Spanish. Hispanics, because of the relatively large percentage of young people in this market, are more likely to purchase contact lenses than non-Hispanics. Even though there are no such things as Hispanic contact lenses, efforts are made to mainstream products and services.

Procter and Gamble has cultivated the Hispanic market with publishing and distributing 4.5 million copies of its semiannual magazine *Avangando con tu Familiar* or *Getting Ahead with Your Family*. Approximately every other Hispanic household has been reached by this publication. Procter and Gamble was one of the first sponsors of *Sabado Gigante*, a Saturday variety show that has been on Spanish language TV for the past fourteen years. The company has also targeted Latino teens with "Explosion Musical," a program that organizes concerts and provides discounted tickets and tie-in CDs.[7]

Language at times creates communication problems. For example, Nestlé had to reconsider its usual single advertising approach for Butterfinger candy. Peanut butter was "montequilla de man" for Hispanics from the Caribbean and "crema de cacuhuete" for those from Mexico. Consequently, Nestlé developed two different sets of copy for their Spanish-language advertisements.[8] Spanish-language advertisements are almost five times more likely to persuade Latino consumers into buying a product than English-language ads.

Hispanic use of the Internet between 1998 and 2000 increased to approximately more than 40 percent. In 1998, Mattel launched BarbieLatina.com to serve this market and it has become one of the top ten online destinations for girls ages two to eleven. The site has become an important branding tool. Visitors to the site can dress Barbie and her friends by selecting different outfits.[9]

Distribution Strategies

Supermarket chains and independents use different approaches to target the Hispanic market. In the Los Angeles area, Vons operates Mexican-oriented stores with its Tianguis stores. Ralph's or Lucky prefer to use the same name as their other units. Sedono's Supermarkets dominates the Hispanic grocery business in Miami which is composed mostly of the Cuban population. Bilingual signage is a positive strategy. As Hispanics assimilate and become more knowledgeable with English, this segment will become more like mainstream Americans in their shopping habits.

Specialty wholesalers and retailers are also aiming at the Hispanic market. For example, the sale of health and beauty aids produced in Mexico to such chains serving the Hispanic market as Tianguis's,

Ralph's, and Albertson's in California have been profitable. Other tactics have been to print credit applications in Spanish and to sponsor Hispanic fashion shows. Shopping malls are also attracting Hispanic customers by hiring music groups to celebrate holidays.

STRATEGY DEVELOPMENT FOR
THE BLACK MARKET

The African-American market is catching up to other markets in importance. The prosperous decade of the 1990s was responsible for soaring black purchasing power to over $500 billion in 1998 when millions of African-Americans achieved middle-class status. Purchasing expenditures amounted to much more than Anglo's on such items as boys' apparel, athletic footwear, automobile rentals, and personal-care products.

Although the largest concentration of blacks is in metropolitan areas such as New York City, Chicago, Washington, D.C., Los Angeles, Detroit, Philadelphia, Atlanta, Baltimore, Houston, and New Orleans, many blacks still live in rural areas, especially in the South. In 2000, African-American households had over $300 billion in earned income and their buying power is expected to reach $700 billion by 2005. The fastest growth areas according to Census 2000 data are the suburbs. The population of blacks who live in the suburbs increased by 5 percent compared to only 2 percent for whites. Blacks tend to shop more at neighborhood stores.[10] This market segment is adopting more affluent suburban lifestyles.[11] Today, more than half of all black households with annual incomes of $50,000 or more have brokerage or mutual fund accounts. The blacks that live in the suburbs own homes and are often well-educated professionals.

The demographics of blacks are changing. Among the more important changes are the following:

- Approximately one-third of blacks are under the age of eighteen compared to 24 percent of whites.
- Approximately 55 percent of blacks reside in metropolitan areas compared to 22 percent of whites.
- Blacks lag behind whites in obtaining a higher education with a bachelor's degree earned by about 15 percent of blacks compared to 24 percent of whites. Black women obtain almost double the number of college degrees as compared to black men.
- While African-Americans have a growing middle-income presence compared to whites earning $75,000 or more a year, they still lag behind about 22 percent to 32 percent.[12]

Personal characteristics reveal that black consumers spend more on pork products, sugar, rice, fish, and flour than do non-blacks. Furthermore, black women use more home permanent products than white women. Black women are household heads in many families and children in these families aid increasingly in making brand decisions. Blacks also rent more television sets and other appliances and purchase more infant accessories than whites. Food products purchased by affluent blacks demonstrate differences not only in cultural backgrounds but social class as well. Refrigerated pizza, pork rinds, beef patties, corn dogs, ramen noodles, melba toast, frozen Italian dinners, frozen green beans, imported cheeses, and bottled water are high on the affluent black's grocery shopping lists.

Regional demographics disclose that about 60 percent of blacks live in the South where they often earn low incomes. The North Central–Midwest states and the Northeast each have about a 16 percent black population. The West contains the remainder. There has been a strong migration from the central cities to suburbs and away from the South.

Lifestyle analysis of activities, interests, and opinions provides marketers with a perspective of consumers and represents the way in which an individual lives and spends time and money. Consumer activities denote how consumers spend their time and interests demonstrate how they feel about things in the environment. Consumer opinions reveal their beliefs about themselves and broad issues. Therefore, lifestyle profiles of blacks could serve as a basis for strategy development. Yankelovich, Inc. offers its syndicated Don Coleman Advertising/Yankelovich African-American Monitor of blacks aged sixteen and older to marketers as a tool to identify forces shaping the consumer lifestyles and behavior of African-Americans, as compared to whites and Hispanics.

A unifying element concerning black women's activities found that some aspect of church participation is present. This involvement takes the form of philanthropic donations and a contribution of time. Religion would seem to have given these women an inner contentment. Leeming and Tripp reported four distinct lifestyle consumer profiles of African-Americans:[13]

- *Contented.* This is the largest group with an average age of about forty-four and approximately one-third are either widowed or divorced. Half are unemployed but the majority have completed their high school education. This group has a preference for remaining at home and does not exhibit impulsive behavior. They are not concerned with status, or social appearances, and are not optimistic about their financial future.

- *Usually mobile.* About one-quarter of the group has materialistic aspirations. This group has a tendency to be impulsive shoppers but are also sophisticated shoppers. Approximately half have completed some college. More than 60 percent are married and are status seekers. Their purchasing behavior reveals a preference for quality goods. This group is financially secure and health conscious.

- *Living for the moment.* This is the youngest group averaging about thirty years of age and number about 20 percent of the black market. This group is mostly single, socially active, and carefree. They are image conscious and have completed high school. More than 60 percent are working but are not concerned with social issues.

- *Living day to day.* This is an unskilled and unemployed group. Price is a consideration in purchases and they are likely to have less than a high school education. Although they are single, divorced, or separated, children are likely to be included in the household. The average age is about thirty-five, they are not health conscious, and are not optimistic about their financial future.

Black women view shopping as a leisure activity and tend to be frequent shoppers. Television viewing is another favorite activity. They are more likely than white women to view daytime programs. Since black women are frequent church goers some manufacturers such as Procter and Gamble have designed "gift bags" with samples of their products for free distribution.

The Affluent Black Market

The upwardly mobile market and affluent segment consists of about 25 percent of the black market. This group could possibly be designated as strivers. The most effective approach in targeting this segment is to use the strategy of aspiration marketing. The hopes, dreams, and desires of the upwardly mobile market segment are similar across American culture groups. A successful family relationship, recognition in work activities, and acceptance with friends and the community are a few examples of core values that permeate from one cultural group to another. Anheuser-Busch and Alberto-Culver have both used these marketing campaigns effectively.[14] The percentage of this market segment investing in the stock market has appreciated from approximately 57 percent in 1998 to 69 percent in 2000.[15] Blacks seem to be more conservative investors than whites. Affluent blacks are heavy consumers of luxury goods. *Savoy Magazine*, launched in February 2001, is targeting affluent blacks with advertisements for upscale automobiles such as the Audi A6 and the Lincoln Navigator SUV. Purchases of affluent blacks also extend to expensive apparel and specialty liquors since there is a need to display success.[16] Black women have risen to the professional and managerial classes faster than black men.

Targeting the Black Market

The size and purchasing power of the black market makes it an attractive target for marketers even though the average black household's income was only 64.9 percent of white household income in 2001. Black men earned 73.9 percent of what white men earned in 2002 as reported by the U.S. Department of Labor. Age, education, occupation, and geographical residency separates this target market into submarkets. Since the black market is sufficiently large and becoming more affluent, special marketing programs need to be designed to serve this target market. Terminology in this market is important. For example, 30 percent of blacks in the United States prefer the term "African-American." Among younger people the term "African-American" is popular but not among older people who prefer the term "black" and therefore demonstrate a pronounced split across generational lines.[17] A possible exception might be blacks from the Caribbean who may prefer the term "Jamaican" or "Haitian Americans." Communicating with blacks in different socioeconomic classes requires different verbal and visual messages. Black unity and Afrocentric identity are important to some groups while black slang is important to others. Another variable is sports. Whether it be basketball with Michael Jordan, or football or baseball, sports would seem to cut across demographic lines and is a popular variable for marketers to use to attract all generations of blacks.

Increases in purchasing power have made the black market more attractive and lucrative for marketers. For example, from 1999 to 2000 expenditures for housing and related expenses increased 9.4 percent from $117 billion to $128.1 billion. Food purchases increased 11.8 percent from $47.3 billion to $52.9 billion. Other categories such as new or used cars and trucks increased 13.4 percent and apparel merchandise spending increased 16.5 percent.[18] Consumption expenditures in the black market are reportedly upward and continue in this direction.

Product Strategies

There is a growing recognition that cultural preference and values are black consumer buyer behavior determinants. Many blacks respond best to products and promotions that reflect an understanding of the black community. For example, Esteé Launders' Prescriptives introduced All Skins, a line of 115 foundation shades spanning the color spectrum from antelope to mahogany. The message that the product matches skin tone exactly was favorably received and sales soared. Dudley Products, Inc., based in North Carolina, offers hair care and beauty products, along with beauty colleges, for African-Americans.

Companies such as Hallmark markets a "mahogany" line of greeting cards that features black characters. Mattel introduced Shani with facial features designed to more accurately resemble African-Americans. Tyco Industries introduced Kenya who wears beads to adorn her cornrows. Both dolls come in a choice of three complexions—light, medium, and dark. Thus, these dolls are more than Barbies in darker plastic. Nike has been selling jogging suits and other exercise wear that feature African prints. Blacks are above average purchasers of compact disc players, jewelry, and watches.

Blacks have been slow to adopt generic and private brands. Brand loyalty is a distinguishing characteristic. Blacks tend to spend more on baby products and breakfast food. Brand preference and purchasing expenditures demonstrate that for some types of products, marketers would do well to segment the black market. Food preferences, in particular, are learned early in life and seem to continue in later life. Education and income may modify many early influences and preferences. As education levels increase, blacks will become more critical and demanding as consumers. Products that demonstrate an understanding of black culture will be especially welcome.

Promotion Strategies

Black consumers tend not to shop by telephone or by mail order. Black upper-middle class women are more fashion conscious. Lower social class African-American consumers tend to make frequent trips to neighborhood grocery stores. Moreover, African-American consumers have a propensity to shop at discount stores compared to department stores.

The most important black-oriented medium is radio. Approximately one-half of radio listening is listening to black radio stations. However, black magazines such as *Ebony* and *Jet* are widely read. These black magazines have a higher readership than general market magazines. Blacks strongly relate to African-American media because black achievements in government, business, sports, and the arts are emphasized. *Essence* magazine was reported as the most influential vehicle for reaching affluent blacks. The most recent data available show that black households on average spend slightly more on newspapers than white households and that black spending on newspapers is increasing while white households have decreased their spending.[19] Another medium that received increased attention by marketers are African-American Internet Web sites in the United States.

Black consumers are split along generational lines as to the use of celebrities marketing their products. Younger consumers prefer the use of celebrity advertising while older African-Americans do not. However, both generations are cynical toward most advertising claims.

Business organizations that are effective in reaching the black market include soft drinks, fast foods, automobiles, tobacco, and liquor firms. Packaged-goods companies are effective but to a much lesser extent.

Unfortunately, many organizations believe that targeting blacks simply means including such black superstars and icons in their advertisements as Michael Jordan, Shaquille O'Neal, Diana Ross, Billy Dee Williams, or Halle Berry. Black buying power is soaring and black consumers are becoming sophisticated consumers.

Distribution Strategies

Many of the largest retailers target black consumers. Shopping habits of black consumers reflect a desire for good prices and stores in close proximity. Affluent female black consumers are more fashion conscious than their Hispanic or white counterparts. J.C. Penney, in order to satisfy fashion demands, opened twenty experimental boutiques call Authentic African with products designed exclusively for black women. *Spiegel* and *Ebony* magazine jointly produced *E Styles*, a quarterly fashion catalog featuring a new merchandise line of apparel for African-American women. The J.C. Penney operation was successful and the retailer has expanded the concept to 100 more stores and will sell merchandise with Afrocentric designs.

A number of organizations have targeted the black market in different ways. Pizza Hut has made minority franchises a priority. It is estimated that Pizza Hut has more than 300 minority-owned stores. Camelot Music has more than doubled its offerings of gospel, jazz, and rhythm and blues music and FootLocker offers styles that sell well in black markets such as suede and black athletic shoes. Since black consumers spend more per capita than white consumers for online services, Web sites such as The Black World Today (www.tbwt.com) and Urban Sports Network have been developed.

MANAGING CHANGE

By 2050, it is projected that the Hispanic group will comprise about 25 percent and the black market segment about 15 percent of the

U.S. population. Since accelerating growth rates focus on Hispanic and black groups, marketers would do well to not only satisfy the preferences of these groups but to maintain ethnic products as well. Cultural sensitivity and language capability are the key to success in marketing to these groups. Since the reactions of Hispanics and blacks are different than whites, it is incumbent upon marketers to use different types of media to reach ethnic audiences. For example, Hispanics and blacks are more influenced by all media (TV, radio, newspapers) for purchasing value-expressive products such as clothing than whites. Hispanics were more influenced by TV and blacks were more influenced by radio than whites for purchasing small electronic products.[20]

Goya Foods uses a new approach to ethnic marketing by developing an all-in-one aisle approach to the placement of the product at Shop Rite supermarkets. Goya offers a shop within a shop that provides an assortment for Hispanic consumers. Goya Foods is not alone in this strategy as the Star Market in the greater Boston area has created "Take a Walk Down the Emerald Aisle" targeting those who are Irish and those who have Irish-food preferences. Ethnic market segmentation has spread across the United States, but not without mistakes. Both Maybelline and Revlon failed in penetrating the Hispanic market. Avon is trying to reach this market with a catalog printed in Spanish and a new cosmetics line aimed exclusively at Hispanics.

There are significant differences in the Hispanic and black markets that relate to language, values, lifestyles, and customs and it would be a mistake for marketers not to acknowledge these differences. Over time, Hispanic and black market segments will integrate and adopt the culture and purchasing behavior of the mass population. Interracial marriages will increase in the future and will also change consumption patterns. This does not, however, mean that either group will move away from their original identities or divorce themselves from their heritage.

NOTES

1. Tobi Elkin, "Product Pampering," *Brandweek*, 16 June 1997, 38–40.

2. Alfred L. Schreiber, *Multicultural Marketing* (Chicago: NTC Business Books, 2001), 1–16.

3. Michael Barone, *The New Americans: How the Melting Pot Can Work Again* (Washington, D.C.: Regency, 2001).

4. Geoffrey D. Paulin, "A Growing Market: Expenditures by Hispanic Consumers," *Monthly Labor Review* 121 (March 1998): 3–21.

5. Susan Juniu, "The Impact of Immigration Leisure Experience in the Lives of South American Immigrants," *Journal of Leisure Research* 32 (Fall 2000): 358–378.

6. Youn-Kyung Kim and Jikyeong Kang, "The Effects of Ethnicity and Product on Purchase Decision Making," *Journal of Advertising Research* 41, 2 (2001): 39–48.

7. Eduardo Porter and Emily Nelson, "P&G Reaches Out to Hispanics," *The Wall Street Journal*, 13 October 2000, B1, 4.

8. Isabel Valdes and Marta Sedane, *Hispanic Market Handbook: The Definitive Source for Reaching This Lucrative Segment of American Consumers* (Detroit, Mich.: Gale Research, 1995); Alf Nucifora, "Hispanic Market No Longer a Sleeping Giant," *Atlanta Business Chronicle*, 3 February 2003, 1.

9. Catharine P. Taylor, "Barbie Latina says 'Hola' to Net," *Advertising Age* 72, 1 October 2001, 54–56.

10. Beth Belton, "Black Buying Power Soaring," *USA Today*, 30 July 1998, 1B.

11. David Whelan, "Census 2000: Black Boom in the Burbs," *American Demographics* 23 (July 2001): 19–20.

12. Robert McNott, "The New Demographics of Black Americans," *Business Week*, 4 December 2000, 14.

13. E. Janice Leeming and Cynthia F. Tripp, *Segmenting the Women's Market* (Chicago: Probus, 1994).

14. Chris Rooney, "Aspiration Cuts Across Racial Lines," *Marketing News*, 26 March 2001, 24.

15. Paulette Thomas, "Investing Survey Shows Race Plays a Part," *The Wall Street Journal*, 6 June 2001, C21.

16. Whelan, "Census 2000."

17. Brad Edmondson, "What Do You Call a Dark-Skinned Person?" *American Demographics* 15 (October 1993): 9–16.

18. "Ethnic," *Marketing News*, 8 July 2002, 22.

19. Mark Fitzgerald, "Spending Data in Black and White," *Editor and Publisher*, 2 April 2001, 9.

20. Kim and Kang, "The Effects of Ethnicity."

CHAPTER 9

Social Class and Targeting the Changing Lifestyles of the Asian, Jewish, and Italian Markets

The American consumer is part of an open class system where there are greater opportunities for social mobility than geographic mobility. It is impossible to find the perfect ethnic mix in any metropolitan area in the United States. The large coastal cities have above average minority and ethnic representation while the cities in the Midwest or South are disproportionately white or African-American with small pockets of ethnic groups such as Asian, Jewish, or Italian. Most consumers view themselves as middle class and often purchase products with the symbols and attraction of the next class up. Occasional splurging and treating oneself to the best or premium brands are methods consumers use to separate themselves from their peers. Marketers frequently design advertisements for premium or status products that are sensual and provocative and express elegance.

There are many determinants of social class than just income alone. They include education, occupation, and housing. Although regional location does develop some disparities, people within a particular social class are more likely to interact with one another than with members of different social classes.

Many Americans do not like to think about social class. However, the distinctions between social classes are becoming sharper since more and more two-income families emerged and there is a propensity for college graduates to marry one another and have higher income occupations. Distinctions between social classes can lead to differences in behavior patterns. For example, middle-class consumers appear to be the market segment most likely to experiment with store brands, whereas low- and high-income shoppers are less prone to purchase store brands. Moreover, some product categories are classless, such as detergent, but many expensive and fashionable possessions such as home furnishings and apparel express class status. Lower to middle-class consumers purchase apparel items that have the name of a famous athlete such as Michael Jordan or a company like Nike where upper-class consumers may care less.

Social class is an important variable in the selection of retail stores for shopping. Nordstrom has targeted upper and upper-middle class consumers whereas Kmart attracts lower-middle class consumers. However, lower-middle class consumers would likely patronize a store like Nordstrom to make a special purchase.

Participation in recreational activities is influenced by social class membership. Upper-class consumers attend the theater, opera, and concerts and play squash. Tennis, racquetball, and playing bridge seem to be middle-to-upper class activities. Lower class activities may include playing bingo, bowling, pool and billiards, frequenting taverns, and professional wrestling matches. Social class based upon lifestyle and not income is a more useful segmentation criterion. For example, income allows a Vanderbilt and the heavyweight boxing champion of the world to purchase a Rolls Royce but it is not likely that they would belong to the same social strata or have similar lifestyle values.

Lloyd Warner divided social class into upper-upper, lower-upper, upper-middle, lower-middle, upper-lower, and lower-lower social structures.[1] Social class has a relationship to shopping and consumption patterns. In addition, social class has a bearing on retail shopping and store choice, savings and investments, product selection, types of services desired, and recreation and leisure activities.

The increasing number of families with two incomes and the greater number of women in the workforce are causing socioeconomic changes that have modified thinking about social class structure. Multiworker families are a growing segment of American society. As the number of these families increases, the impact on the economy of their income and level of consumption will grow as well. Dual-income families are able to withstand the impact of inflationary pressures and tough economic times. Furthermore, dual-income households enable a family to purchase, within a relatively short period, the material goods that their parents worked for years to acquire. Marketers will find families with working wives welcome labor-saving appliances. Moreover, working wives are interested in life insurance, credit cards, rental cars, and travel. The working wife also wants home furnishings that are easy to maintain.

The motivation to look well dressed at work will help to increase sales of such items as clothing, cosmetics, costume jewelry, toiletries, and footwear. Childcare services are also in demand among working wives with children under age six. Many stores and service establishments find it important to remain open later in the evening to accommodate customers who find it difficult to use their services during the day. Restaurants, fast-food chains, and take-out organizations profit from the increase of multi-income families. Suburban markets continue their growth in purchasing power.

Social class has a strong impact on preferences in cars, clothes, home furnishings, leisure activities, reading habits, and store choice. For example, the middle class is more likely to purchase imported cars while the working class favors domestic cars. Consumers with a higher social class background may prefer to purchase expensive cameras. Upper class consumers prefer to eat out in restaurants with table linen as opposed to fast food. Members of each social class impart certain values and behavior norms to their children. Some working-class families are content with their lifestyles and do not aspire for higher social class membership.

More people have turned to a component lifestyle whereby their attitudes and behavior depend upon particular situations rather than overall lifestyle philosophy. Cross-shopping behavior is a manifestation of lifestyle segmentation. There is a trend away from social conformity, demonstrating changes in consumer attitudes. Consumers seem to be less constrained by social custom. Individual style and taste appears to combine social class with the desire for convenience. Whether marketers consider the social class system in the United States classified on the basis of occupation, education, income, residence or other variables, there are no sharp lines that separate the classes. This is a change from Lloyd Warner's social class system. There is a merging of each class with those adjacent to it such as upper-middle with lower-middle class which now comprises the vast majority of consumers.

The Lloyd Warner taxonomy of social class was devised in 1940. It might be convenient for marketers when attempting to target various social classes to reconceptualize the categories of wealthy, affluent, upper-middle class, middle class, lower-middle class, and poor. Possessions may be used as a symbol of class membership— not only the number of possessions but also the nature of the choices. A middle-class family may select wall-to-wall carpeting for their homes whereas an affluent family might choose oriental rugs.

SHIFTING PATTERNS WITHIN SOCIAL CLASSES

The first immigrants to North America were predominately white Protestants from a western European culture perpetuated by an upper class. Subsequent waves of Germans and Irish had to assimilate in a culture basically influenced by British aristocracy. As the Germans and Irish moved upward in social class standing other immigrants from southern and eastern Europe immigrated. A great wave of immigrants arrived in the United States between the years 1880 to 1910. These immigrants were generally unskilled. As generation succeeded generation, these groups assimilated and moved up in social class standing. Consequently, there tends to be an ethnic variable in social class hierarchies. Although ethnic communities were established, this did not prevent the development of subclasses in communities of Italian, Polish, Russian, Scandinavian, or other ethnic extractions.

A similar process appears within Asian groups. Although recent immigrants tend to hold on to their homelands' culture and language, their offspring tend to adopt the social and economic ways of mainstream America. A common factor present in the assimilation of ethnic groups has been language barriers.

When assimilation has taken place, there are generally feelings of status anxiety. This may take the form of conspicuous consumption. Thorstein Veblen coined the term "conspicuous consumption" and it was meant to characterize individuals who obtain products simply to visibly display them. But certain items can express social class status and might be important to an individual who desires or has achieved social class mobility. Cultural tastes, values, and attitudes learned early in life tend to resist change, while information acquired later in life is more subject to change. Purchasing behavior is powerfully linked to acculturation levels.

There are numerous factors that enter into the selection of a particular subcultural group as a target market. While size is a significant variable, there are other variables to consider when developing marketing strategies aimed at subcultural groups. For example, the number of Jewish people in the United States who insist on kosher products is small. Yet, marketers have extended the preferences of this subculture group to the total population with marketing campaigns that state, "You don't have to be Jewish to like Levy's rye bread." Firms that sell kosher hot dogs and meat products have used this strategy. Marketing campaigns have linked the word "kosher" with quality. Although the Chinese population is relatively small in the United States, Chinese restaurants exist in all metropolitan and even rural areas and shelf space is given in supermarkets for the sale of Chinese products. The United States is characterized by cultural assimilation and structural pluralism. Cultural assimilation means that the major ethnic groups in the United States tend to share a common culture. Structural pluralism means that each of these groups retains a sense of identity.

Ethnic groups are referred to as a subculture or microculture because they have values, customs, traditions, and engage in other activities that are particular to their group within a culture. Asian Americans, for example, make up less than 5 percent of the U.S. population, but 93 percent of this population, estimated to be about 10 million people, live in urban areas. The concentration of Asians and other ethnic groups in specific geographical locations provides a cost efficient use of print and broadcast media.

The middle class in previous generations seemed to encompass almost everybody in the United States. Currently, there is expansion in both the top and bottom ends of the social class system. The increase in educational levels, two-income families, and the growing ranks of professional women are some reasons for growth in upper-class ranks. On the other hand, those in the lower classes have not attained the education needed to gain well-paying jobs. The gap is widening between the "have and the have-nots."

Although divorce rates are spiraling and unconventional alternatives to the traditional nuclear family have emerged, the survival of the family is not in question. Childrearing functions and the need for economic and emotional support sustain the importance of the family unit. However, trends such as working married women, smaller-sized families, increased life expectancy, more formal education, and the women's movement have influenced shifting patterns within the social class structure.

The middle and upper-middle classes constitute the vast majority of consumers and have received an influx from two important minority segments. The first group, consisting of the Italian and Jewish markets, is a more established segment that emerged in the 1950s and 1960s when economic growth occurred and opportunities presented themselves. The second group consists of Asians, Hispanics, and African-Americans. Jobs within these groups may be relatively insecure in economic slowdowns since many were the last hired and therefore will struggle to maintain their hard-won middle-class gains.

The bottom-end of the social classes find themselves challenged by high educational and skill requirements. For Asians, language barriers need to be overcome in order to gain higher social-class status.

There is a growing class of individuals accumulating a disproportionate amount of wealth. These are people with college degrees and knowledge of the Internet. They form a technological market segment.

CONSUMPTION BEHAVIOR
AND CULTURAL ASSIMILATION

Along with social class, ethnic identification is one of the most fundamental distinctions among consumer segments. These distinctions are closely tied to cultural differences. Ethnic differences between groups, actual or perceived, are an important determinant in designing a marketing strategy. Major ethnic groups in the United States are differentiated by race, religion, and nationality. In the United States these groups constitute 31 percent of the population up from 24 percent in 1990.

There are a variety of Asian subcultures depending upon region (West Coast versus North), rural versus urban residence, and social class. A West Coast urban, college-educated Asian with origins from Japan leads a far different life than a Korean small grocery-store owner in New York City. There is no single Asian market. Early immigrants from Asia came to the United States from China and Japan. Many members of these groups are third or fourth generation Americans. Newer Asian immigrants come from the Philippines, Vietnam, Cambodia, Hong Kong, and Korea. They have a strong preference in communicating in their native language. Asians are living in more heavily Asian neighborhoods than they were ten years ago. Asian Americans consume products like everyone else but have special needs. For example, they are interested in skin care products and products related to stomach ailments and indigestion due to their liking of spicy foods.

Cultural assimilation develops when a common culture is shared in the United States and minority groups are absorbed into this culture by adapting to and subscribing to many of these cultural characteristics. Structural pluralism is present when each of these minority groups retains a sense of identity. Until the 1970s, there was little intermarriage between ethnic groups and social relationships and contacts were largely restricted to members of the same ethnic group. While some of this structural pluralism is evident, the rate of intermarriage has grown considerably and many people have friendships with individuals unlike themselves. There is evidence that ethnic groups prefer to cluster together rather than integrate into the community. This is true of Jewish students who join Jewish fraternities and sororities. There are also neighborhoods known in various cities as Italian areas. Ethnic enclosure can be fostered by national origin and religion. Italian Catholics have a spirit of identity with the Vatican as do Jewish Americans with Israel.

The acculturation process has exposed both Jewish and Italian groups to new cultural patterns. Native-born Jews at various social-class levels are very similar to native-born non-Jews of the same social class in purchasing behavior. Working-class Italian Americans have acculturated to an American working-class pattern.

Nevertheless, there are some ethnic cultural differences. Jews, for example, have become independent entrepreneurs and self-employed professionals. Jews are also important audiences for cultural events such as opera, ballet, poetry readings, and subscribe to intellectual publications. Jews are also receptive to purchasing new paintings, new homes of advanced architecture, and are more likely than some other ethnic groups to be among innovators or early adopters in the purchase of new products.[2]

Italian Americans tend to be strongly attached to their neighborhoods and families. Italians, as they become more prosperous, choose to rebuild or renovate their homes in neighborhoods that are presently occupied by other Italians. The family is envisioned as all-important. Success is prized because it makes the entire family stronger. The old-fashioned Italian mother, like the Jewish mother, tends to overfeed and overprotect their children.

Second and third generation Italians and Jewish Americans tend to be almost indistinguishable in manner from the core group members of the same social class. Many bear little physical resemblance to the stereotyped pictures developed of earlier generations of Italians and Jewish immigrants. In contrast, physical appearance is still a striking difference when describing the assimilation of Asian Americans.

The following is a list of the experiences and assimilation of Jews and Asians, Hispanics and Italians, blacks and Irish:

1. *Asian and Jewish similarities.* High average level of education. High median income. Business expertise. Strong identity. Interest in cultural events.

2. *Hispanic and Italian similarities.* Strong interest in preserving the family. Interested in preserving food consumption habits. Strong identity associated with ethnic background.

3. *African-American and Irish similarities.* Strong interest in preserving ethnic background. Both groups had to overcome prejudices.

Early Irish, Italian, and Jewish immigrants were regarded as other races. Many East Asians who arrived from 1965 to 2000 were like many European Jews who were leaving their countries because of authoritarian governments. Many Asians, like Jewish immigrants before them, have successfully climbed the ladder of social mobility because of education.

Many Italian immigrants preserved a sustaining trust in family structure. This is also true of many Hispanic arrivals. Both groups had a distrust of their governments in their native countries. Hispanics still remain the most family-oriented ethnic group.

Irish immigrants had primarily rural backgrounds and, like blacks migrating to the North, were not well equipped for urban living. The Irish and blacks suffered the consequences of family disintegration. Many Irish people gravitated toward working as law enforcement officials.[3] The immigrants from Europe took two or three generations to leave the ghettos they first settled in to adjust to American culture.

Like the Italians, Jews, and Irish before them, Asians, Hispanics, and blacks are becoming assimilated into the American culture. For the last twenty years, the number of businesses owned by African-Americans increased by 26 percent, Hispanic Americans and Asian Americans by 30 percent, and Native Americans by 84 percent. More than 4 out of every 100 minority Americans in the United States own a business. The economic position of these business owners will have an impact on their social class and buying patterns. Consequently, the melting pot metaphor is operating again.

Intermarriage in the past two decades has become a striking force for cultural assimilation. Such notables as Senators Philip Gramm from Texas and Mitch McConnel from Kentucky have both married individuals of Asian descent. Governor Jeb Bush of Florida has married a woman of Hispanic origin and Linda Chavez, formerly Head of the Civil Rights Commission and of Mexican descent, has married a Jewish man. Justice Clarence Thomas, an African-American, has married a white woman.

LINKING PRODUCTS TO SOCIAL CLASS AND ETHNIC GROUPS

Consumer purchasing behavior patterns respond slowly when dependent upon cultural and social changes. While consumer resistance to products dependent upon cultural and social change may be difficult to overcome, Berelson and Steiner maintain that whatever was learned early in life tends to resist change and whatever was transmitted late in life is much more receptive to acceptance.[4] Therefore, it is not surprising to learn that early food habits are difficult to surmount. Learning what wines go with fish or meat and the different types of wine for various occasions leads to a measure of sophistication.

There would seem to be a linkage between the consumption of food products to social class and ethnic groups. When John F. Kennedy occupied the White House, French food and other delicacies were frequently served. In contrast, when Lyndon Johnson occupied the

White House, cookouts prevailed and roast beef was served frequently. Stories abound about successful people who return to their "old neighborhoods" to purchase food or eat in restaurants that serve the food of their early years. For example, White Castle was established in 1921 and is considered the original fast-food hamburger chain. Although now only operating restaurants in ten states, market coverage is achieved through mail order and telemarketing operations for the sale of its hamburgers and cheeseburgers in the frozen food sections of supermarkets. Singer Frank Sinatra once had White Castle ship him frozen hamburgers at a concert site.

Religious Jewish Americans have practiced fusion cookery. Hasidim are the most devout, orthodox Jews and are able to accommodate themselves by eating in kosher, Italian, Chinese, or French restaurants situated in their neighborhoods.[5] There is a linkage of food to social class and ethnic groups. Some ethnic groups have maintained their food preferences into American society. Bagels and rye bread have been Jewish favorites, while pasta, fresh vegetables, and fruits have been Italian food preferences. Many groups have maintained their identity through food. Such food as kasha, kugel, and knaidlach, while not mainstreamed are an inherent part of the diet of many East European Jews.

As a new generation of Jews and Italians emerges some of the old ethnic foods do not remain favorites. Instead, new ethnic food such as sushi, salsa, burritos, and Thai foods have become popular. Italians and Jews are following the eating patterns of established generations of Americans.

An understanding of Jewish and Italian mothers is necessary to comprehend marketing to these segments. There is a devotion to food preparation and family dining that is not only traditional but an all-consuming part of life. Eating is a joyous festival. The family meal is an important occasion in the lifestyle of these groups. Although family dining is not as ritualistic among Asians, it is still an integral part of family life.

TARGETING THE ASIAN MARKET

The Asian-American market is exploding. This market has high brand loyalty and communicates by word-of-mouth. The segment has a high family orientation. Asian Americans are more likely than whites, blacks, or Hispanics to own a credit card, to own three or more different credit cards, and to use credit cards more often each month. More than two-thirds of Asian-American credit card holders avoid finance charges by paying off their balance every month. Asians live in multigenerational households, which puts the average size of Asian-American households at 3.8 per household compared to 3.2 per household for the average of the population. The majority of this market still speaks their native language at home and sends their children to language schools in addition to their regular schools. Asian consumers are composed of different nationality groups. Filipinos, Chinese, Korean, Vietnamese, Asian Indian, and Japanese, in that order, will be the largest groups in the Asian population by 2010. The Asian-American market represents $225 billion in purchasing power with a population of 11 million. Asian consumers have settled in primarily five states: California, Hawaii, New York, Illinois, and Washington. Filipinos are currently the second largest Asian subgroup in the United States after Chinese. Their numbers have grown more than 700 percent since 1960.

Education is highly prized by Asian Americans. They are more likely to obtain a college degree than the average American. Thirty-eight percent hold a bachelor's degree or higher. They also aspire to managerial and professional status. Marketers would do well to position luxury goods to this market in the future. Asian Americans prefer to shop as a family. Traditional Asian culture demonstrates deep respect for family elders. Shopping decisions are influenced by older family members.

Once Americans ate Asian food only outside the home and it usually was Chinese, but now they want to cook the items eaten in restaurants in their own kitchens. Asian items placed on supermarket shelves include the familiar soy sauce, fried noodles, fresh ginger, wonton wrappers, oyster sauce, and Vietnamese fish sauce. Hunt-Wesson, under its La Choy label, sells frozen egg roll entrees. Asian food is on the supermarket shelf with significant penetration and is a mainstream food.

Nearly one-third of the Asian restaurant market is located on the West Coast. Another third of the restaurant market is located in the Middle-Atlantic and South-Atlantic states. Asian restaurants comprise more than 6 percent of total U.S. restaurants. Although Asian food has grown increasingly popular with Thai food and Vietnamese cuisines, a national Asian food chain that would be a counterpart to Domino's Pizza has not been successful and significant time may elapse before such a chain of Asian restaurants emerge. Health and dietary concerns can be turned into an advantage for Asian food and national Asian restaurant chains. Already portions of the menu entrees have been designated by diet with low caloric intake, low fat, and/or low sodium and this has done much to ease the minds of those who are health conscious. As long as consumers have options between healthy entrees, this should be beneficial in mainstreaming Asian food.

As minorities become successful they choose to move to the suburbs from the cities, forming suburban versions of ethnic enclaves that have shaped cities for much of the past century. Whereas more affluent minorities are choosing to live among themselves, this trend is less evident among Asians. While the reasons for this rational choice may be debatable, assimilation of Asians into the culture of the United States has been faster than other minority groups. Although Asians are the smallest minority group, they constitute the fastest growing group and they have made significant inroads into Hawaii and California. Nevada, New Jersey, and Maryland are also experiencing significant increases of Asians.

One of the most important reasons responsible for population changes was the 1965 Immigration and Nationality Act. The 1965 Act, for the first time, treated Chinese immigrants equally with other nationalities, thus concluding years of bias against the Chinese. This opened immigration and the boundaries of Chinatown in New York City were extended. In 1960 the female ratio was 2:1 and by 1980 had become almost equal.[6] Eventually, this legislation opened immigration from Korea and Hong Kong.

A high proportion of post-1965 Korean immigrants have established small businesses. Jewish immigrants at the beginning of the twentieth century developed small businesses to advance in American society. Korean immigrants have settled in large metropolitan areas in the United States. The largest Korean population is found in Los Angeles, followed by New York City and then Chicago. Once Koreans become successful, they usually move to the suburbs. Koreans came to the United States with a "success ideology" and with financial resources. Even though many Korean immigrants came to the United States with high levels of education, employment opportunities were limited and they turned to establishing small businesses. Among immigrant groups there is usually a generation split. Vietnamese Americans appear to be divided by generations.[7] Orange County and southern Los Angeles represent the largest concentration of Vietnamese in the United States.

Many of the offspring of the original immigrants are now college students or have graduated from college. The generations are divided by language, political memories, music, and dress. For example, at a wedding many women wear *ao dais*, costumes that are traditional and older immigrants prefer music from their country of origin rather than music from America. Marketers will find that there are opportunities through the Internet to reach Asian Americans. Chinese Americans have the highest personal computer ownership and the highest rate of Internet connection in the United States.[8] This market segment is targeted online and tends to be younger and wealthier than other users. Asian Americans do well economically as both husband and wife work. Almost three-quarters of Asian Americans are employed with 80 percent of those employed in white-collar positions. They represent the fastest growing and most affluent demographic segment among all ethnic groups. They are described as intellectually gifted, mathematically skilled, technically competent, and hard working. The importance of this market should not be underestimated.

TARGETING THE JEWISH MARKET

The successful application of product differentiation should result in an increased horizontal share of a generalized market. Product differentiation refers to marketing efforts to distinguish a product from competitors' products. Methods used to accomplish this would be to alter the product's physical characteristics or to use branding, advertising, and packaging. These methods are especially successful in an affluent society. Market segmentation should increase the market share of specific carefully defined submarkets. Product differentiation and market segmentation should be used together.

The general public appears to believe that kosher certification is a sign of quality and purity. The term "kosher" may be the equivalent of the Good Housekeeping Seal of Approval. For the health conscious, a kosher designation is important. Kosher-certified packaged-food products represented about $150 billion in retail sales in 2000 with 20 percent of the market for these products being Jewish, 30 percent Muslim, 28 percent were those with special dietary requirements, and 25 percent view kosher as higher-quality items. Since 1990, more than 1,000 new or newly certified kosher items have been placed on the marketplace.

Although Jewish Americans number approximately six million in population, their higher-than-average incomes and concentration in key major markets make this group a sought-after target. For example, Gerber Products Company acquired the kosher designation for its dry baby cereals. The Dannon Yogurt Company found that the Circle U label placed on a number of its products added $2 million in annual sales. This helped Dannon gain shelf space in smaller stores and generated free publicity in the Jewish media. The number of kosher-certified products has increased rapidly in the 1990s. Growth is estimated at more than 5 percent annually. There are 60,000 kosher-certified packaged-food products. Kosher foods are in about one-half of the nation's supermarkets and nearly 75 percent of Hebrew National customers are non-Jews. This is also true of Empire Kosher that sells mostly chickens and turkeys.[9]

The kosher designation means that sources of ingredients and processing equipment are checked to ascertain that no food is processed with derivatives of animal fat such as gelatin. Beef and fowl must be slaughtered humanely and then completely drained of blood before processing. Periodic inspections are scheduled once kosher standards are certified. The control over the use of animal fats is the main reassurance that consumers find in a kosher endorsement.

Companies that have had kosher endorsement over the years include H. J. Heinz, Best Foods, the makers of Hellmann's mayonnaise, and Kraft for such products as Breakstone dairy products and Post cereals. Maxwell House coffee has targeted this niche for generations. Both *Food & Wine* magazine and *Rolling Stone* declared the kosher designation as one of the leading trends of the 1990s. Such brands as Coors Beer, Pepperidge Farm cookies, Nabisco's Grey Poupon mustard, and Ben and Jerry's ice cream were certified in the 1990s.

As an older generation disappears, kosher food companies like Hebrew National need to reach out to a new generation. For example, a small company has been marketing kosher Oriental pot pie and kosher Mexican pie. Both cultural integration and a high rate of intermarriage has changed the traditional population base. The traditional Hebrew companies must change or there is a risk that other companies will enter the marketplace. The Empire Kosher Poultry Company sells its chicken products at a higher price than competitors. One reason is that the observance of kosher standards costs more. Empire believed that its brand can compete on the basis of taste. In a blind taste-test performed in a study by Penn State University, Empire was chosen as the tastiest and most tender chicken over four leading consumer brands. Marketing efforts have targeted a market that desires a premium brand and this strategy appears successful as non-Jewish consumers have become more quality conscious.

Many traditional values have been changing over the years. Kosher-goods companies have been long associated with matzo and gefilte fish but are now endeavoring to enter the mass marketplace. Kosher linguine, kosher frozen pizzas, kosher frozen yogurt, and kosher baby cereal are the results. However, some old-line kosher companies are slow to adapt to these trends like Manischewitz and Rokeach Foods who have each experienced sales declines for their product lines.

TARGETING THE ITALIAN MARKET

Most Italian immigrants migrated to the United States during the period from 1880 to 1910. Many of these immigrants settled in New York City, Philadelphia, and Chicago. The older generation tended to preserve the customs and language from Italy. As generation succeeded generation, fluency in the Italian language diminished. Food habits and recipes passed from one generation to another.

The Italian ethnic food market ranks first followed by preferences for Mexican and Oriental food. Hershey Foods, Borden, and CPC International are the three largest pasta producers according to supermarket sales. Healthy Choice dominates Italian frozen entrees. Italian sauces are dominated by Classico, Ragu Today's Recipe, Ragu Fino Italian, Progresso, and Francesco Rivaldi. The most popular new food product introductions in the 1990s were Italian and Mexican.

The Hershey Pasta Group is the number one company in its category and includes brands such as San Giorgio, American Beauty, Ronzoni, Skinner, and Light'N Fluffy. The profile of a typical pasta user is a female, married, most likely between the ages of eighteen and forty-four, with an annual household income between $25,000 and $50,000, with one child living at home and has three or more packages of pasta in the cupboard, but eats spaghetti more than any other type of pasta. This pasta user eats pasta one-third of the time when dining out and believes that pasta is a good source of complex carbohydrates, that it is economical, convenient, and filling.

Pasta has had positive media coverage. Since 1975, the volume of pasta consumed in pounds has more than doubled. Pasta is a food high in complex carbohydrates and for those consumers concerned with proper eating habits this is a factor that gets consumers to buy the product. Pasta has a long shelf life. Other reasons for consumption are that consumers have grown up using pasta products. There is a loyalty element and pasta is viewed as inexpensive.

Italian food is ranked as healthy and beneficial. This is true of pasta but not necessarily true of pizza because of the high fat and salt content of some of the types of cheeses used. However, there are cheese alternatives that are beneficial to good health. Although the offerings of many American chain pizza restaurants only remotely resemble Italy's pizzas and pastas, the popularity of pizza in America is evidenced by Pizza Hut with more than 8,000 units in the United States and Domino's Pizza with more than 4,000 units. There has also been an increase in Italian restaurants catering to both casual and fine dining. America's enthusiasm for Italian food has transcended ethnic background.

One of the most notable aspects of growing preferences for Italian food is by looking at America's heartland. The fastest growing markets are Cincinnati and Dayton, Kansas City, Missouri, Wichita, Peoria, Columbus, Toledo, and Green Bay, Wisconsin. Anyone who has traveled across the United States realizes that there are many regional differences in consumption behavior. For example, in the

South and Midwest white bread is preferred, while on the East Coast, rye, whole wheat, French, and Italian are preferred. Although these geographical preferences remain, there is a preference for Italian food that is spreading to other regions of the country. The increasing demand for Italian food has contributed to the growth of restaurant chains such as Olive Garden, owned by General Mills and Sbarro. The acceptance of Italian food is not a fad. This ethnic food preference has staying power. Italian restaurant distribution is the strongest in the Mid-Atlantic, Pacific Coast, south of the Mid-Atlantic, and East–North Central states.

One of the best neighborhoods for Italian food shopping is in the Bensonhurst section of Brooklyn, New York, which many believe feels like Italy. Many immigrants and their offspring remain in the old neighborhood and some resist moving to the suburbs because the neighborhood feels like home. Many of the retail stores are family owned and operated. There is still a strong Italian ethnic identification even though there has been an influx of Russian immigrants in recent years. Strong family ties and enjoyment of food are intertwined.[10]

In the future, food marketers need to transcend local and regional ethnic food preferences and make these food preferences national. The penetration of Italian entrees in restaurants serving primarily American food with lasagna, spaghetti with sauce, and ravioli has grown. Even the sale of spaghetti sauces in food stores such as Ragu, Prego, Hunt's Classico, and Healthy Choice have grown. To some extent, the producers of Jewish ethnic food are making their products national in scope. Some years ago, a slogan was expressed that "You don't have to be Jewish to eat Levy's bread." This slogan should serve as a guideline for producers of ethnic food to market their products to a broad spectrum of consumers. Consumers have a propensity to experiment by eating different ethnic foods.

Italian, Asian, Jewish, and other subcultures and their food preferences represent definable target groups for specific products and logical units for segmentation. Sales of Italian food, for example, are well beyond this group's population numbers in the United States. Therefore, food preferences of this ethnic group have achieved acceptance among mainstream America. With the influx of new immigrant groups into the United States, sophisticated consumers appear more inclined to sample new ethnic foods.[11] Throughout the United States, small independent ethnic restaurants are springing up that are satisfying consumer demand to eat different ethnic foods. For those Americans who enjoy travel, there are eight Italian schools that offer cooking vacations such as the International Cooking School of Italian Food and Wine or Venetian Cooking in a Venetian Palace.

MANAGING CHANGE

As the immigrant returned from work in an alien America, the smells of familiar cooking greeted him and were links to his or her past. Food has served to link individuals to groups, to family, and to friends. Ethnic food patterns helped to establish and strengthen ethnic communities. For Italians, Eastern European Jews, and Chinese, an important staple of their diet was not a conventional part of American cuisine and ritually prepared food was essential. Ethnic food stores, in ethnic neighborhoods, functioned like ethnic churches or like community centers. Credit was extended and neighbors shared gossip, recipes, and advice. Women shopped every day. Ethnic food was linked to religion and helped to strengthen the ties of communal identity. For Italians and Jews, it is not possible to understand their family structure until one has understood the role of the mother in food preparation.

The connection with mainstream America was established by the ethnic restaurant. These ethnic restaurants were places for men who had come to the United States to earn enough money to send for their families who remained abroad. Later, these restaurants were patronized on special occasions—for anniversaries, birthdays, or marriages. Finally, these restaurants served mainstream Americans looking for their roots. Today, the customers of Italian or Asian restaurants are rarely Italian or Asian.

The challenge remains to attempt to explain how Italian, Asian, and other ethnic food has become accepted into the culture of mainstream America. The past twenty years have witnessed an acceleration of open housing patterns, increased travel, education, and intermarriage. Therefore, no single factor is responsible for consumer interest in ethnic foods but rather a combination of factors.

The disappearance of traditional housing patterns where individuals of similar ethnic groups clustered in neighborhoods has opened up new horizons. Schools have integrated allowing children to sample one another's lunches and become familiar with a variety of different foods. Neighbors of different ethnic backgrounds have exchanged recipes.

Educational attainment is one of the reasons that explain the maturity and sophistication of the consumer. More educated consumers create demand for such products as books, art, travel, and the curiosity and willingness to try different foods. Food manufacturers are already responding to pressure to specify the balance of ingredients in their products. As education increases, consumer tastes may likely reflect this trend and may heighten the current interest in ethnic and health foods. Travel is another variable associated with education and high-income families. Travel both within the United States and abroad has introduced consumers to a host of ethnic foods. Luxury cruises have allowed passengers to briefly see different ports and also try different foods. Wendy's envisioned the increased interest of ethnic food by adding Mexican food to its salad bar. Travel and education lead to a desire to try and enjoy different ethnic foods.

Intermarriage has also increased consumer awareness of different foods. The extended family is another dimension to the enjoyment of new foods. Christmas and Hanukkah may be observed in new kinds of family structures and the exchange of favorite foods is at the center of these celebrations.

Many Asian, Italian, and Jewish consumers will hold on to some of their food preferences for generations. Their purchasing behavior will broaden and new foods will be accepted as members of these ethnic groups strive for assimilation. Consumer behavior is influenced by social pressure and consequently if ethnic group members desire to identify with middle-class culture they will behave in ways acceptable to mainstream Americans. If integration is desired, then members of these ethnic groups will be assimilated and this will be reflected in purchasing patterns. For some members of these ethnic groups, some elements of their identity will be preserved and transmitted to subsequent generations.

Social class affects lifestyle and influences buyer behavior. A new system called geodemographics is able to relate many large-scale databases with multiple levels of small-area geographics such as zip codes or census block groups. This new system should enable researchers to better understand the role of social class in influencing buyer behavior.[12] Social class is an important variable in understanding the development and maturity of Asian, Jewish, and Italian markets creating greater opportunities for marketers to use market segmentation strategies to reach these markets.

Subcultural analysis enables marketers to segment markets to satisfy the needs, attitudes, activities, interests, and values that are shared by members of a specific subcultural group. There is not any single ethnic group market any more than there is a single European-American market segment. A heterogeneous group of segments within ethnic groups exists just as in European-American markets. These patterns can be described in terms of environmental influences on consumer behavior. The important distinction between a lifestyle and a subculture is the latter's capacity to endure.

Ethnic food marketers would do well to use a strategy known as benefit segmentation. Benefit segmentation is a form of market segmentation that classifies buyers according to the different benefits they seek from the product. Benefit segmentation usually implies that the marketer should focus on satisfying one benefit group. Benefit segmentation is allied with psychographics and product usage information. As consumers' attitudes, values, lifestyles, and past purchase habits are altered, benefits sought in specific purchasing situations change.

NOTES

1. Lloyd Warner, *Social Class in America* (Chicago: Science Research Associates, 1949).

2. Nathan Glazer and Patrick Moynihan, *Beyond the Melting Pot* (Boston: MIT Press and Harvard University Press, 1963).

3. Michael Barone, *The New Americans: How The Melting Pot Can Work Again* (Washington, D.C.: Regency, 2001).

4. Bernard Berelson and Gary A. Steiner, *Human Behavior: An Inventory of Scientific Findings* (New York: Harcourt, Brace and World, 1964), 653.

5. Alan Mintz, "Sushi and Other Jewish Foods," *Commentary* 106 (October 1998): 43–48.

6. Nancy Foner (ed.), *New Immigrants in New York* (New York: Columbia University Press, 1987).

7. Mike Tharp, "Divided by Generations," *U.S. News & World Report* 129, 17 July 2000, 42.

8. Matt Ackerman, "Sites Target Wealthy Chinese-Americans," *American Banker* 166, 27 March 2001, 8; and Laurie Freeman, "Stunning Loyalty," *Advertising Age* 70, 29 November 1999, 6.

9. Yochi Dreagen, "Kosher Food Marketers Target Non-Jews," *The Wall Street Journal*, 30 July 1999, B2.

10. Michele Soicolone, "A Slice of Italy Reached by Subway," *The New York Times*, 5 October 1994, C4.

11. Donna R. Gabaccia, *We Are What We Eat: Ethnic Food and the Making of Americans* (Cambridge: Harvard University Press, 1998), 215–218.

12. Eugene Sivadas, Goeorge Mathew, and David J. Currey, "A Preliminery Examination of the Continuing Significance of Social Class to Marketing: A Geodemographic Replication," *Journal of Consumer Marketing* 14 (December 1997): 463–479.

Epilogue

Changes in the approaches taken by marketers to lifestyle market segmentation strategies are rapid as companies seek more effective ways to know their customers better. New approaches to identifying market opportunities and defining customer groups have made it easier for marketers to develop strategies to reach specific customer groups. The Internet allows more precise and faster quantification of data. At the same time, more is known about using the behavioral sciences to explain buyer behavior. Companies can now reach their customers in a way the customer wants to purchase. Marketing is becoming more of a science than art. Using marketing research, the company can know what the customer wants, how to reach the customer, what the customer is willing to pay, and even when the customer will become a repeat buyer. The company is now able to put a value on its customers. Market segmentation permits the company to build equity with each customer based on the variables selected to define the market.

Marketing in the past emphasized selling. Efforts were focused on stimulating demand and increasing sales volume with little emphasis on profitable sales or on customers' long-term needs. Research was not conducted on customer buyer behavior because of the cost, the lack of sophistication of marketing personnel on how to use the information, and the time it took to collect the information. When the marketing concept philosophy—a customer orientation, profitable sales, or other long-term objectives, and using an integrated organizational effort to achieve these—was introduced, new terms like culture, values, and beliefs were considered by the organization in making decisions. Long-term planning, distribution cost analysis, and information systems became operational. Although there is still confusion in the minds of many business executives between marketing and selling, today's emphasis has moved from customer orientation to customer equity.

Market segmentation groups potential buyers by demographic characteristics such as geographical areas, lifestyle and usage patterns, and other factors. Submarkets can then be established on the basis of income, age and sex, occupation, behavioral dimensions, and ethnic factors among other variables. The term product differentiation referred to marketing efforts to distinguish a homogeneous product from competitors' products by altering the product's physical characteristics, using branding, advertising, and packaging or other components of the marketing mix, namely, distribution and pricing. Segmentation and differentiation must work hand-in-hand for the marketer to achieve his or her objectives.

Strategic management and its emphasis on customer orientation and market segmentation, targeting, and positioning are now the focus of marketing activities.[1] Strategic management looks at positioning and customer value as important success factors for a company. Lifestyle market segmentation is an integral part of the positioning strategy and customer value orientation. An analysis of changing consumer lifestyle activities focuses on how to create and dominate markets using segmentation strategies.

An important decision to consider is whether subcultures such as singles, young people, seniors, and ethnic groups can be approached by using a single strategy or if different strategies need to be developed for each subculture. Companies that are successful treat each subculture as a distinct market and engage in micromarket segmentation; namely, aiming at a market of one. By taking this approach, the company can be engaged in relationship marketing and establish a monetary value on the lifetime buying behavior for each of its customers. Whether one strategy is used or many, there are certain variables common to all subcultures such as word-of-mouth, the self-concept, the buyer-decision process, the adoption process for new products, motivation theory, the brand-decision process, reference group influence, and the impact of culture and social class on purchasing behavior. Each of these variables can be useful in describing what takes place in the market. On the other hand, each variable must be explored separately to reach and communicate with the appropriate subculture. For example, word-of-mouth marketing is used effectively in reaching 57 percent of African-Americans and

48 percent of Hispanics. Furthermore, family members are an instrumental source of information for 62 percent of Hispanics and 44 percent of African-Americans.[2] The importance of word-of-mouth marketing will vary from subculture to subculture. A way to increase word-of-mouth exposure is to promote the product among local opinion leaders who are considered a reliable source of information. Another tactic is to sponsor special events within the community and a third method is to use local ethnic media.

The extent of information search by the customer will depend upon the degree of risk involved in the purchase. Thus, the nature of the product, the lifestyle of the purchaser, reference groups and sources of information used and other behavioral variables vary. There will be more time spent in the purchasing process as the perceived risk increases. Promotional appeals for specific brands may concentrate on particular motives. Culture, social class, and social performance are among the exogenous variables that direct buyer behavior.

Motivation theory is useful in lifestyle market segmentation. Buying motives may be rational, emotional, or based upon patronage factors. A particular brand of orange juice may be purchased because it is the private label offered by a neighborhood supermarket where most of the family purchasing takes place, due to advertising, packaging, or other promotional instruments, because the family likes its taste, because it is the lowest or highest priced brand or because of a combination of rational, emotional, and patronage motives.

Strategic marketing management is built around lifestyle market segmentation, targeting, and positioning strategies. Recent advancements in strategy that involve technology are real-time marketing and emotional product positioning. Real-time marketing is dissimilar to earlier marketing strategies inasmuch that it adapts itself over time to the customized needs of customers.[3] Real-time marketing has developed from mass customization and relationship marketing and is reflected in products such as a washing machine that selects its wash cycle based on the weight of dirtiness and type of wash load and a vacuum cleaner that adjusts its suction pressure based on dirt level on the carpet. Creative positioning uses emotional appeals based upon product characteristics, benefits, usage occasions, user category, and contrasts the product against a competitive product.[4] These strategies direct themselves to participation by the customer. Creative positioning also includes the emotional reaction of individual customers. These advances in strategies are only the beginning of satisfying individual customer needs.

Recently, cultural variables have reflected changes in lifestyle market segmentation strategies. Age compression has been an important issue facing marketers in the past two decades. Although codependency has been extended because of the educational process, children, tweens, teens, and college-bound youths are assuming older roles and behavioral patterns. Young people have altered their appearance to reflect older ages. Senior citizens feel and act much younger than their counterparts did years ago. The singles market is finding that their lifestyles are being served by ski lodges, tour organizations, and other types of marketers' direct products and services to them. Intermarriage is breaking down many ethnic barriers as compared to earlier generations. An affluent market has created a new demand for upscale housing, recreational activities, apparel, and household goods.

Opportunities to satisfy changing lifestyles exist. Advances in generational marketing, usually taking twenty to twenty-five years, and cohort marketing usually taking five to six years, have allowed marketers to experiment with changing lifestyle market segmentation strategies. As consumer needs emerge, customer priorities will change as a result of the environment, technology, and daily living activities. Customer value will be considered a company asset. Customer relationships may be on Web sites. New ways of generating information about consumers will be used to create databases. There is no doubt that new developments in lifestyle market segmentation will lead to better and more profitable ways to build relationships with customers.

NOTES

1. Frederick E. Webster, "Marketing Management in Changing Times," *Marketing Management* 11 (January–February 2002): 18–23.

2. Deborah L. Vence, "Word of Mouth," *Marketing News* 36, 22 July 2002, 19.

3. Richard W. Oliver, Roland T. Rust, and Sajeev Varki, "Real-Time Marketing," *Marketing Management* 7 (Fall–Winter 1998): 29–37.

4. Viiay Mahajan and Jerry Wind, "Got Emotional Product Positioning," *Marketing Management* 11 (May–June 2002): 36–41.

Bibliography

BOOKS

Atchley, Robert C. *Aging: Continuity and Change.* 2d ed. Belmont, Calif.: Wadsworth, 1987.

Barone, Michael. *The New Americans: How the Melting Pot Can Work Again.* Washington, DC: Regency, 2001.

Black Americans. Ithaca, NY: American Demographics Books, 1994.

Blattberg, Robert C., Gary Getz, and Jacquelyn S. Thomas. *Customer Equity.* Boston: Harvard Business School Press, 2001.

Engel, James, Roger Blackwell, and Paul Miniard. *Consumer Behavior.* 7th ed. Chicago: Dryden Press, 1995.

Guber, Selina S., and John Berry. *Marketing To and Through Kids.* New York: McGraw-Hill, 1992.

Hanson, Ward. *Principles of Internet Marketing.* Cincinnati, Ohio: South Western College, 2000.

Horner, Louise L., ed. *Hispanic Americans: A Statistical Sourcebook.* Palo Alto, Calif.: Information Publications, 1995.

Hughes, Arthur M. *Strategic Database Marketing.* 2d ed. New York: McGraw-Hill, 2000.

Keller, Kevin Lane. *Strategic Brand Management: Building, Measuring and Managing Brand Equity.* Upper Saddle River, N.J.: Prentice-Hall, 1998.

Kotler, Philip, Durak Jain, and Suvit Maesincee. *Marketing Moves.* Boston: Harvard Business School Press, 2002.

———. *Marketing Management.* 11th ed. Upper Saddle River, N.J.: Prentice-Hall, 2003.

Meredith, Geoffrey E., and Charles D. Schewe. *Defining Markets, Defining Moments.* New York: Hungry Minds, 2002.

Miller, Daniel. *A Theory of Shopping*. Ithaca, N.Y.: Cornell University Press, 1998.

Moschis, George P. *Marketing to Older Consumers: A Handbook of Information for Strategy Development*. Westport, Conn.: Quorum Books, 1992.

Oliver, Richard. *Satisfaction: A Behavioral Perspective on the Consumer*. New York: McGraw-Hill, 1997.

Ostroff, Jill. *Successful Marketing to the 50+*. Englewood Cliffs, N.J.: Prentice-Hall, 1989.

Richardson, Paul. *Internet Marketing: Readings and Online Resources*. New York: McGraw-Hill/Irwin, 2001.

Robinette, Scott, and Claire Brand. *Emotion Marketing: The Hallmark Way of Winning Customers for Life*. New York: McGraw-Hill, 2001.

Rust, Roland T., Valerie A. Ziethaml, and Katherine N. Lemon. *Driving Customer Equity*. New York: The Free Press, 2000.

Schrieber, Alfred L. *Multicultural Marketing*. Chicago: NTC Business Books, 2001.

Seybold, Patricia P. *The Customer Revolution*. New York: Crown Business, 2001.

Sheehy, Gail. *New Passages: Mapping Your Life Across Time*. New York: Random House, 1995.

Taylor, Jim, and Watts Wacker with Howard Means. *The 500-Year Delta*. New York: Harper Business, 1997.

Underhill, Paco. *Why They Buy: The Science of Shopping*. New York: Simon and Schuster, 1999.

Zaltman, Gerald. *How Customers Think*. Boston: Harvard Business School Press, 2003.

ARTICLES

Aaker, Jennifer, Anne Brumbaugh, and Sonya Grier. "Non-Target Markets and Viewer Distinctiveness: The Impact of Target Marketing on Advertising Attitudes." *Journal of Consumer Psychology*, Volume 9, 3 (2000): 127–140.

Aaker, Jennifer, Anne Brumbaugh, Sonya Grier, and Patti Williams. "Empathy versus Pride: The Influence of Emotional Appeals across Cultures." *Journal of Consumer Research*, Volume 25 (December 1998): 241–261.

Ackerman, David, and Gerard Tellis. "Can Culture Affect Prices? A Cross-Cultural Study of Shopping and Retail Prices." *Journal of Retailing*, Volume 77 (Spring 2001): 57–82.

Albonette, J. G., and L. Dominguez. "Major Influences on Consumer-Goods Marketers' Decision to Target U.S. Hispanics." *Journal of Advertising Research*, Volume 29, 1 (1989): 9–21.

Ariely, Dan. "Controlling the Information Flow: Effects on Consumers' Decision Making and Preferences." *Journal of Consumer Research*, Volume 27 (September 2000): 233–248.

Arjona, L. D., R. Shah, A. Tinivelli, and A. Weiss. "Marketing to the Hispanic Consumer." *McKinsey Quarterly*, Volume 3 (1998): 106–114.

Arnett, J. "Adolescents' Uses of Media for Self-Socialization." *Journal of Youth and Adolescence*, Volume 24, 5 (1995): 519–532.

Bazerman, Max H. "Consumer Research for Consumers." *Journal of Consumer Research*, Volume 27 (March 2001): 499–504.

Beatty, Sharon E., and Salil Talpade. "Adolescent Influence in Family Decision Making: A Replication with Extension." *Journal of Consumer Research*, Volume 21, 2 (1994): 332–341.

Belch, Michael, and Gayle Ceresino. "Parental and Teenage Child Influences in Family Decision-Making." *Journal of Business Research*, Volume 13 (1985): 163–176.

Berman, G. "The Hispanic Market: Getting Down to Cases." *Sales and Marketing Management*, Volume 143, 2 (1991): 65–74.

Blattberg, Robert C., and John Deighton. "Manage Marketing by the Customer Equity Test." *Harvard Business Review*, Volume 74 (July–August 1996): 136–144.

Braus, P. "What Does Hispanic Mean?" *American Demographics*, Volume 15, 6 (June 1993): 46–49.

Brenkert, George G. "Marketing to Inner-City Blacks: PowerMaster and Moral Responsibility." *Business Ethics Quarterly*, Volume 8 (January 1998): 1–18.

Bristor, Julia M., R. Gravois Lee, and Michelle R. Hunt. "Race and Ideology: African-American Images in Television Advertising." *Journal of Public Policy & Marketing*, Volume 14 (Spring 1995): 48–59.

Burkauser, Richard V., Greg J. Duncan, and Richard Hauser. "Sharing Prosperity Across the Age Distribution: A Comparison of the United States and Germany in the 1980s." *The Gerontologist*, Volume 34, 2 (1994): 150–160.

Campanelli, Melissa. "The African-American Market: Community, Growth and Change." *Sales and Marketing Management*, Volume 143 (May 1991): 75–81.

Carbone, Lewis P. "What Makes Customers Tick?" *Marketing Management*, Volume 12 (July–August 2003): 23–27.

Childers, T., and A. Rao. "The Influence of Familial and Peer-Based Reference Groups on Consumer Decisions." *Journal of Consumer Research*, Volume 19 (September 1992): 198–211.

Christenson, Peter. "The Effects of Parental Advisory Labels on Adolescent Music Preferences." *Journal of Communication*, Volume 42, 1 (Winter 1992): 106–113.

Cohen, Judy. "White Consumer Response to Asian Models in Advertising." *Journal of Consumer Marketing*, Volume 9 (Spring 1992): 17–27.

Cui, Geng. "Marketing to Ethnic Minority Consumers: A Historical Journey (1932–1997)." *Journal of Macromarketing*, Volume 21 (June 2001): 23–31.

———. "Marketing Strategies in a Multi-Ethnic Environment." *Journal of Marketing Theory and Practice*, Volume 5, 1 (Winter 1997): 122–134.

Delener, R., and J. Neelankavil. "Informational Sources and Media Usage: A Comparison of Asian and Hispanic Subcultures." *Journal of Advertising Research*, Volume 30, 3 (1990): 45–52.

Deshpande, Rohit, Wayne Hower, and Naveen Donthu. "The Intensity of Ethnic Affiliation: A Study of the Sociology of Hispanic Consumption." *Journal of Consumer Research*, Volume 13 (September 1986): 214–220.

Donthu, N., and B. Yoo. "Cultural Influence on Service Quality Expectations." *Journal of Service Research*, Volume 1, 2 (1998): 178–186.

Epstein, Jeffrey H. "The Net Generation is Changing the Marketplace." *The Futurist*, Volume 32, 3 (1998): 14.

Fournier, Susan. "Consumers and their Brands: Developing Relationship Theory in Consumer Research." *Journal of Consumer Research*, Volume 24 (March 1998): 343–373.

Friedman, Hershey H. "The Impact of Jewish Values on Marketing and Business Practices." *Journal of Macromarketing*, Volume 21 (June 2001): 74–80.

Garbarino, Ellen, and Mark Johnson. "The Different Roles of Satisfaction, Trust and Commitment for Relational and Transactional Consumers." *Journal of Marketing*, Volume 63 (April 1999): 70–87.

Goodwin, Cathy, and James W. Gentry. "Life Transition as a Basis for Segmentation." *Journal of Segmentation in Marketing*, Volume 4, 1 (2000): 71–83.

Grier, Sonya A., and Anne M. Brumbaugh. "Noticing Cultural Differences: Ad Meanings Created by Target and Non-Target Markets." *Journal of Advertising*, Volume 28, 1 (1999): 79–93.

Hall, Owen P., Jr. "Mining the Store." *Journal of Business Strategy*, Volume 22 (March–April 2001): 24–27.

Herbig, P., and R. Yelkur. "Hispanic and Anglo Differences in Consumer Behavior." *Journal of International Marketing & Marketing Research*, Volume 23, 1 (1998): 47–56.

John, Deborah Roedder, and Catherine A. Cole. "Age Differences in Information Processing: Understanding Deficits in Young and Elderly Consumers." *Journal of Consumer Research*, Volume 13, 3 (1986): 297–231.

Kang, Yong-Soon, and Nancy M. Ridgway. "The Importance of Consumer Market Interactions as a Form of Social Support for Elderly Consumers." *Journal of Public Policy & Marketing*, Volume 15 (Spring 1996): 181–201.

Kaufman, Carol, and Sigfredo Hernandez. "Barriers to Coupon Use: A View from the Bodega." *Journal of Advertising Research*, Volume 30 (October–November 1990): 18–25.

———. "The Role of the Bodega in a U.S. Puerto Rican Community." *Journal of Retailing*, Volume 67 (Winter 1991): 375–396.

Kim, Youn-Kyung, and Jikyeong Kang. "The Effects of Ethnicity and Product on Purchase Decision Making." *Journal of Advertising Research*, Volume 41, 2 (2001): 39–48.

Kinley, Tammy, and Linda Sivils. "Gift-Giving Behavior of Grandmothers." *Journal of Segmentation in Marketing*, Volume 4, 1 (2000): 53–70.

Kivetz, Ran, and Itamar Simonson. "The Effects of Incomplete Information on Consumer Choice." *Journal of Marketing Research*, Volume 37 (November 2000): 427–448.

Koslow, Scott, Prem N. Shamdasani, and Ellen E. Touchstone. "Exploring Language Effects in Ethnic Advertising: A Sociolinguistic Perspective." *Journal of Consumer Research*, Volume 20, 4 (1994): 575–585.

Lee, M., and E. Ulado. "Consumer Evaluations of Fast-Food Services: A Cross-National Comparison." *Journal of Services Marketing*, Volume 11, 1 (1997): 39–52.

Leonhardt, David. "Hey Kid, Buy This." *BusinessWeek*, 30 June 1997, 62–67.

"Lifestyle Marketing." *Progressive Grocer*, Volume 76 (August 1997): 107–110.

Longino, Charles F., Jr. "The Comfortably Retired and the Pension Elite." *American Demographics*, Volume 10 (June 1988): 22–25.

Mangleburg, Tamara F., and Terry Bristol. "Socialization and Adolescents' Skepticism Toward Advertising." *Journal of Advertising*, Volume 27, 3 (1998): 11–20.

McCarthy, Michael. "Stalking the Elusive Teenage Trendsetter." *The Wall Street Journal*, Volume 19, November 1998, B1–B10.

McDougall, Gordon. "Customer Retention Strategies: When Do They Pay Off?" *Services Marketing Quarterly*, Volume 22, 1 (2001): 39–55.

McNeal, James U. "Tapping the Three Kids' Markets." *American Demographics*, Volume 20 (April 1998): 34–39.

Menendez, T., and J. Yow. "The Hispanic Market: An Overview of the Major Markets." *Marketing Research*, Volume 1 (June 1989): 11–15.

Moschis, G. P., A. Mathur, and R. B. Smith. "Older Consumers' Orientation Toward Age-Based Marketing Stimuli." *Journal of the Academy of Marketing Science*, Volume 21 (Summer 1993): 195–205.

Naumann, Earl, Donald W. Jackson, Jr., and Mark S. Rosenbaum. "How to Implement a Customer Satisfaction Program." *Business Horizons*, Volume 44 (January–February 2001): 37–47.

O'Guinn, T. C., and L. J. Shrum. "The Role of Television in the Construction of Consumer Reality." *Journal of Consumer Research*, Volume 23, 4 (1997): 287–284.

Otnes, Cele, and Mary Ann McGrath. "Perceptions and Realities of Male Shopping Behavior." *Journal of Retailing*, Volume 77 (Spring 2001): 111–137.

Penaloza, Lisa. "Immigrant Consumers: Marketing and Public Policy Considerations in the Global Economy." *Journal of Public Policy & Marketing*, Volume 14 (Spring 1995): 83–94.

Pham, Michel Taun. "Representativeness, Relevance, and the Use of Feelings in Decision Making." *Journal of Consumer Research*, Volume 25 (September 1998): 144–159.

Price, Linda L., Eric J. Arnold, and Carolyn Folkman Curasi. "Older Consumers' Disposition of Special Possessions." *Journal of Consumer Research*, Volume 27 (September 2000): 179–201.

Ratchford, Brian T. "The Economics of Consumer Knowledge." *Journal of Consumer Research*, Volume 27 (March 2001): 397–411.

Reichheld, Frederick F., and Phil Schefter. "E-Loyalty: Your Secret Weapon on the Web." *Harvard Business Review*, Volume 78 (July–August 2000): 105–113.

Seybold, Patricia B. "Get Inside the Lives of Your Customers." *Harvard Business Review*, Volume 79 (May 2001): 81–89.

Shin, Dooyoung, and Kevin M. Elliott. "Measuring Customers' Overall Satisfaction: A Multi-Attributes Assessment." *Services Marketing Quarterly*, Volume 22, 1 (2001): 3–19.

Shoemaker, Stowe. "Segmentation of the Senior Pleasure Travel Market." *Journal of Travel Research*, Volume 27 (Winter 1989): 14–21.

———. "Segmenting the Market: 10 Years Later." *Journal of Travel Research*, Volume 39 (August 2000): 11–26.

Smit, Edith G., and Peter C. Neijens. "Segmentation Based on Affinity for Advertising." *Journal of Advertising Research*, Volume 40 (July–August 2000): 35–43.

Smith, N. Craig, and Elizabeth Cooper-Martin. "Ethics and Target Marketing: The Role of Product Harm and Consumer Vulnerability." *Journal of Marketing*, Volume 61 (July 1997): 1–20.

Speer, Tibbet L. "Older Consumers Follow Different Rules." *American Demographics*, Volume 15 (February 1993): 21–22.

Spreng, Richard A., Scott B. MacKenzie, and Richard W. Olshavsky. "A Reexamination of the Determinants of Consumer Satisfaction." *Journal of Marketing*, Volume 60 (July 1996): 15–32.

Steele, Jeanne R., and Jane D. Brown. "Adolescent Room Culture: Studying Media in the Context of Everyday Life." *Journal of Youth and Adolescence*, Volume 24, 5 (1995): 551–574.

Stevenson, Thomas H., and Patricia E. McIntyre. "A Comparison of the Portrayal and Frequency of Hispanics and Whites in English Language Television Advertising." *Journal of Current Issues and Research in Advertising*, Volume 17 (Spring 1995): 65–74.

Taylor, Charles R., and Barbara B. Stern. "Asian-Americans: Television Advertising and the 'Model Minority' Stereotype." *Journal of Advertising*, Volume 26, 2 (1997): 47–61.

Teaff, Joseph D., and Thomas Turpin. "Travel and the Elderly." *Parks and Recreation*, Volume 31, 6 (1996): 16–20.

Urban, Glen L., Fareena Sultan, and William J. Qualls. "Placing Trust at the Center for Your Internet Strategy." *Sloan Management Review*, Volume 42 (Fall 2000): 39–49.

Webster, Cynthia. "The Effects of Hispanic Subcultural Identification on Information Search Behavior." *Journal of Advertising Research*, Volume 32, 5 (1992): 54–62.

———. "Effects of Hispanic Ethnic Identification on Marital Roles in the Purchase Decision Process." *Journal of Consumer Research*, Volume 21, 2 (1994): 319–331.

Wellner, Alison Stein. "The Forgotten Baby Boom." *American Demographics*, Volume 23 (February 2001): 46–51.

Wilkes, Robert, and Humberto Valencia. "Hispanics and Blacks in Television Commercials." *Journal of Advertising*, Volume 18, 1 (1989): 19–25.

Williams, Jerome D., and William J. Qualls. "Middle-Class Black Consumers and Intensity of Ethnic Identification." *Psychology and Marketing*, Volume 6 (Winter 1989): 263–286.

Williams, Jerome D., William J. Qualls, and Sonya A. Grier. "Racially Exclusive Advertising: Public Policy Implications for Fair Housing Practices." *Journal of Public Policy and Marketing*, Volume 14, 2 (1995): 225–244.

Winsberg, M. "Specific Hispanics." *American Demographics*, Volume 16, 2 (1994): 44–53.

Wolfe, D. B. "Targeting the Mature Mind." *American Demographics*, Volume 16 (1994): 32–36.

Wyner, Gordon A. "Beyond Customer Understanding." *Marketing Management*, Volume 12 (July–August 2003): 6–7.

Wyner, Gordon A. "Segmentation Architecture." *Marketing Management*, Volume 11, 2 (2002): 6–7.

Zimmer, Zachary, Russell E. Brayley, and Mark S. Searle. "Whether to Go and Where to Go: Identification of Important Influences on Seniors' Decisions to Travel." *Journal of Travel Research*, Volume 33 (Fall 1995): 3–10.

Index

Working class, 201
Working wives, 17, 200–201
World War II, 16–17
World War II cohort (Great Depression Generation), 110

Xers. *See* Generation X

Yankelovich, Inc., 149, 186, 191
Yers. *See* Generation Y
Young and Secures, seniors, 162, 164

Young-again market segment, seniors, 154, 155, 156
Young people. *See* Children, tweens, teens, and college markets
Youth and seniors, 156
Youth segments, 129
Yuppie attitudes, 37
Yuppies, 30–31, 94

Zany Brainy, 37–38, 56
Zip code (markets), 21, 22

ABOUT THE AUTHORS

Ronald D. Michman is Professor Emeritus of Marketing, Shippens-burg University, Shippensburg, Pennsylvania. He is the author or coauthor of nine books, including *Specialty Retailers: Marketing Triumphs and Blunders* (Quorum Books, 2001), *The Food Industry Wars: Marketing Triumphs and Blunders* (Quorum Books, 1998), and *Lifestyle Market Segmentation* (Quorum Books, 1991).

Edward M. Mazze is Dean of the College of Business Administration and holder of the Alfred J. Verrecchia-Hasbro Inc. Leadership Chair in Business at the University of Rhode Island. He is co-author with Ronald D. Michman of *Specialty Retailers* and *The Food Industry Wars*.

Alan J. Greco was formerly Associate Professor of Marketing at the School of Business and Economics at North Carolina A&T State University in Greensboro. He is the co-author with Ronald D. Michman of *Retailing Triumphs and Blunders: Victims of Competition in the New Age of Marketing Management* (Quorum Books, 1995).